Yukon Passage

YUKON PASSAGE

RAFTING
2,000 MILES
TO THE
BERING SEA

KEITH TRYCK

Times
BOOKS

Published by TIMES BOOKS, a division of
Quadrangle/The New York Times Book Co., Inc.
Three Park Avenue, New York, N.Y. 10016

Published simultaneously in Canada by
Fitzhenry & Whiteside, Ltd., Toronto

Map adapted with permission from *National Geographic* magazine.
All photographs not otherwise credited are by Robert Clark.

Library of Congress Cataloging in Publication Data

Tryck, Keith.
Yukon passage: rafting 2,000 miles to the
Bering Sea.

1. Rafting (Sports)—Yukon River.
2. Yukon River—Description and travel.
I. Title.
GV776.15.Y83T79 1980   797.1'2'097986   80-5135
ISBN 0-8129-0926-7

Manufactured in the United States of America

CONTENTS

1

Following Grandpa's Footsteps

3

2

A Raft is Built in Buccaneer Cove

33

3

Trials on the Yukon: Pole Trolls and Tempests

63

4

Wipeout, Whitehorse, and Plans for a June Reunion

91

5

The Rafters Rejoin and Meet the Can-Can Queens

129

6

From Raft to Cabin; By Skis to the Bering Sea

179

Epilogue

213

(Color illustrations appear between pages 90 and 91)

Yukon Passage

1

Following Grandpa's Footsteps

Tracing the origins of our adventure is like tracing the origins of the Yukon River. It sounds like a simple problem to follow the Yukon to some crystalline lake high in the mountains, a lake with no great tributaries, a timeless emerald cradle. But cascades and rivulets bound down to the lake from higher still, each in itself a miniature river whose headwaters may seem to be a tarn no larger than a millpond. Yet trickling into the tarn . . .

"I'm ready to go home," I said, turning to Bob.

We sat cross-legged on the hot steel deck, our backs against a hatch cover on one of five barges the Sudanese stern-wheeler was pushing up the Nile through the endless swamp, the Sudd. As far as one could see, no earth rose to break the horizon. The Nile was a thin channel hewn through thousands of square miles of lush vegetation. It was the Sudd that held modern explorers at bay, guarding the legendary Mountains of the Moon, thought to be the Nile's headwaters since antiquity. Late in the nineteenth century, explorers did gain the Mountains of the Moon, but only after struggling two thousand miles upriver through desert Africa to chop their way through this seemingly limitless, disease-choked, crocodile-infested swamp.

A century later we made our way steadily against the sluggish current. With each day I was more deeply mesmerized—the African people leading stoic but full lives, bartering with us at the landings; the land that seems endlessly the same, yet is ever-changing to patient eyes; the ceaseless beat of the paddles pummeling the waters of the imperturbable river.

The sun grew damask as it closed the horizon, forced by the slowly turning earth to ease its merciless stare. Bob and I stayed unmoving, waiting for the evening coolness. It seemed time had taken a vacation along the Nile.

"The river's got you, hasn't it?" he asked quietly.

"I don't know what's got me," I responded, "but I know what I'm going to do. I want to live like I am now, without schedules, unbound by the clock, feeling things at the pace of the life around me, allowing myself to be a pebble, to feel the wash of the tide. I want to do it at home, in Alaska, in the North Country.

"In 1899 two young Swedes, my Dad's father, Oscar, and his brother, Charlie, stepped off the steamer in Skagway, behind them an all too recent memory of the Michigan iron mines and a future as black as the tunnels and shafts they slaved in. From Skagway they packed their outfits over the White Pass to the headwaters of the Yukon. They couldn't have known what lay ahead of them, other than a lot of work. What they were accustomed to. They couldn't have had much money, either: They backpacked through the pass on the railroad bed rather than taking the train to Lake Bennett, where they built a scow by hand and floated down the Yukon to the Klondike goldfields in Dawson City. That was in early 1900. Dawson was an established city by then, being all of three years old, but not the boomtown of its youth. The action had moved to the shores of the Bering Sea and the new gold strike at Nome.

"They worked a winter as teamsters in Dawson, freighting for the miners on the creeks. In the spring of 1901 they were back on the Yukon with a new grubstake, headed downriver for the Nome goldfields. Nome, Fairbanks, Tenderfoot, Ruby, Iditarod, Livengood—they hit them all at one time or another, sometimes prospecting or mining, sometimes freighting or cutting wood or what have you.

"Grandpa married and had a family, Uncle Charlie stayed single and lived in Ruby on the Yukon from the strike in 1912, I think it was, until he passed on in the fifties. Grandpa moved to the Willow Mining District to take a job as superintendent of the Independence Mine. That was after World War I. The story goes that he refused the job; he didn't feel the mine was safe and the owners wouldn't change it. He must have been a Wobbly! Anyway, he stayed in the district freighting with horse teams to the mines. When the Alaska Railroad

4

reached the road from Knik to the mines, he built his home there in the new town Wasilla.

"Dad was born there, his mom passed away there, and when I was young I spent a lot of time with Grandpa in Wasilla. He was truly independent. He lived alone, except for family visits and my longer stays, cut his firewood alone, tended his gardens alone, and he liked it that way. I can see him as clearly as yesterday, quietly, contentedly rocking back and forth, back and forth in his chair, rubbing oil of wintergreen into one gnarly hand then the other, trying to drive out the aching rheumatism he earned in his youth, when his hands, rocking a gold pan, were plunged in countless icy streams and numbed senseless."

I paused, reflecting on my own image. In a way I felt like I was confessing from the pit of my being. Bob didn't stir, he was listening attentively, so I went on.

"I saw a stern-wheeler on the Yukon once, when I was a boy. I can remember it clearly, the tall stacks and stately pilot house and the flashing orange paddle wheel. It was sunny, but windy and cold, and my eyes were watering. The steamer was turning around in the river in front of Whitehorse. Dad and I stood on the bank and watched. Forward then back, forward then back, it worked its way around in the narrow river.

"'Remember this,' he said, 'you won't see it again.'

"I'd just turned five. We were driving up the Alaska Highway (it was the Alcan then), the first time any of us except Mom had been outside Alaska. Dad was right, the stern-wheelers are gone now, a part of the past, a page in history that I remember."

I kept talking. "Bob, Lord knows how I've thought about heading down the Yukon, but it was always through some sort of time tunnel, with me living in the past, during the gold rush, prospecting and mining spiced with lots of hardy living and adventure. But that time is gone, so it stayed a dream. But, you see, it wasn't the gold that kept them there, the few like my granddad who came during the rush and stayed. It was the North and the full lives it provided them. I miss it, the North. I miss the blueberries and the infuriating alder brush, the muskeg and the surly rivers. I don't miss Anchorage—the city with its smell of exhaust smoke and asphalt and its roar of forest-chewing machines that leave landscaped subdivisions behind them, but I miss its setting—mountains in every direction, sea at its foot, its temperate climate. I don't miss my work there, the countless subdivision lots I've staked, the roads I've surveyed, but I miss being out-of-doors and free from office hassles, climbing some mountain alone to put a sight on its summit for triangulation. I miss commiserating with the surveyor before me. Did he choose the same route as I as he climbed this mountain? Did he use the same handholds in the rock? He must have laughed like I did that someone was actually paying him to be there, miles and miles of beauty in every direction, to set the brass monument that I, years later, would erect my sight over. I guess I'm saying Anchorage is no longer my place.

"The gold rush has passed into memory but the river, the Yukon, is as ageless as the Nile. Along its banks deserted cabins and ghost towns squat in the brush with their memories. Well, I want to go north through that door that I've only read about and I want to record everything I see, everything I find—write it down, make maps, talk to the old-timers and listen to their stories. I want to make my contribution to the North, in the North. That's where I belong."

Bob hadn't said anything during my spiel, and I finally looked at him out of the corner of my eye. I knew I was throwing a monkey wrench in our round-the-world trip. Almost exactly half way from home I was ready to jump ship.

"You know," he said, feeling my gaze, "I could spend some time here in Africa in one area, seeing more than just a passing glimpse. We could rest up a bit, look around, relax. It won't be warm up north for three or four months anyway. Then I'd kinda like to get into photography. I've been thinking about that a lot lately. You know, if you had pictures of everything, your records would be much more complete. Besides, you wouldn't want to do all that adventuring alone would you?" He slowly turned to face me, smiling.

"No way!" I exclaimed. "Pardner!"

My memories of high school Anchorage, Alaska-style, where Bob Clark and I met during that *American Graffiti* year of 1963–64 are sort of embarrassing. All I see really is a big day-care center where I had to go because that was the way to get to college, and if you didn't get to college you'd probably end up a wino or something. I was there most every day, too, because so was everybody else, especially girls. Except for a couple teachers who somehow held my attention for a full fifty minutes, I was more concerned with whether that was a real whisker standing up in the fuzz on my lip or whether I should

6

unbutton her blouse real cool like or snake my hand ever so slowly around from the back. Anyway, that's where Bob and I met, during our senior year.

At first our friendship was probably based on the fact that he was a transfer student from California, and in 1963 the sun never set on California with its beach boys and golden-tanned surfer girls. Bob also had better access to his folks' new Impala, one with a stick shift, even if it was an automatic, than I had to my family's (ugh!) station wagon, especially after I customized Dad's company car, drilling the exhaust manifold full of holes, thinking it could at least sound like a hot rod even if it wasn't one.

On Good Friday, 1964, the earthquake hit us, pretty much rearranging a lot of things. Thankfully, none of our close ones were hurt, though my grandfather barely made it a month before tossing it in. In its aftermath Bob and I were "drafted" by my father's engineering firm and put to work as surveyors. There wasn't any school to go to for a while anyway, it had fallen down, and the experience was good for us. Surveying became our trade.

College took us in different directions, but every summer we were back in the field again, brushing line and turning angles. We were rarely on the same crew, going where we were sent. But we were always outside, sometimes seeing a new part of Alaska.

Our first meeting was eight years past now, and we were good, close friends, the best kind of friends. We hadn't made some vow to "stay close," but rather went our own ways, and they turned out to be similar directions. We were friends through time to the point that we each decided there had to be something better than an office job and nine-to-five on the one hand, and being bound by a nose ring to surveying and the construction industry on the other. So we teamed up for a grand look-see that we figured would take us around the world.

The sun was all but gone, and we talked on in the closing light. By not continuing from Africa to Asia and beyond, we could save money, return to Alaska in the spring, and head for the Yukon in May or June, giving us at least two more months for Africa and the journey home.

We wanted our voyage down the Yukon to be similar to our African trip; it would be open-ended. We would form our itinerary on a daily basis, overcome obstacles as we faced them. Our surveying

7

experience would be an asset when it came to following long-overgrown trails and recording what we found. We would seek out the old-timers and listen to their tales; perhaps some of them had known my grandfather or his brother. We hoped the accumulated information would be a contribution to the North, a record of what still remained, in 1972, of the gold era and the way of life that went with it.

A lone African tree stood out as the sun set, its branches flat black wisps of a cloud tied to the swamp by a thick trunk. What its roots held I hadn't any idea.

Our four-month overland odyssey of patient hitchhiking, crowded buses, and wheezing trains was compressed into ten hours of a jet's whispered sleekness to return us to London, our European starting point. After a short tour of northern Europe we separated, each to follow his own whims for a while before returning to England and the last leg, the long nonstop flight from London to Anchorage. A rendezvous was agreed on, in Paris, but when I reached the French capital Bob was nowhere to be found, nor was there any word from him, so I proceeded to England alone. Two days, no Bob, I was broke; it was time for me to exit.

I handed my passport to the immigration officer at London's Heathrow Airport. He thumbed through it briefly then stamped it with a thump, "Embarked. 19 May, London Airport."

"Here you go, lad," he said, nodding me through the gate as he handed my passport back. I was no longer in England but a resident of the international in-between. Almost as an afterthought he added, "Come again," as if I were just leaving his corner pub!

"How about Friday?" I retorted, and we both laughed as I clanked my way toward the plane, thirty pounds of what should have been excess baggage rubbing me everywhere.

I settled heavily into my seat. Before the hour hand could make a circuit of the dial I would be in Anchorage, a hemisphere away.

I tried to picture the Yukon River in my mind, for itself rather than as a distinguishing feature of Alaska, and saw the map of Alaska and the Yukon Territory that hung on our wall in Corvallis, Oregon. We'd put it just above our kitchen table, Jerry and I, where we could see it from almost anywhere in the apartment. Jer had spent some good times in Alaska, logging, and we both liked to listen just a little less than we liked to talk, so we hardly needed an excuse to put off our

8

college studies. The map was more than sufficient. Many an evening begun in diligent study collapsed in an affable swapping of Alaskan experiences, mostly humorous, or a sharing of curiosity for places we hadn't seen. The map seemed to be our catalyst. In fact, looking back, I think too many evenings started that way. It got so bad that getting caught just looking at the map would spark some remark, such as, "Big country, isn't it?" That was all it took.

Well, I got to know the map. The Yukon headed into a number of thin, pale blue ink lakes tucked away in the far northwest corner of British Columbia. The chain of lakes and connecting pieces of river moved quickly into the Yukon Territory, passing Whitehorse before entering Lake Laberge.

Whitehorse—the memory of the stern-wheeler returned, and I saw the clear green river I'd crossed a number of times on subsequent trips up and down the highway, but I remembered the bridge and the road more than the Yukon. Whitehorse itself didn't register anything.

I had an image for Lake Laberge, though I'd never seen it. I pictured a great field of snow with a shadow of a forest shore and poor Sam McGee cooking away in his "Cre-ma-tor-eum," in Robert Service's poem about luckless Sam.

After Laberge I was back to the map. Now more lakes and large rivers joined the Yukon: the Teslin, the Pelly, the White, the Stewart. Though they were only ink lines with names to me, they seemed to give the Yukon the resolve and confidence to take a straighter course to the northwest, past Dawson.

Dawson I knew something about. As a boy I'd spent part of a carefree summer there, on one of the annual Crews plus Tryck summer outings. Paul Crews, Sr., and Dad, professional engineers, were pretty busy during the summer construction season, so our mothers would pack us kids into two dilapidated station wagons and haul us all around Alaska. It became a yearly institution, and, while other boys honed their arms for baseball and keened up eyes for batting, we caught fish, climbed mountains, and roamed the forests and ghost towns of Alaska. In 1959 we went international, to Dawson in Canada's Yukon Territory.

The Yukon was immense. Murky, ominous, and alive, it was like nothing I had ever seen. A ferry carried us across it to Dawson.

Dawson was weathered and gray. Most of the houses and buildings were boarded up and there didn't seem to be many people, not even kids to play with. We stayed in a pair of slanty-floored cabins at the end of town. One day somebody showed us where Robert Service had lived, and I was in awe of the humble cabin; for me his poems were the living story of the gold trails. Another day an old man, maybe a caretaker, let us into the old Palace Grand Theater. It was dark and eerie, with velvet-cushioned railings and heavy curtains that you ran into before you saw. If it didn't have ghosts, it should have. I caught strep throat in Dawson and had to go to the hospital to get a shot. The fact that I negotiated its destination up to my arm was victory enough, but on top of that was the matter-of-fact statement from the doctor that in Canada they used very thin needles, much thinner than in the States (Alaska became a state that year) so that shots wouldn't hurt more than a pinprick. It didn't, either, and I still don't know what to think about that.

Paul Crews, Jr., got forever up on his older brother Dave and me in Dawson. He was twelve; we were two years older. I guess he was tired of being the underdog when he took on age and numbers in a struggle for the rope swing we'd slung over a branch in a birch tree. He held the swing and from then on was no longer a minor third wheel.

The Yukon turned below Dawson, just past the dump where we shot bottles with our BB guns. We'd throw them in upriver and race along the muddy bank as far as the dump, plinking at them. Green bottles, pink bottles, purple and blue bottles, all different shaped bottles—we asked around town for them after we'd picked the dump clean, and most people were happy to have us pack them away. Only one bottle survived our marksmanship. Its fragile neck defied tremendous odds and a lot of BBs and, like a periscope, guided it out of range and off toward Alaska.

I was back to the map after Dawson, where the river changed to blue printer's ink with neat white banks. It kept its straight course, a little west of north, past the dots for the cities of Eagle and Circle. Just below Circle the thickened line splayed over the map in a wire macrame of islands and channels—the Yukon Flats. About halfway through the flats and just north of the Arctic Circle, Fort Yukon rests at the mouth of the Porcupine River. The Yukon takes in the Porcupine, marking its farthest northing, then it arches south and west across Alaska, gathering the Tanana, a great river in itself, and the Koyukuk, and passing a number of villages, among them Ruby, before closing within fifty miles of the Bering Sea. Then, as if enjoying its will with the land, the Yukon plunges south, almost to the latitude of its headwaters, forcing itself through another five hundred miles of western Alaska before meeting the Bering Sea in a last twist northwest. That was it for the map, so I turned to what I'd read.

The first people to leave written records were the Russian and British fur traders. The Russians, working for the czar's Russian America Company, pushed their way upriver from the delta on Norton Sound as far as Nulato, during the first half of the nineteenth century. On the other side of Alaska, Fort Yukon, the most westerly link in the chain of Hudson's Bay Company posts across the continent, was doing business by 1850. The Hudson's Bay Company voyageurs portaged from the Mackenzie River to the Porcupine and traveled down the latter to its mouth on the Yukon, establishing their post there. Traders and not surveyors, they had inadvertently crossed into Russian America.

In the footsteps of the fur traders came the missionaries, to save the heathens from perdition. Representatives of the Church of England followed the Hudson's Bay men, while bearded scions of the Russian Orthodox faith offered their brand of eternal reward for mortal obedience, as they preached their way upriver.

In 1867 Alaska changed owners: The czar sold his North American Colony to the United States government for $7,200,000, the Russian America Company was sold to San Francisco interests, becoming the Alaska Commercial Company, and frontiersmen and prospectors replaced cossacks and convicts.

And I knew about the big event and the era it ushered in. In late August 1896, gold was discovered on a nondescript brook a half a day's walk from the Yukon.

GOLD! Gold from the Klondike! What had been rumor during the winter of 1896–97 along the waterfronts of Seattle and San Francisco became incredible fact when the steamers *Portland* and *Excelsior* docked in July 1897, with their cargoes of boisterous miners and gold, gold from the Klondike. They were inundated with questions by newsmen as they came ashore, lugging their precious metal in pokes, jars, valises, crates, and even wheelbarrows. As fast as the stories could be tapped out in Morse code they were telegraphed to the world. Every newspaper on the continent set a new word in its type—Klondike, or Klondyke, or Clondyke, it didn't matter which they chose, all seemed to be cast in gold. The papers sold like wildfire; no matter how outlandish or unbelievable the stories, their proof lay in the handful of miners gloriously "blowing 'er in" enthroned in the grand hotels of San Francisco, floating in champagne and the best of everything money could buy.

It was everywhere instantly; a pollination of hope. Industrialists formed combines overnight, tossing millions into their capital accounts. Merchants and professionals were just as quick to hang up their "Gone to the Klondike" signs. Farmers and nurses, washerwomen and clerks, loggers and entertainers, teachers and whores, tailors and gamblers and greengrocers hurried their preparations for the journey north and the Klondike gold harvest. Some took the tools of their trades; most spurned them for pick and shovel. Few even knew where the Klondike was, other than "way up north," but everyone knew what it was and what it could mean for them. The North American economy was suffering; the Gay Nineties hadn't been gay for all. And it was hurry, hurry, hurry. It stood to reason that the first ones on the scene could stake the best ground, pick the biggest nuggets. No bones about it, it was "first come, first served." The Klondike Stampede was on. I bet a lot of men didn't even kiss their wives good-bye.

That summer and fall the army of Stampeders converged on Puget Sound. Seattle had been quick to establish itself as the premier launching point for the Klondike and points north. A Klondike hopeful had a decision to make in Seattle, after he'd been through the mill of a thousand merchants all of whose goods had been "proved" in the goldfields. If he'd survived being scalped and could still see his way north, he had two main routes to choose from.

Money would book him passage on a steamer to St. Michael, the former Russian fort on the Bering Sea, sixty miles from the Yukon's mouth. All goods and passengers were transfered to stern-wheelers for the journey through the shallow delta then up the Yukon. At St. Mike's, once more doling out his money, the prospector could book passage on one of the handful of steamboats in service, or on one of the many being feverishly rushed to completion for the boom ahead. Whichever boat he chose, however, he would be forced to wait for the river to clear itself of ice in the spring before the wheezing 1500-mile voyage upriver to the Klondike and Dawson City. It was a long journey, fully 4000 miles from Seattle, and, while it was the easiest way to the goldfields, it was neither the quickest nor the cheapest.

There was another route, for the man without great resources, a route with epidemic appeal. Two "cities," Dyea and Skagway, only a thousand miles up the rugged Pacific Coast from Seattle through the scenic inland passage, clung to the shins of the Coast Mountains that lay less than forty miles from the Yukon's headwaters. At either town, boats could be built for the journey to the Klondike. Steamship lines abounded. Their brochures still wet from the printers extolled images of stately steamers providing full service on regular schedules. Nowhere was it written that many of the ships were leaking, worn-out tubs, little more than relics. Food was bad, and service was worse. Some boats sank, and the others, bloated with people, ran up and down the coast long past their seaworthy days. Citizens of Dyea and rival Skagway worked the Seattle dockside. Like barkers on a great fairway, they drew the Stampeders to the quickest, shortest, cheapest routes to the goldfields—through their booming communities that had taken little longer to blossom than circus big tops.

Skagway offered a better port and unloading facilities, and the route through the White Pass was lower, if a bit longer. Dyea boasted a shorter route to the Yukon headwaters through the Chilkoot Pass, but the Chilkoot summit was higher than the summit of the White Pass, and the trail was more difficult, especially for pack animals. But they were both right. Each offered the shortest, cheapest, quickest route to the Klondike. And they were unquestionably equal in hardship.

Far back in that human tide, my grandfather disembarked in Skagway. We would do the same.

I turned to the Japanese businessman sitting to my right. The captain, in a crisp British accent, had just announced that we were crossing the Yukon River.

"Excuse me, do you mind if I take a look?" I asked. I didn't know how much English he spoke, but the association with the announcement must have been made, as he smiled and jammed back in the window seat.

The Yukon emerged from the distant horizon confident and strong, sweeping across the land in staggering arcs and bends. I followed its course, pressing my face against the cool plastic window to catch it passing under us, seven miles below.

Easing back from the window, carefully so as not to fall on my still smiling neighbor, I lowered myself into my sweaty, sticky seat, stretching my legs into the aisle. The plane was quiet, the engines muttering softly to themselves as we began the descent into Anchorage.

Now all I could think of was home. I missed my brothers and sisters, I missed my parents, and I remembered the excitement of other homecomings, the evenings of sharing lives and re-establishing intimacies. But on those occasions, as the discussion caught up with the present and pressed into the future, my plans were usually clear.

Eight years previous I had left Alaska for Oregon and college, beginning an erratic style of life. Summers, I was usually in Alaska surveying to help pay for my education. When I wasn't in either place I was off gallivanting about, sometimes as far away as Europe. That sort of life, I've found out, is passed off by parents as the last flings of a young person before he dons the more predictable behavior of an adult with responsibilities. The rub was, I didn't stop living that way after graduating from college, but hid under the "respectable" excuse of paying my university debts off by working again with transit and chain. But when my debts were paid I realized I could hide under no more excuses and had to face the fact that I was pretty confused about my goals. I knew I didn't want anything to do with a glassed-in job, a twenty-year apprenticeship toward one of a million vice presidencies spread across the land. I was a surveyor; my degree in economics was already collecting dust.

And so I was off to Africa, to seek and learn and think and perhaps return with some new insight, some new resolution. Well I had, and I felt I was finally on track, even if only by the slim margin of an idea, an idea that seemed to lead backward through time rather than forward. I was going to the Yukon. Mothers have to love their kids, I reasoned, no matter what. But Dad? I didn't know how I would present it to him.

I made it through my homecoming with flying colors. We'd shared experiences till the wee hours of the morning on the one hand, and I took the chicken's way out on the other. I simply ducked the issue. There had to be a better time to tell Dad, even if I wasn't sure when. I would at least wait until there was no turning back.

And there was a boon. My income tax refunds were waiting,

enough money to keep me going for a while, for try as I had to save, I stepped off the plane with a single pound note in my pocket. There was one hitch. Bob hadn't reached Anchorage before me, nor was there any word from him.

Before separating we had discussed whether or not we wanted anyone else along. Paul Crews, Jr., was our only real candidate, but we decided to wait until we returned to Anchorage before making any decision. I was alone in Anchorage now, and the way I figured it I might be an expedition of one, so I wasted little time making tracks to Paul's, hopping in my VW microbus and heading across town. I knew Paul was around, he'd left word at the house less than a week before my arrival. To make sure, I phoned.

While Paul and Bob had only known each other for half a dozen years, I'd grown up with Paul. We were both members of the brood of nine that had roamed Alaska under our mothers' wings. Paul was twenty-four, two years younger than Bob and I, and like me he had graduated from college with a degree in economics. But grass hadn't grown under his feet either, for while I'd been off to Europe and Africa he had been traveling as a member of the U.S. National Alpine Ski Team. The last time I'd seen Paul, Bob and I had dropped in unexpectedly on him in France in December, just before the downhill at Val D'Isere. I thought we'd been really slick, just happening by in the French Alps, but the surprise was mine. On seeing us he laughed and without batting an eye said, "About time you showed up, I've been expecting you. I've been saving a bottle of wine for us!" We had a fine weekend together.

Now Paul was camped at home, facing another summer on a construction site. While my ace in the hole was surveying, Paul's was construction; he was a laborer.

He was waiting in the drive as I pulled in, eyes gleaming above a reddish-gold beard. I knew in an instant I sorely wanted him to come. We'd done too much adventuring together not to share the biggest one of all.

"Howdy stranger!" he said, grinning as I hopped out of the bus. Paul offered me his muscled hand with its thick, keglike fingers. Everything on that guy was hard, solid muscle.

"We've been here before!" I said, as our hands locked solid. It was our eighth replay of the same annual scene. We talked a bit about the highlights of our winters, then I asked, "How come you're not working yet? You've been home more than a week. Maybe you're not broke!"

"Well, not quite," he sighed, "but close. You know, it isn't something I look forward to. Have you been by your dad's office yet?"

"No, and I don't think I'm going," I replied. "I've got a better plan for the summer than working—see what you think of it. I want to head for the Yukon River, go down it like they did in the old days, living on bacon and beans while recording what remains of those times. It's all going so fast. It should have been done long ago, but today is better than ten years from now, better than next year, even. I want to talk to . . ."

But his nodding head and beaming face interrupted me. "All right! Let's go for it!"

The afternoon drifted away, lost in a whirlpool of dreams. We fed like wolves on each other, returning often to our adolescent summer in Dawson.

"Remember the time we went across the tailing piles to the other side of the Klondike valley and found that plank flume all overgrown, and we followed it back into the hills?" he asked.

"Sure, when we found that old cabin hidden in the brush," I answered excitedly. I remembered well. Though it was a bit dusty and dank inside, the cabin had looked like the last tenant had just stepped out for a walk. The ornate coal-oil lamp, the silverware, matches that flared when struck—all were in their carefully selected places waiting patiently for someone's return. On the door was a typed letter saying the cabin was no longer occupied. The note, dated 1914, was left by the Mounties.

"There must be places like that along the Yukon," Paul continued. "We could travel off the river, up some of the streams in the middle of nowhere, relocating the old trails and marking them down. Who knows what we might find."

That evening we began forming mental inventories of gear we'd need—cooking utensils, hardware, tent, sleeping bags, rifle, fishing gear, ropes, saws, and axes, not to mention food for the summer.

"We'll never get it in a canoe, not even two canoes," I finally stated flatly, halting our planning. Bob and I had planned on using a canoe.

16

"No," Paul concurred, "that's for sure. OK, how did your granddad travel?"

"He and his brother and their partners built a scow by hand at Lake Bennett and floated downriver," I answered trying to get the drift of his thinking. A scow, I figured, was out of the picture; we didn't have time now to build one.

"Well, it's too late to build a scow," he said reflectively, "so let's build a raft."

A raft! I started laughing. It was so obvious I hadn't been anywhere near it. My mind started racing, gears meshing cleanly everywhere at once.

"We could live right on it." I was talking and thinking at the same time. "We wouldn't have to make and break camp, packing and unpacking all the time—that's a real hassle. We could carry all kinds of stuff; we'll just build the raft to fit our needs!"

"Sure," Paul said, "and we would just slide along quietly, so quietly. . . ." The last words he drew out in a soft, soft whisper. I could see us drifting along. What a way to go.

The next morning we were off to the library. Had the river been traveled by raft? Could it be done? Surely during the gold rush . . .

The original peoples of the Yukon, the Indians and Eskimos, both used similar craft for travel along the river. The materials available to them dictated the vessel's construction. Toward the mouth of the river, the Eskimos lashed together sturdy but light wooden frames which they covered with sealskins. Upriver, the Indians covered their lashed frames with birch bark, found all along the interior reaches of the Yukon. These boats could carry their occupants downstream and in turn could be poled or pulled by rope back upriver. The Russian traders called the boat of the Eskimo "birdaka" and used it extensively, while the Hudson's Bay Company men were accustomed to the Indian boat, the canoe. The Europeans brought a third kind of boat, the most sturdy and lasting. With their axes and saws they could shape boards from trees and make boats from them. This was the vessel of the later traders and prospectors, and it allowed them to carry heavy loads of tools and equipment that would have soon worn out the native craft. The roaming prospector only needed to carry his ax, saw, and auger. Whenever a portage of his boat was impractical he could leave it, travel across the portage with his outfit, construct another boat, and carry on.

Nothing was said of rafts, and I could see why. Rafts have the unfortunate characteristic of being altogether impractical to take upstream. Using one for river transportation would be about as practical as having a car that would only go downhill in the mountains. However, if returning the way you came wasn't an issue . . .

"Here we go," Paul said, laying an old volume in front of me, *Along Alaska's Great River* by Frederick Schwatka. It had been done. In 1883. A United States Army expedition led by Lieutenant Schwatka crossed the Chilkoot Pass and built a raft at Lake Lindemann, connected to Lake Bennett by the Lindemann River, about a mile long. They sailed the lakes at the Yukon's head, ran through Miles Canyon, Whitehorse Rapids, and Five Finger Rapids—though they thoughtfully carried their gear around the dangerous sections. They had done it, therefore we could do it; it was back to the dream mill.

We were up another rung on the ladder, with clear skies ahead. Then gray wisps of doubt crept into view. Could we find wood at Lake Bennett for raft building? Maybe it was barren and treeless today, stripped for lumber then perhaps for firewood during and after the Stampede. What kinds of permission would we need to cut trees in Canada? Were there more barriers of the red tape variety, that hadn't existed during the gold rush? Dams and bridges that made rafting unrealistic?

We tried for a couple of days to locate the answers, but they weren't to be found in Anchorage. We were stymied. The string of days heralding summer were yet to come; the north wind continued to blow. Dad was wondering when I would go to work; I hadn't even been by the office. Bob had apparently run aground somewhere; still no word. Schwatka had had seven men on his raft. I didn't see how we could run ours with two.

After dinner one evening Paul and I ducked the table discussion and retreated to my room. It was chaos; I was neither packed nor unpacked but living out of stacks that had mostly found their way to the floor. I kept the door closed. We sat in the jumble for a long time, contemplating. I spoke first.

"We've got to go to Whitehorse, there's no other way. Is there timber at Lake Bennett? Do we need special permits or licenses of any kind in Canada? How long can we stay? Can we hunt and fish for

18

food? What should we purchase there and save transporting from here? We have to get closer to the horse's mouth to find answers."

"I guess so," Paul said. "Can we leave tomorrow?"

"I don't see why not," I answered. "I've been thinking about something else. Would you mind having another guy along?"

"No, there'll be plenty of room in your bus for . . ."

"No," I interrupted, "for the whole trip. We'll definitely need another hand if Bob doesn't show. Jerry Wallace . . . he and I were roommates at Oregon State. You and I know we want to build a raft, but we're not sure how we'll do it, and it'll take a lot of work. Well, Jer is a third-generation logger. He was studying forestry, and if there's any problem that can be solved by a logger, he'll know how to solve it. He was runner-up collegiate logging champion on the West Coast when we were in school. More important, he's one hell of a fine fellow and I know we'll all get along."

"Fine," Paul answered. "He sounds like just the ticket. Give him a call."

I traced Jerry through his folks; he was logging out of Randall, Washington. I had the operator place the call.

Jerry and I had hit it off well in college. We had lived next door to each other for a winter before deciding to toss our gear in a common pile. We had similar views on many things, including higher education. Our serious work centered first on ensuring that there was always excellent food on the table—and plenty of it. (Dorm food was fine for those who hadn't known better.) Our other priorities were chasing girls and completing our schooling. We did the best at eating, second best at chasing, and third best at getting through college.

"Wallace here!" he boomed into the receiver. "Who wants him?" Bad connection.

"This is Keith, Jer!" I yelled.

"Who?" he smarted back.

"Keith! What's the matter, got sawdust in your ears?"

"Hmm [mumble, mumble]. What's up?"

"Listen. We're going down the Yukon on a raft this summer if we can get it together—Paul and I and maybe Bob. Paul, my skiing friend I've told you about, and I are going over to Whitehorse to check on the legalities and see if there are any insurmountable obstacles. If it's a go, what do you think?"

19

"I can be on the plane tomorrow," he answered quickly. "Make that day after tomorrow. What'll I need?"

"Hold tight where you are," I replied. "I'll let you know for sure after we get back from Whitehorse. But to answer your question, we're doing everything by hand, like during the Klondike gold rush, and you'll be responsible for our wood-working tools—axes and saws and such. Bring anything you want for yourself, as long as you can get it all into one pack. And bring six hundred bucks. That's what we'll each have."

"I'll be waiting for your call. I sure need to get out of here. I had a dream the other night that I felled a big Noble Fir on my head, and this gal I've been seeing is getting to be too much."

The highway climbs and dips through mountains out of Anchorage, reaching the high interior plateau. Miles and miles of plateau, dwarfish spruce shouldering the road, another mountain pass, a gaunt forest fire scar, a right turn at Tok, across the Tanana River, and we were 350 miles from home—about halfway to Whitehorse, and closing in on the Canadian border. Northerners, Alaskan and Canadian, grow accustomed to the great distances. We have a lot of them between places, broken only once or twice by small road hamlets like Glennallen and Tok, Beaver Creek and Watson Lake. Between the hamlets a fistful of people run the roadhouses where a tire can be repaired, or gas and oil topped off while you have a cup of coffee and stretch your legs. The crisp air, after riding cramped in a car for hours, is scintillating, and the steady, forlorn thump of the roadhouse's generator is a part of the highway—a part of the North.

I tried to recall which roadhouses ahead would be open twenty-four hours. I used to know. During college many of us were spread out all over the states and a winter in school was often prefaced by the drive south, which we tried to make in record time. Roadhouses became pit stops during the round-the-clock race. Three people—one driving, one keeping the driver company, one sleeping, and all rotating—were the optimum number. If you showed up late in the night with a flat tire or needing gas from a roadhouse that was closed, so went the race for that trip. Anchorage city limits to Seattle city limits, 2400 miles or so. The guys who had the fewest breakdowns, the fewest flat tires, lowered the mark.

No record this time, I thought, as I shifted my Volks up every hill, a rubber-tired "little engine that could." It was a warm, sunny day, the forest was greening. I hunched over the steering wheel, driving with my elbows. Paul sought some distant point, whether with his eyes or with his mind I didn't know. At any rate he was somewhere else. Paul's friend, Ruthie, who came along for the scenery, was sitting on a duffel bag jammed in the corridor between the two front seats. It kept squishing down lower and lower and she'd given up adjusting it. Unable to see over the dash, she was content to gaze at lofty cumulus clouds and the azure sky. We were silent. It was as if talking about our raft trip would bring us bad luck in Whitehorse. At the border we dropped off the asphalt, leaving the potholed, frost-swollen road in Alaska for the Yukon Territory's smooth, well maintained gravel highway.

Most of Whitehorse, a growing city of ten thousand and capital of the Yukon Territory, rests in a spacious earthen canyon that the swift Yukon carved out long ago in its rush to leave the stone gorge of Miles Canyon, three miles above the city's center. A mile or so below Miles Canyon, the rapids that choked the river in rolling, spuming waves resembled the manes of great white horses. Miles Canyon and the Whitehorse rapids chewed up many a Stampeder and his outfit and didn't always spit them out. But that's another part of the past. The rapids are buried under a hydro dam, and its reservoir restrains the river's rush through the gorge.

"Turn here," Paul said. Whitehorse was only a couple of miles ahead. We bumped and lurched up a narrow gravel lane out of sight of the highway. The lane opened into a gravel pit, peppered with worn-out tires and the tin-can remains of past oil changes. The forest, mostly lodge-pole pine, crept to the edges of the pit.

"It'll do," I said, optimistically looking around. The moss was deep and soft in the forest, making for nice beds. If it rained we could all squeeze into the bus. We headed for town, our lodging secure.

We had little difficulty locating the federal building on Main Street, and it was as good a place to start as any. We didn't really know where to go for the answers to our questions: First, could it be done? And, if so, under what conditions?

A very cheery lady operates the elevator in the federal building. In the exchange that freely followed our asking her where to get maps, we mentioned we were contemplating floating down the Yukon.

"Go in and see Alan Innes-Taylor then," she insisted. "He's the Yukon River authority around here. His office is just down the hall."

We stepped out of the elevator and walked slowly down the hall. I wasn't sure this was what I wanted to do, but when a really helpful person answers your half-thought questions, correctly second-guessing you, it isn't easy to say thank you, step out of the elevator, and turn in the opposite direction from the one that person has suggested. I looked over my shoulder—no way. She wanted to be sure we knocked on the right door.

"This one?" I asked feebly.

She smiled and nodded, helpful to the last. I wondered what we'd gotten into. True, we wanted to find out about the river—we had to. I guess I didn't want my dream to be dashed just yet, to get that firm "No, you can't do what you're planning, to travel down the Yukon, because, blah, blah, blah." I was still holding back as Paul tapped on the window part of the door, one of those frosted kind that light penetrates but that you can't see through, the kind the government always seems to buy.

"Come in."

I imagined Alan Innes-Taylor would be a recent graduate of an established Canadian University—gung ho and totally oblivious to his shortcomings as an authority on the Yukon, having read a few books over a couple of years.

We stepped through the door into his office, a maze of filing cabinets, sheaves of papers, picture portfolios, and shelves jammed with books. Crates of what I guessed to be even more of the same were stacked wherever room could be found. The one spare part of a wall, other than for the desk where he sat, was occupied by a map table, with rolls of maps stacked on top. The walls were a montage of interesting photos, mostly old: a stern-wheeler in Five Finger Rapids, a sailing ship caught in pack ice, a dog team with its fur-clad musher. Above the map table hung a sign, framed and glassed over, its message simply

A Journey of a Thousand Miles Begins with One Step
— Chinese Proverb

Innes-Taylor turned in his chair, leaving for a moment what he was writing.

"What can I do for you?"

He was at once imposing. He was trim, wide-shouldered, and tall, even sitting down. I guessed him to be in his early sixties, and he looked fit as a fiddle. He wore casual clothes, chosen for comfort rather than formality. I pictured him kneeling, stirring the coals of a campfire, and I sensed he had done that many times.

We introduced ourselves. He remained seated, we stood.

"We'd like to go down the Yukon and were told you're the man to see," I offered.

"The three of you?" he asked. "What kind of boat, canoe?"

"Well, no," I answered, "Ruthie's not coming. We'll be three or four guys. Paul and I are just checking everything out. We're hoping to cross the Chilkoot Pass to Lake Bennett and build a raft there, then go down the Yukon making a record of all we find of historic interest. We'll be doing everything by hand, like they did in the old days during the Stampede." I paused, then continued. "I guess what we really need to know is if it can still be done today."

The silence, however short, was unbearable. My heart was throwing a rod.

"Yes, it can be done," he said, removing his glasses deliberately. Then, pointing to two folding chairs and a large wooden chair by his desk, he asked us to sit down. "Tell me, where are you from?"

Many more questions followed. At first they were basic, such as whether or not we could swim, but they became much more complex. I enjoyed answering them and soon saw their gist. Alan Innes-Taylor, while acknowledging the Yukon could be rafted, hadn't decided whether or not he thought we could do it. His questions then, sought information on our potential for such an undertaking. Following that line, he was suggesting that to do what we planned would require a change in our ways and thinking. His only way to guess whether or not we could make the changes was to mine our backgrounds for information, for clues. It was exciting. Boy! In a situation like that, confronted with knowledge and experience far superior to your own, all you can do is lay yourself wide open and soak up every drop of knowledge that falls your way. I sure hadn't reckoned on anything like that when we knocked on the door!

In turn we learned a bit about Alan Innes-Taylor. He'd come to Whitehorse in the early 1920s, as a constable in the Royal Northwest Mounted Police. He was in Whitehorse for a number of years and was a veteran of the long winter dogsled patrols in the Arctic before he left

23

the police to sail the West Indies for a year, alone in an open boat, living off the sea. He sailed before the mast and whaled in the Antarctic. He was with Admiral Byrd on his first two Antarctic expeditions and journeyed in the Arctic with the great Canadian explorer Vijhalmar Steffanson. He served during World War II as an Allied expert on Arctic survival and equipping. In the 1950's he returned to the Yukon River with his family, making his home in Eagle, Alaska, before coming full circle to Whitehorse. Now he was working for the Yukon government doing a historical retracement on the Yukon River, marking the locations of former settlements. Our plans meshed with his.

"Now, then, what can I do to help you on your way?" he asked. He was offering to help us! At least we hadn't flunked our test. Whether we had passed it or not could only be proven by time and the river.

We wanted only the answers we needed to get our expedition moving, yet the questions poured out. Firearms? Royal Canadian Mounted Police. He referred us to Staff Johnson. Hunting? Fishing? Game Branch. Timber at Lake Bennett? White Pass. And so on. He was a complete clearing house for the Yukon wilderness.

We were in a frenzy for a couple of days, following down our leads. The roadblocks I feared would end our trip had only surfaced in my imagination.

We could have no handguns in Canada, which was just fine with us; none of us had them or really believed in them. We wanted firearms for two basic reasons: to hunt for food and to protect ourselves against bears, which, on occasion, unfortunately, can be dangerous. We would be a floating open-air market with dried, salted, and smoked meats in profusion. We might also stop in one place long enough for any critter in the area with a good nose to home in on us. Yes, the proper firearm and the ability to use it can be a good thing in the bush. We always had one in surveying camps in the forests, and twice we needed to use it.

We could have rifles, said Staff Johnson, but the conditions were dependent on Game regulations. Check Game Branch he said. Aha—we could not hunt, being nonresidents and Yanks, but a rifle, kept properly packed, could be transported through Canada in our vehicle. We got permission to cut our trees at Bennett, in British

24

Columbia, by phone from Atlin. The folks at McBride Museum in true northern spirit offered us all the help they could, including a place to stay on our way back through. It was like that. I've never slid through bureaucracy in such a pleasant or expedient fashion. The phone was actually an asset.

Somewhere along the line Dan Johnson, chief of the Carcross Indians, was suggested as the best source for information concerning timber at Lake Bennett's head. He could tell us, for example, if there was any! We piled in the bus and drove the forty miles to Carcross, eager to talk to the chief but just as eager to get a glimpse of Lake Bennett. Carcross, a small community on the White Pass and Yukon Route Railroad, sits astride the channel of a river that connects the foot of Lake Bennett to Nares Lake.

We sat with Dan in the old Caribou Hotel and learned that he trapped out of Bennett, at the head of the lake. There was timber all right, second growth was replacing the harvest taken at the turn of the century.

"Best logs are up King River," he said, speaking softly, soothingly. "I don't know what its name is on the map." He thought about it, then went on, "Homan, I think, but we call it King River, since the old days. You can't mistake it, it's only a mile or so from Bennett." He was a small man, and very unassuming. Gray had just begun to touch his temples. Another walking encyclopedia, I thought, for the right questions.

Dan invited us to visit with him and his wife on our way back through, and pointed out his house across the "river." Nares Lake and Lake Bennett were hardly a mile apart. We prepared to leave. We were in a hurry to be gone so we could return all the sooner.

We were at the north end of Lake Bennett and at the foot of the mountains. Bennett Station was somewhere back in the heart of the Coast Mountains at the lake's head, twenty-six miles away, under massive, ugly gray clouds. The wind whistled down the lake, whitecaps garnishing its translucent green water. It was as if the lake, like a troll, was a mountain creature, filled with disdain for the land beyond. It was ominous, yet exciting! Soon we would return and voyage the lake on a raft!

We walked out on the railroad bridge. Our raft would have to go under it. The distance between its single pier and the pilings along the shore measured something like twenty-five feet, by pacing. The water-weathered pilings suggested high water would be about three and a half feet below the bridge girders. Things to remember.

Four days after arriving in Whitehorse, Ruthie and I were on our way back to Anchorage. Paul flew; he had to start working that Monday for his grubstake. On the way out of town we stopped to check out with Alan Innes-Taylor and thank him for his invaluable assistance.

"I don't know how you'll get around the hydro dam here," he said, half musing to himself. "Did you check the railroad bridge at Carcross?"

I smiled and answered, "We have the green light; let's see if we get this far before we worry about it too much." He nodded and we left. The sign in his office, "A Journey of a Thousand Miles Begins with One Step," would linger in my memory.

Back in Anchorage we could finally begin, really begin, and we could plan on four. We called Jerry, who was waiting for the signal to move out, and our lost partner finally broke cover with a four-word postcard from Switzerland. "Wait for me," it said almost beseechingly. It was signed simply, "Bob." Jerry was first to arrive.

"Here, here, where's this Yukon River?" greeted us at the airport, coming from a bearded, long-haired man who vaguely resembled the clean-shaven fellow I'd lived with in college. But then, I was sporting a beard now too.

"Bet you didn't recognize me," Jerry said as we shook hands.

"Oh no!" I answered in mock agreement. He was a full head taller than anybody who got off the plane, and but for the lack of "cork" shoes, the smell of oil, and a liberal dose of sawdust, he might have just stepped out of the crummy, home from a day of falling timber. Red suspenders, well-used and faded to near-pink, held up his equally faded denim jeans, and crossed over the ubiquitous hickory shirt, hallmark of the Pacific Coast logger.

Paul leaned back roaring with laughter. "Well Wallace, it's about time we met, let's go have a beer!" The rest of the evening—and it was a long one—we filled Jerry in on our adventure.

Now, Mom and Dad knew Jerry; it was going to be hard to hide him in the house without some sort of explanation, so I finally had my "confrontation" with Dad. I told him about our plan and tried to show him it wasn't harebrained by explaining all that had transpired to date.

To my surprise there wasn't any criticism, just a smile that stretched all the way up to ruffle his brow and a shake of his head that made me think he was wondering what he was ever going to do about me! Whew! I could live with that. Then, by golly if he didn't offer to let me paint the house in case I needed just a little bit more money! I did!

Jerry offered to help me paint the house so we became a house-painting duo. We'd paint and talk and talk and paint, generally catching up on each other's lives. Jerry had just finished circling the globe with a pal of his. Paul was working, so we were back in a holding pattern waiting for Bob, though we still devoted our evenings to planning, mostly how to get out of Anchorage as quickly as we could. We didn't wait long for Bob.

He was all smiles and tanned from the European spring. He hadn't been kidnapped or anything else as exciting, the rat. He'd been traveling with a geology class from AMU in Anchorage. It so happened a girl friend of his was in the class. He'd arranged to meet her in Copenhagen. Some guys have all the luck! But he was ready to go and got right into putting the picture-taking gear together.

For the next couple of days Jerry and Bob worked together gathering this and that and generally getting to know each other. I was left to finish splashing paint on the house, with only myself to talk to. I was done just about the time Paul had his grubstake together. June was slipping away.

A cacophony of activity preceded our departure from Anchorage. Every permutation of the four of us worked simultaneously on a dozen projects, always at full speed. In the morning each outlined what he wanted to do, and Bob's VW bus was allotted accordingly. My bus, alas, friend and faithful companion for three years, had been sold in a major effort to arrest the unexplainable yet continual erosion of my funds.

We were in need of a canoe to give us access to regions and areas where we couldn't take a raft. Purchasing it would leave us low on funds, so we sought local support to the tune of a canoe and paddles. We got it, from an Anchorage wholesaler who I thought at the time must have wondered if he was truly a champion of lost causes. I was sure he wasn't, but how could he know?

Everything, I mean everything, found its way into Dad's garage: ropes, tent, tools, cooking gear, boxes of supplies, not to mention a case of mosquito repellent. Every night Dad checked our growing pile of junk and reminded us there weren't steamboats anymore to haul it for us!

The morning of June 27 we were packed, ready for the road to Whitehorse. Bob's bus squatted forlornly, stuffed to the max, even with the personal limit of one pack each. To boot we would be five in the bus, the members of the Klondike-Yukon Expedition (as we now called ourselves, somewhat humorously since the confusion that was us in no way resembled the nicely organized, efficient operation that name evoked) and Jim Isbell, a friend who would drive us over and return with the bus.

I wasn't sure who solicited whom, but my mother would drive her car to Whitehorse with our overflow, including the canoe tied on top. The last thing a twenty-six-year-old wants as he begins a journey of this kind is his mother—what with the normal amount of beer drinking and girl chasing to be done—yet she was excited for me and always up for a bit of adventure. Really, I think she just wanted to see that I was properly fed and had clean socks before I started. Whatever the case, her help was needed and much appreciated. Jim's mother would ride along to keep her company.

So we tore out of Anchorage sometime around the crack of noon. We talked about our adventure along the way, but everything was too conditional, like stacking blocks. There wasn't any sense in worrying about the third block if the second one fell off the first. At least we had the first—we were on our way—so we concerned ourselves with having a good time. Mom and Mrs. Isbell drove slowly but we couldn't keep up, not with visiting certain innkeepers and their waterholes along the way!

The next day we were miles apart, and at the border there was a message. The Canadian customs man, after looking us over wonderingly, asked, "Which one of you is Keith Tryck?"

"Right here," I answered, wondering why he picked on me.

"Your mother says to hurry on, she can't wait forever!" Ha! Big explorers were we, with Mother leading the way. But we did hurry a bit.

We arrived in Whitehorse on June 29. The Yukon had been free of ice for more than a month; the lakes we had to sail before reaching the Yukon had been free of ice for two weeks. That afternoon I cracked a new surveyor's transit book, the waterproof kind that floats, and made the first entry in my log:

McBride Museum is letting us use one of their old log exhibit buildings to pack and rearrange our gear in. It used to be the telegraph office in the old days. They're fixing it up, but it isn't open to the public yet. I guess we'll sleep here too.

Alan Innes-Taylor is getting maps for us and he's trying to arrange for the City of Whitehorse to help us move our raft and equipment around the hydro dam above town. We'll know when we get this far.

There's a dam at the bottom of Marsh Lake, something like 25 miles upriver from the hydro dam. It's equipped with a lock for boats and we now have all kinds of dimensions for the lock, each different. The best way, as usual, to find out about the lock will be to go there and measure it ourselves.

Bob left his wallet a hundred miles back up the road, and we're still waiting for the canoe, so Bob headed back in the bus looking for both.

Jerry and Paul are purchasing food and equipment, probably at the Whitehorse Inn Tavern. I'm sitting here in the telegraph office trying to make some sense and order out of the piles of junk. And Jim—Jim thinks everything is hilarious and is taking pictures of it all. Which reminds me, it's time to set up the photography record books, survey-style. . . .

Bob returned with his wallet all right, and the van, but he hadn't found Mom and Mrs. Isbell back along the road with the canoe, broken down and fuming about our absence, as I feared. Instead he found them in a motel room fuming about us ignoring them. You try putting an expedition together sometime and see if it's any easier. It worked out, though. We let them cook dinner for us in the campground above Miles Canyon that night. Sort of the last supper.

After dinner Jim and I dropped the guys off at the tavern, took the bus, and headed south for Marsh Lake. The highway crosses the river at its foot, just above the dam and lock, so we could drive to it.

Crazy, I thought. Skagway is only 120 miles from Whitehorse by rail, yet our return would be one hassle after another: first the Chilkoot Pass (we'd agreed on it as our route to avoid the railway through the White Pass), then building a raft. Would it be made of dry logs or green logs? What size would it be? After the raft was built we had to sail it through a seventy-mile chain of inland fjords—Bennett, Nares, Tagish, and Marsh Lakes—just the five-mile stretch between Tagish and Marsh Lakes could be considered river. We had heard tales of storms hammering out of the mountains, too, storms that brewed as the ocean winds and moist air currents hit the Coast

Mountains and that came screaming down over the lakes in gales that sent three-deck lake steamers scurrying for shelter. We wouldn't be able to just scurry away though; we'd have to tough it out. We had a sail, a surplus Spanish Army parachute with instructions for its use in both Spanish and German. It was probably made in Hitler's factories before we were born. The directions didn't say anything about the parachute doubling as a storm-tested sail.

The sail and its holding mast would have to come down to go under the railroad bridge at Carcross, go up again to sail Nares and Tagish Lakes, come down for the bridge crossing the short stretch of river between Tagish and Marsh Lakes, go up for Marsh Lake, then down again for the highway bridge at its foot—not to mention the dam there, the first dam we'd encounter and the one Jim and I were on our way to check out. From there we had a river for twenty-five miles or so to Miles Canyon, a rushing channel barely a hundred feet wide between rugged columnar basalt walls. During the gold rush it gave the Stampeders nightmares, some of them terminal. It has been tamed by the hydro dam below it and is navigable for boats, but it still sports a powerful current and the sharp turn into it is just as sharp, the rugged stone walls just as hard. How would a raft fare without power for easy maneuverability? If we ever collided with the canyon, something would have to give. And if we made it through Miles Canyon into the calm reservoir behind the hydro dam, we could completely forget any thought of running around or over it with the raft in the water. From the spillway the river drops, drops, drops, nearly straight down, and then arches back up, spewing tons upon tons of green Yukon River into foam on the stone riverbed. Nothing could come through it intact. We had to go around the hydro dam. How? Truck? Log by log?

It was too much, too much to think about, too much to worry about. The lock. We pulled off the road behind the steel highway bridge, bumping a quarter mile to what looked like an old railroad trestle with doors of heavy planks that could be raised and lowered, filling the narrow gaps between the log pilings. The dam was used to control the water level of the hydro reservoir. It seemed there were only five or so feet of difference between the water levels above and below the dam, yet the current was very strong, and the water boiled through the trestle and its latticelike bracing when the doors were up. The lock was on our side, we would have to pass the dam through it, no way through the trestle. Jim and I climbed over and around the lock taking measurements then checking them before coming up with its inside dimensions: 38 feet by 11.6 feet. Then we checked to make sure the lock worked, and the gates wouldn't move. Perhaps it was jammed. The third time we tried, we read the directions first. Success.

2

A Raft is Built in Buccaneer Cove

"I think we're slowing down," Bob said.

I'd noticed it too. For a while, on leaving Whitehorse, we'd roamed up and down the train exploring. We were riding on a freight–passenger combination train, six coaches with a string of ore cars between us and the locomotives. The coaches were small and quaint, each named for a local lake—Tagish, Tutshi, Bennett—and had open walkways between them, where you weren't supposed to stand but did anyway, until the chill numbed the novelty and romance of exalting fresh air and wind tossed hair. According to the conductor, the coaches had been built in the 1870's, when Britannia ruled the seas and Queen Victoria was in her prime. They'd been in service on the White Pass since completion of the railroad in 1899. Many of the Stampeders must have ridden the same coaches, I thought, headed for the stony draw to Skagway in comfort, the same canyon so many had fought so hard to claw their way up. As near as I could tell the coaches hadn't changed much in the three-quarters of a century they'd been in use, either, except that in days past the oil-fired Yukon stove in each had burned wood.

The end of the lake was in sight.

"That must be the King River over there," I said, pointing to a wooded valley a mile or more across the lake.

Since leaving Carcross, where we'd had just enough time to race out and measure the two bridge spans at twenty-two feet each, we'd ridden south into the mountains on a winding railbed, a chiseled ledge of stone along the east shore of Lake Bennett. Crystalline water lapped at the foot of the railroad embankment on the one side and a wall of sheer rock rose up on the other, so close to the train it was dizzying to focus on.

We'd angled our chairs to face Lake Bennett (nobody sat on the other side of the coach) and turned the register on the Yukon stove down so our coach would be comfortable. Most of the people on the train were elderly tourists. Why are they always so cold? No one seemed irritated though; the people who wanted a warmer coach left for one of the others. Those who preferred a cooler seat moved to ours or to the one Paul and Jerry were in, where they were temporarily holed up in deep conversation with two blonde Swedish girls from Whitehorse.

We joined Jerry and Paul as we entered the yard at Bennett and were off the train before the unnerving chorus of steel brakes choking steel wheels had died. We were in the mountains all right; it felt like it, smelled like it. But it just didn't seem right. We hadn't come up one bit in elevation, just south from Carcross along the lake.

The train from Skagway, a twin to ours, was already at the station; we could see its passengers eating in a large dining hall, one of the two wings to the station. We were ushered into the other wing by a matronly hostess and her brood of young waitresses, all smiling in their trim white uniforms. We were then seated boarding-house-style at rows of tables with settings in place, and served with heaping platters of roast beef and gravy, potatoes, and tinned vegetables. We were famished and ate accordingly, and in the process of asking the girls for second, third, and (by now it was embarrassing) fourth platters of food, we found the solution to a very pressing problem.

One of the waitresses, an attractive, dark-haired gal from Vancouver, after hearing our plans, offered to let us store the gear we wouldn't be carrying over the Chilkoot Pass in front of the trailer she shared with another girl. We left the dining room early, though not before polishing off a couple apple pies, and unloaded our gear from the baggage car, stacking it in front of the pink trailer and placing the canoe on top of the gear to serve as a rain cover. All that remained aboard were our packs for the trail.

We returned to the dining room and chatted with the girls, who were busy clearing tables under the watchful eye of the hostess. We helped, in a way, by finishing off uneaten pieces of pie while the

34

railroad crews and their locomotives swapped trains, each to return the way they had come.

Our visit was short; there would hopefully be more time later.

"Might not be too bad building our raft near here," I said in a low voice as we filed aboard the waiting train.

"Mmm, precisely what I was thinking," Jerry answered. "I spotted six girls, counting the one who just peeked at us from the kitchen."

"Six? That's great!" Paul responded as we crowded down the aisle. "That leaves two for the section crew!"

We climbed steadily from Bennett to the White Pass summit, then descended magnificently through tunnels, under avalanche sheds and finally onto latticework trestles, delicately suspended over foaming cascades. The shadow of the old trail was sometimes traceable in the valley below.

The more excited you are to reach your destination, the slower a train seems to go. Pulling into Skagway was no exception. The tracks skirt the town to the east along the valley wall, where we could see the bare backsides of the false-fronted buildings that flank the streets. We picked an abandoned building to spend the night in, just in case we could find nothing better, finally pulled into the depot, cleared customs, and headed for town.

It was Saturday night; the evening was ahead of us. We decided, unanimously, to send ourselves off on the proper footing. We would "blow 'er in"—party it up good one last time before hitting the Chilkoot trail. Ah, and that we did, splitting our time between Skagway's two night spots, our packs stacked in the corner of one, Moe's Tavern. It was a dandy night; there was a hometown crowd of perhaps fifty souls between the two bars, and a handful of out-of-towners, most preparing to catch the Sunday ferry for Juneau and points south. We alone of the late revelers were heading for the Chilkoot in the morning. There were people to visit with and girls to dance with and challenges to be made at the pool table. Except for the couple of times one of the local wives clobbered her husband (hard, too) for dancing too close to another man's wife, there were no awkward moments. Jerry and I even managed to add twenty dollars to a husky gent's pocket in an ill-fated attempt to strike it rich in a 4–5–6 game at the bar.

Sometime after midnight, when Jerry and I started thinking about sleep, and Bob and Paul were still going strong but not in sight, we started spending more time with two gals from Inuvik, in the Canadian Arctic. They were teachers, headed south after the long winter. At just the right moment we mentioned we didn't have any place to sleep, and they obligingly suggested we join them at the stately old Golden North Hotel, where they had a room with two spacious canopied beds. What could we say? Now if we could just get there before Bob and Paul spotted us. . . .

2 July 1972

Sunday, Skagway, on a clear, gorgeous day, about 70°. Skagway is a beautiful old town, with boardwalks, a handful of gravel streets, old cars, old people, and many personable buildings dating from the gold rush. Jerry and I are lying on a nice big lawn, a vacant lot on the corner of Fifth and Broadway. Surrounding us are buildings and warehouses that have been here long enough for all the gravel around them to be covered with green; the shrubs and trees have had years to grow and spread, making their tenancy permanent. It's a funky town; nobody's in any great rush. The mountains on either side, split by the sea and a long wharf, narrow swiftly to the White Pass. The mountains are exquisite with the heavy forest mantle flowing up to alpine mosses that give way to hard rock and snowy peaks.

Paul and Bob found us just after noon, asleep on the lawn, and after purchasing food for the trail we shouldered packs and strode out of Skagway on the gravel road that snakes along the Lynn Canal ten miles to Dyea. We were there by supper time. We were warned there was little to see at Dyea but were still not quite ready for what we found.

Where Dyea had been, with streets and boardwalks and power poles, where once the din of creaking wagon wheels, the whinnying of pack horses, the bellowing of oxen responding to yelling, cursing teamsters, and voices from restaurants, saloons, gambling and dance halls, sawmills and laundries and machine shops had all filled the air, there was now hardly a sign that men and women had ever built a city there. Nothing stood but the forest, a new forest of youthful spruce and hemlock. Dyea's last remains were flat on the ground, snow-mashed jumbles of gray, rotting lumber and rusting scraps of iron. Where the lumber was gone, scavenged through the years for this and that, only holes, one-time cellars and basements, remained. What now were faint trails, too straight to belong to the forest, were once Dyea's streets. All other incongruities in the land from far back in the forest to the tide flats were hidden under a blanket of dark azure velvet—waist-high fields of the blue plant lupine.

On the tidelands, where tons and tons of Stampeders and their outfits had been piled unceremoniously by the workers who feverishly unloaded the steamers, two parallel rows of rotted piling stumps, like old couples standing side by side, stretched forlornly a quarter of a mile to the sea.

Dyea and the Chilkoot trail got the jump on Skagway in 1896. Healey's trading post was there and Indian packers were available for hire, on a trail that had been in use for years. For a couple years Dyea kept its lead, but Skagway, the site of Billy Moore's homestead and the stone wharf he'd built with considerable foresight, offered a better port. During the thick of the rush the two boomtowns were neck and neck, but Skagway, even with its Soapy Smith and his gang of frontier con men, won in the end, absolutely and mercilessly, because the "Irish Prince," Michael J. Heney, elected to build his railroad through the White Pass. It was finished by early 1899—and so was Dyea.

We camped that night along the Taiya River, where the road from Skagway bridges it. It was past midnight by the time each of us had ambled back to our camp in the forest, satisfied with his roaming of Dyea. We slept in the open, sharing two mosquito bars pitched crosswise over our heads and shoulders. The sky was cloudless, but we kept our ponchos handy in case nature played a trick on us.

The sun was high overhead when we left camp the next day. Again, not a cloud marred the sky. A scorcher of a day was on us. The one thing you are never truly prepared for in the North is hot weather, uncomfortably hot weather, especially along the coast where varying degress of gray, misty, or rainy days are more common. We could at least look forward to crossing many mountain brooks with their cool, bubbling waters.

The trail led out of Dyea on the west side of the Taiya River. At first it was a road more than a trail. It was excellent going, but hot. We should have started earlier. The valley was a huge reflector oven, preheated and ready for baking. In short order we were facing the Taiya River, a rushing power in the valley too deep and swift to ford. A tram for crossing was suspended on pulleys below a cable stretched

37

taut between two trees on opposite banks. We loaded ourselves and our packs on it and crossed two at a time in three trips, almost as complicated as the old riddle of how you get the duck, the fox, and the grain across the river intact! On the far bank, close against the valley wall, we intersected the trail that was apparently most often used by Chilkoot travelers today.

Our road was excellent hiking; an easy grade continued up the valley, but for the most part it was open to the beating sun. Jerry and Paul were setting a blistering pace, one of them right out of a logging camp, the other coming off a season of world-class skiing. I was buying every mile at that rate with blisters, yet I was foolish enough to keep the pace. The crossings of small streams were a relief, a chance to soak a steaming head, a chance to drink cool, clear water, true mountain dew. But the relief was only temporary. I continued to be bathed in tepid salty sweat, my feet continued to cook without relief.

The devil must have started working in my brain. As we crossed brook after brook on single- or double-log foot bridges I began wondering how nice it would feel to dunk my feet, boots and all, then walk along in a cool bath. I tried it. It felt heavenly.

About three miles out we passed an abandoned sawmill and soon lost our road, entering the rain (ha!) forest, on a well-beaten trail. Now my boots were really heavy—leaden, full of water. My feet softened right up and were soon just as hot as before. I dunked them again; some guys never learn. Instead of a couple of hot spots rubbing into blisters, my feet when wet seemed to be blistering everywhere. And I thought I had problems before. Soon it was easier not to think about my feet. I slowed my pace and began to enjoy the forest.

We were on an elfin trail, a fantasy trail in the forest. Luxuriant spongy moss made even the steepest and roughest sidehills pour instead of jut. From above, a kaleidoscope of sunlight and shadow drifted through the tall hemlock and spruce. We walked along through the flashing contrasts. The trail bore little resemblance to the road of mire and muck churned by a hundred thousand footsteps into black reeking ooze, the trail of 1898. For us there were only subtle reminders: grades too even, too consistent for nature's hand, grooves in the trail too deep to have been made by the packers of today, the rotted out abutments of once substantial bridges, stretches of old corduroy wagon road crossing bogs.

A Raft is Built in Buccaneer Cove

Bob had fallen back with me and we pulled into the Canyon City shelter as Jerry and Paul were stirring soup into boiling water. We had gained something like four hundred feet in elevation in just about eight miles.

"Feet bothering you?" Jerry asked.

I didn't really need to respond, the way I hobbled into camp was evidence enough, but I answered optimistically, "Yes, but as soon as I dry them off, change socks, and tape some blisters I'll be in action again. That wet business is for the birds!"

"Did you guys find Canyon City?" Bob asked.

"I figure it's up the trail a piece," Jerry answered. "We can look it over when we pull out. Soup's ready, give me your cups."

The Canyon City shelter is the first of two log cabins the state of Alaska has built along the Chilkoot trail, in addition to opening it and laying log bridges across streams. It lies in an idyllic hollow with a clear, bubbling brook running through the site into the Taiya River. An hour's rest there was like a full night's sleep.

On the trail again I felt like a new person. Dry feet and dry socks made all the difference in the world, especially with the feet beneath them wrapped in adhesive tape like a mummy's!

We took a side trip to the ruins of Canyon City, crossing the Taiya about half a mile from the shelter on a beautiful miniature suspension bridge. During the rush, Canyon City was a humming community of more than twenty permanent log buildings, including a steam plant for generating electricity. It was located on the Taiya's rocky flood plain, now an alder jungle where one solitary building, already fallen to its knees, continues to fight the relentless forces of nature. The huge boiler was there, all that remained of the power plant, and it would outlast us all. Seventy-five years had only painted its thick iron hide with rust. Rearranged stones indicated where wagon roads and trails had been. Along them, through the dense foliage, wagon wheel rims, sled runners, and bits of lumber grasped for the surface below layers of leafy humus. Clumps of rust proved to be the remains of cast-iron cook stoves, a filigreed "Monarch" or "Imperial" once emblazoned on oven doors. Rusted out and far beyond useful, they had nevertheless outlasted the buildings that once housed them. There were stoves with single ovens, double ovens, and hot water reservoirs, stoves that had smelled of baking bread, or had dried

39

stinking socks, stoves that bleary eyes had focused on while wet, cold hands, chalk-white and pruney, were turned slowly, absently, in front of them.

We returned to the trail and began the five-mile ascent to Sheep Camp, the second and last shelter on the Alaskan side of the boundary, and immediately embarked on a steady, steep climb, for above Canyon City the valley pinches the Taiya into a narrow, deep canyon, and the trail seeks its east shoulder. We crossed stretches of exposed glacier-smoothed rock for the first time in our climb and began to encounter cast offs of long ago: a "granite" or porcelain cook pan, a coffee pot, a basin that had grown into the moss where it had fallen. On achieving the canyon's shoulder, the trail leveled off.

Bob and I, trailing behind again, arrived at the Sheep Camp shelter in the early evening, after a final, gradual two-mile ascent over a stony trail that once more paralleled the Taiya, but above the canyon. For the first time the mountain tops were occasionally visible, blue glacier ice and enamel snowfields covering rocky peaks. The air was blessedly cooler. A breeze suggested timberline was at hand.

A group of packers had preceded us at Sheep Camp, led by a lean, rangy Skagway guide, Skip Burns. He was a likable fellow with an easy-going manner and we commiserated about this and that but mostly the trail—which he'd crossed many times—and the weather, which all agreed was unusually hot. Skip and his group were staying the night in the shelter cabin, a one-room, log bunkhouse with wood stove and overhanging porch, a mate to the Canyon City shelter. I looked inside the cabin, where his youthful charges, from fifteen to fifty were laying out their bedrolls.

"Check out the table," Skip suggested.

I did. It was a simple, weathered table with what looked like a bite out of one side that made little sense to me.

"It's an old gambling table," Skip informed me. "That's where the dealer sat. I guess they found it around here when they built the cabin."

Sheep Camp, named for a hunter's camp before the gold rush, was the last good spot for shelter and firewood before leaving the forest on the Chilkoot trail. A sheep camp: It was synonymous with inhospitable heights, the bastion of the sure-footed sheep.

We moved out after dinner, which was a concoction of

macaroni, cheese, and blood-and-tongue sausage, the remains of which not even Skip's dog would eat. We elected to reach the pass that night, though night you could hardly call it. We were only a fortnight past the longest day, and night was a long, glorious twilight.

The tunnel forest was behind us, with the tall conifers consigned to lower, lusher elevations. What conifers that did venture into the land above Sheep Camp were few and far apart, twisty and stunted. It was the undisputed realm of the alder, small trees and shrubs of the birch family. The trail became more determined, climbing almost constantly, with only a few short downhill stretches for relief. Patches of snow lay in the hollows.

"Hey guys, there's a grave over here," I called. For some reason I had looked in the right place at the right time. Cradled in a cleft of stone twenty yards off the trail was a weathered plank headboard.

"Can you make out the name?" Paul asked.

I ran my fingers slowly over the coarse wood grain. Just the faintest hint of lettering remained in raised wood that had defied the weathering of the wind, snow, and sun because of its now-gone protective paint.

"Maybe Hugh or John," I answered, "but I can't be sure."

What an immense cradle to rest in. No trees of any kind to shade the stars, a niche to snuggle into for eternity, facing the sunset not from the horizon but from high above, on a rim of blue ice and jagged stone braided with threads of trickling water.

Who could it have been? Man? Woman? Had foul play taken a hand, or was nature alone responsible? All kinds of things to think about as we quietly returned to the trail.

I was still conjuring up possibilities when a muffled report from the skyline reached us. I turned in time to see a colossal chunk of glacier falling silently as the sound of its release echoed around us. In an instant it met the valley's flanks, and in two tremendous bounding collisions was riven to pieces. By the time the sound reached us—two titanic crunches and then one great roar—we were viewing a Niagara of icy slush spewing from the rock face, spilling and ricocheting down stone battlements. As the slush river reached the valley floor (perhaps a quarter mile from the wooden gravemark) burying three or four acres of alder forest under a blanket of soggy pulp, we could still hear its trail on the stone.

We entered the world of snow for the last two miles to the pass.

The well-worn trail shortly disappeared under a white crust, as did the rusty Chilkoot Railroad and Transport Company tram cable, the bent iron telegraph poles and sagging wire, and the youthful Taiya River.

We moved steadily upward to the foot of the pass. We could see it now, and halted near where the "scales" had been, where men willing to pay packers to carry their outfits over the top weighed their loads. Twelve hundred and fifty feet above us and 3,700 feet above sea level was the notch that had once daily swallowed armies of men. Somewhere nearby, enterprising men had collected their tolls, fifty cents a head, for the use of the 1500 steps they had carved in the ice that stretched to the summit.

We started our ascent just after midnight. The sun was toying with the horizon far beyond the mountains to the north. We were in shadow, in a vast empty bowl incredibly silent and still. We could whisper to one another from hundreds of feet apart, and nature's acoustics carried our voices perfectly. The snow was a luminous white, the stone that jutted through it dull and dark. The valley's stark contrasts had a weird effect. We were moving up the back side of a gargantuan ladle, its white enamel chipped by the bare rock below.

We took turns kicking in sturdy steps and reached the summit at 2 A.M., passing a group of passive mountain goats barely two hundred feet away on rocky ledges. They alone watched us achieve the pass.

Dropping our packs on a rock outcrop straddling the divide, we scouted the summit, taking in its views. In the stone declivities and benches, hidden from the wind that must roar through the pass most of the time, were soft alpine mosses, covering the bedrock. A stone's throw into British Columbia, a log crib filled with rock appeared to have been some sort of anchor for the tram that in 1898 boasted the longest single aerial span in the world, over 2,200 feet between two of its log towers.

The Northwest Mounted Police post must have been close by, but certainly its remains were buried in snow now. More than 20,000 people were checked through here by the Mounties during the winter of 1897–98, each required to have supplies for a year, the amount Inspector Steele set as mandatory to ensure against a reoccurrence of the famine that Dawson, with thousands of new mouths to feed, was experiencing that very winter. The last steamboats into Dawson in the fall had come loaded not with food but with hardware, frills, and whiskey.

Depending on your tastes and pocketbook, a year's supply in those days weighed between 1200 and 2000 pounds. I sat on a ledge to do some figuring. Twenty-five hundred feet below me (two Empire State Buildings stacked on top of each other), was the valley we'd so recently left, and four miles away from that, Sheep Camp was hidden in the shadows of the forest, the Taiya singing nearby. If my outfit weighed 1500 pounds, it would take me twenty trips at seventy-five pounds a load to carry my outfit over the Chilkoot. In the course of doing it I would have to walk more than 1300 miles on the Chilkoot trail—enough to take me twice to the top of Mt. Everest from sea level with an excursion to the 16,000 foot level of Mt. McKinley thrown in as a side trip. One way or another, in the winter of 1897–98 thirty million pounds of freight came through the notch where I now sat.

I made my way back to our packs. Bob and Paul had unrolled their sleeping bags on patches of moss and were already inside them. My own body ached at the sight of their comfort, and I found a mossy spot for myself. The sky was coloring with the sunrise; we hadn't seen a cloud for two days. It was a far cry from the blizzard-wracked winter summit of 1897–98.

"Happy Fourth of July," Jerry said as he rolled his bed out near mine. I smiled; it was easier than answering. I was dog tired. I wondered if by some quirk of fate I was lying on the International Boundary, my feet in Alaska, my head in British Columbia.

The view from our summit was spectacular the next day, sun-bathed mountain and glacier, snowfield and rock everywhere we looked. The journey to the pass was behind us, the memories of the Stampede buried under tons of sun-reflecting snow. The day was exquisite and our hike would be Elysian. Before us stretched a broad white valley. Half a mile away and seven-hundred feet below us lay Crater Lake, the highest in the receding tiers of lakes, connected by brook and stream, that would lead us to Lake Bennett, sixteen miles away and 1600 feet below us. Crater Lake was still protected from the high summer sun by its thick winter ice, which blended smoothly into the snowfield we would traverse. At the center of the lake and on top of the ice, a large dish of melt water, a tiny lake on top of a lake, mirrored the light blue sky, lensing it aquamarine. The edges of Crater Lake were marked in places by fissures through the thick ice that reflected slivers of the emerald lake below.

Sore feet were ignored and bent into cold, stiff boots. They would warm up soon enough; it was a day for shirt sleeves and sunglasses. Our bellies were filled—with bread, butter, cheese, and sausage swilled down with tea made from melted snow cooked over our tiny gas stove—and we were off.

"All Yukon water from here!" Bob called out. And so it was. Spit anywhere now, and it would somehow find its way to the Bering Sea.

The hard summer snow made for excellent hiking, though Paul more than once longed openly for his "sliders," his skis. We followed the boot prints of other hikers along the side of the valley in a gradual descent to the foot of Crater Lake. We followed a stony brook from Crater Lake to Long Lake in an open defile. Snow line was near. In the sun, mosses and lichen were open to the air, yet in shadowy areas heavy drifts of snow persevered. Likewise the brook was sometimes open and burbling, but at other times it disappeared under ice and snow. We made our own trail down the rocky creek valley, sometimes on snow, sometimes on stone. We crossed back and forth on great ice arches, the stream beneath us dripping through blue grottos.

We found the Chilkoot trail once more at snow line and followed its worn stone track above Long Lake, an infinitely clear loch incapable of hiding anything in its crystal waters. At the foot of Long Lake we crossed the brook (now running in a neat bedrock notch), on a fine footbridge, newly built with handrails and all. By whom? I wondered.

We were in the forest once more as we traversed along the shore of Deep Lake, on what had been a wagon road. It was overgrown, the trail a one-lane path that dodged back and forth from one old rut to the other. The lake seemed to take on the color of the forest, more evergreen than it was emerald. The forest was different from the one we passed through on our way to the Chilkoot summit; now it was predominantly pine and spruce, lacking the coastal rain forest lushness. Hardly twenty miles from the Pacific we were entering the fringe of the vast interior forests, a different world. At the toe of Deep Lake our freshet of a stream dropped into a shadowy canyon of plunging rapids and misty waterfalls.

"Whoa for a look!" Paul called, and we dropped our packs on the trail and made our way along the rock to the rim of the canyon. The mist felt good, but the rushing water was too far below us so we returned to the trail thirsty.

44

"Here we go," I said, spying some sprouts along the trail's edge. "Fresh, succulent greenery from nature's garden." I picked a handful, popped two in my mouth and offered the rest around.

"How do you know they're edible?" Jer asked, looking one over. He seemed to be my only taker.

"Kids on the Kenai gave me some once when I was surveying down there," I answered. "Tasty, too."

"Ah, I'll wait till lunch," Jerry said, handing the buds to me. "Lindemann can't be too far away."

We were off again and soon striding down a long, magnificent grade to the rumbling accompaniment of the canyon. The grade was such that if you leaned forward and literally tossed your feet out in front of you you could really move. Long-legged Jerry had the best of it, too, and it was such good going I forgot the unpleasant acidy aftertaste from the buds. As I strode along, I remembered reading somewhere that an American soldier who escaped the Japanese takeover of the Philippines during World War II and spent the duration of the war with the guerillas said he could walk downhill indefinitely without sleep or food, or something to that effect. I mulled that for a while. It made sense, but just how long could you go down before you have to go up?

"Lindemann!" Jerry called from up front.

About time, I thought. I was really hot and feeling a bit queazy, possibly a touch of heat prostration. We'd really been smoking along.

In a moment I saw it too. The lake was silver-green and opaque, a big lake, not a mountain tarn. Glacial silt, which came to the lake from a different stream than the one we followed, was the cause of its color, I guessed.

I was truly relieved when I dropped my pack next to the cabin at the head of the lake. We were in the center of what had been Lindemann City, head of navigation and boat building for Chilkoot travelers. From here to Bennett, seven miles away, the Stampeders sought stands of timber to whipsaw into boards for boats that would carry them to the Klondike. I cared little. My blood seemed to be boiling, sweat oozed out of me, my stomach rolled with hunger to the point of nausea.

Something in the way I sagged down on the shady porch brought a quizzical look from my partners.

"I think I might have a touch of heat prostration," I answered confidently. "After I cool off and eat I'll be all right."

We had a good feed, the last of our trail food, and it seemed to help, even if the aching feeling I had in my stomach didn't disappear. I rested while the others looked about. Our building, a log cabin, was relatively new, and the only one I could see from where I lounged.

Paul, Bob, and Jerry returned one by one and I learned from them in bits and pieces that Lindemann, but for a rusty boiler and a lonely graveyard atop a hill, was what I saw—sparse forest, rusty tin cans, and multicolored shards of broken bottles. The Yukon Department of Corrections, with a camp just off the trail, was responsible for the improved trail, the bridges, and the cabin.

"Last hump ahead," Jerry called out, shouldering his pack. It was my signal and I followed, bringing up the rear as we moved out of Lindemann City. I was not well, I was sure of that now. I strained to keep up, even though we weren't burning up the trail as before. At the first creek we crossed, hardly a half mile from Lindemann City, I called a halt.

"Hang on, I gotta have water." I stumbled down to the creek, filled my cup, and drank. It was tepid, revolting. It seemed to release rancid gas from my stomach. I crawled back up to the trail wondering what was wrong with me. I stood up to shoulder my pack but I was waving around like a tree in the wind. I felt strange, disconnected, but I had just an instant to wonder what was happening to me. The next thing I knew I was lying on the ground! I was flabbergasted! I'd lost contact with my body and it had collapsed out from under me.

"What the hell. . . ?" Bob said, plainly shocked. He was staring down at me from way up in the sky.

I knew. "The buds I ate," I gasped, "wrong ones, poison." My thinking was clear, and I felt no pain, but my stomach was a cesspool of ilk . . . and up it came. The vomiting made me feel better, sort of.

Paul was kneeling beside me.

"Maybe it was skunk cabbage or something," I said, guessing his question. "I must have mistaken the buds."

I vomited again. I was running out of stuff in my stomach, yet the wracking convulsions continued.

"I'll be all right when I get my system cleaned out," I muttered to no one in particular. Jerry and Paul were shouldering their packs.

46

"We'll head into Bennett and call a doc in Whitehorse," Paul said, as they started out.

"Bring back some food," I called after them, "I've gone and wasted my lunch!" That brought a snicker. "A tin of fruit, I can use the sugar."

I vomited again while they watched. The relief I felt the first time was gone. It hurt, dry wracking heaves. I felt stupid too.

I tried for a parting jest, somehow to lighten the situation, which I felt terrible about. "Find out if I'm going to die!" I thought it was really funny. Nobody else did. Then it hit me. What if they thought I might?

I vomited again, and again, and again. My stomach was long dry, yet I felt like I had swallowed a gallon of battery acid. If my stomach hadn't been hooked to my insides it would have come up too. Convulsions consumed my whole body, exhausting me. Slimy strings of brown moss came up; I knew it was blood. Bob brought me water but my stomach rejected it. My insides had turned to acid; cramps knotted me from my knees to my shoulders.

I was like that for two hours before something clicked. In the end it reaffirmed my faith in education. Somehow I remembered studying in chemistry that bases neutralize acids. Base? Baking soda!

"Bob! Go back to that corrections camp and get some baking soda," I asked, mustering up enough energy for the words, but no more.

He was off at a trot, and I think I already felt better. I could at least hope for an end to the convulsions when the magic powder arrived.

It seemed he was gone forever, but it couldn't have been half an hour. He poured some of the soda in a cup of water then held it to my lips. I was too shaky to hold anything.

"Ahhhhh," he said, as he held the cup to my lips, opening his mouth wide like he was feeding a baby. Nothing like picking on a guy when he's down! I would have laughed, but a smile was all my body could muster.

That baking soda was water to a parched wanderer in the desert, morphine to a shell-blasted infantryman. Blah! Up it came; my stomach didn't trust it, but oh, it felt so good. The second load I kept down. It was like drinking a tiny genie who lovingly began massaging my body from the inside out. Peace at last.

I woke up to the soft buzz of voices. Paul had returned.

"Doctor says you're not going to die if you ate skunk cabbage," he said. I laughed, we all laughed. I felt like a million bucks, but very hungry.

"Where's the fruit?" I asked.

Paul handed me the opened can and I gulped it down, making short work of whatever it was.

"I'll be ready to go as soon as the fruit hits my system," I said. As if to verify my words I stood up and took a step. Wham! I was back down.

"Uh, maybe not," Bob said, smiling.

"Uh, maybe not," I mimicked, feeling rather foolish.

"Well, I'm tired," Paul said. "How about in the morning?" And so it was. We slept there, three heads under one mosquito bar.

Next morning I felt great, if a bit weak, and we took the trail to Bennett, winding through a high-altitude pine forest, a paper-thin covering of forest over stone, stone that jutted out regularly like kids' knees through trousers.

Paul and Jerry, I learned, had run the six miles into Bennett and the railroad station to use the phone to contact a doctor in Whitehorse. Paul ran back out with the fruit and the baking soda the doctor suggested, while Jerry remained in Bennett.

We met Jerry, though, three miles out of Bennett, where the trail left the forest to join the railroad tracks. Paul, Bob, and I each had a turn at describing the events of the previous evening, bringing Jerry up to date. As we resumed our walk along the tracks, I stepped up beside Jerry.

"How'd you make out with the girls at Bennett last night, you dog, trying to steal a march on your partners? Let's hear it," I asked jokingly.

"Well we've got to get our gear off their property immediately. I had to move it all across the tracks last night, by order of the White Pass section foreman. Man, I had a strange night," Jerry answered. Uh-oh. He was serious.

"Whatever you did to get us all booted out must have been good," Paul said. "All was quiet when I left."

"That's just it, I didn't do anything," Jerry responded. "After we got the call through to the doctor in Whitehorse and Paul headed back up the trail, I left the station house and walked tenderly over to our gear to get the first-aid kit and fix my feet up. I blistered them pretty bad running in with a full pack, that's why I stayed in Bennett. Anyhow, one of the girls, Melody, the tall brunette, saw what I was up to and offered to help, inviting me into the trailer where I could clean and dry my feet and do the job properly. I'd hardly gotten my shoes off when that big redheaded gal who runs the dining room came by and saw me in there with my shoes off. She made a terrible uproar about me being in the girls' quarters, went storming out and came back with the railroad foreman. I wasn't allowed to explain anything and was unceremoniously booted out and had to move all our gear across the tracks from the quarters, sore feet and all.

"Melody was really mad but had her job to consider. I just shook my head and told her we'd come back and visit some evening after things cool down. That old bag Mary runs that place with an iron hand, she reminds me of the Big Nurse from *One Flew Over the Cuckoo's Nest*. We are persona non grata with her and I personally want to get out of there as soon as possible."

There wasn't much discussion the rest of the way in; we would depart the railroad premises immediately. We plodded along in silence.

I have never perfected an easy way to walk along railroads. There is just no way to establish any kind of stride where you consistently hit the ties. About every third step my foot would come down in the hole between the ties unless I altered my stride. I'd get mad and walk outside the rails, on the edge of the embankment, but then, soon enough, I'd be tripping over the ends of the ties in a struggle to avoid having to pick my way along the side of the embankment. Back inside the rails I'd go, looking for greener pastures, step-and-a-half my way along again until I'd get mad and move back out to the shoulders. It's infuriating, to say the least. The only thing I can figure is some smart coolie back in the heyday of western railway building established tie spacing to fit the minced steps of Chinese laborers!

We didn't look twice at Bennett, but moved through the yard to our gear and launched the canoe. All four of us climbed in and stroked across the tip of Lake Bennett, past the mouth of the Lindemann River, the mile-long connector between lakes Lindemann and Bennett, then along the shore of the grass flats delta that separates the mouth of the King River and the Lindemann.

We entered the King River, calm and slow moving and about

fifty yards wide. We had little trouble paddling in the peaceful water along its banks. About half a mile up the King and out of sight of Lake Bennett we landed on a small island along the forest limit and chose it for our camp. While Bob and Jerry arranged camp, Paul and I returned to Bennett Station for more gear. Three trips it took, and the rest of the afternoon. On our first return the fire was going, the coffee was on, and the bean pot was being filled. Second trip we saw a makeshift kitchen under construction, and our canvas-wall tent, 12 by 14 feet, was shaping up, and by the end of the third trip it was time to eat beans and bacon!

The days that followed were like one of those flashing card machines in a penny arcade, the forerunners of motion pictures. Each day was like enough to the one before and the one after, but the first and last bore little resemblance to each other. Days and dates lost their meaning. Wind, clouds, and rain, the sun, the river, and the night orchestrated our actions as we came to grips with building a raft.

A quarter-mile up the King was a set of foaming rapids, the end of the road for our canoe. From there we traveled on foot. We didn't find any log jams, or any standing dead trees, as we had hoped. We would have to horse heavy green logs from the forest. Jerry located the best trees for our purposes in groves near the rapids.

Once more the sharp report of axes and the sweet singing of handsaws echoed through the forest along the King River. Jerry fell the trees while we limbed and bucked them into thirty-seven or eighteen-foot lengths. The logging was an efficient harvest; Jerry was in his element. Wherever he could, he chose diseased or otherwise imperfect trees—they all float the same—and felled them leading to the river. They were matchsticks to him as a logger, but formidable to us as hopeful rafters. We had to move them by hand as far as two hundred yards through the brush and to the water. Some weighed between one-half and three-quarters of a ton—we had no army of Stampeders or brace of oxen to move them with. Each log was a project in itself. We laid down skids and rollers of slick green alder to ease their deportation to the river bank, but no matter what we did to make the journey easier they all got there one way, pulled through the woods by block and tackle, log on one end of the line, human donkeys on the other, obeying hoarse cries to "heave . . . HEAVE!" When we were tired and hungry and had had enough for one day we fell into the canoe and floated to camp.

A Raft is Built in Buccaneer Cove

Saw a black bear about 300 feet from our island, just upstream and across the river. Decided to leave one man in camp from here on out, just in case. Can't afford to feed the bear too. Moved grub into a hole dug in the river bank, then at night we put the canoe upside-down on top. If he comes snooping while we're asleep he'll surely knock the aluminum canoe over, making lots of racket. I hope he just scares himself right away!

Leaving a man in camp proved to be a multifaceted boon. It was nice knowing camp was secure from the local four-footed grub thieves, but it was heaven knowing that after a tough day of logging you didn't have to somehow drag yourself through the motions of preparing dinner. Nobody looked forward to coming home weary to the bone then going right back to work in the kitchen. Consequently our first dinners, though ample (we had lots of beans), were to the point. They were all right mind you, but they just couldn't hold a candle to the meals prepared by a full-time camp cook, who had all day to strut around and whip up some culinary delight from our store of staples.

We had flour and rice and pinto beans; we had corn meal, oatmeal, and kidney beans; wheat cereal, dried fruit, and navy beans; canned ham, slab bacon, and lima beans; tinned vegetables, canned milk, and large white beans; potatoes, onions, and red beans; and for a while we had eggs. We had baking powder and small white beans, split peas, lentils, and spices—all kinds, that generally boiled down to salt, pepper, and garlic—and we had a sourdough pot going.

We rotated staying in camp on a daily basis and, surprisingly enough, our output in the forest increased, because when the work day ended it was truly over, so we stayed at work longer, knowing a fine meal waited in camp to lift the spirits. And if the meal couldn't erase thoughts of the tough job ahead, it sure eased them. Food was incredibly important and we went through it like a wood-fired boiler eats cordwood. Our meals jumped right in there with the elements as a major influence in our lives and each of us did his best to ensure the influence was positive!

I looked forward to my day in camp. Hand logging left little time for taking in the forest all around or ruminating on the nature of things.

My day came and I eased out of the tent early to start breakfast. I brewed up a big pot of oatmeal, throwing in a half pound of raisins, sliced off some slab bacon and fried up about half a pound, and cooked up a pot of coffee.

"Grub's up!" I called, and Jerry was first out of the tent, still in a fog. He had the habit of getting on his feet before he could weigh the sense in leaving his warm bed.

He was still trying to get his suspenders on the right arms when I handed him a steaming bowl of mush.

"Yeah oatmobile," he mumbled to the bowl.

"What?" I asked, not sure I'd heard right.

"Yeah oatmobile," he repeated flatly. "I'm hungry."

From behind the mosquito bar we safety-pinned across the door of the tent to keep the little blighters out at night, another one stumbled out, Paul. He looked kind of sideways at Jerry, then Bob called from inside, "What's for breakfast?"

"Oatmobile," I answered, eyeing Jerry.

"What's that?" Bob hollered back.

"I don't know. Better ask Jerry, he's got some."

Well, Jerry finally woke up, but to his credit, he woke up thinking.

"Why," he paused, "it's this stuff right here. You know, like cornmobile or wheatmobile. Yah, and I can see it's got rabbit turds in it."

It came out over breakfast and after some good ribbing, that before my reveille Jerry had been involved in a bit of derring-do in Portland with his brother, Mike. They were making good their escape in an ancient Oldsmobile that wasn't the clunker it looked thanks to Mike's timely, brilliantly executed engine overhaul in Spokane. Even so, during the pursuit, two carloads of toughs from Sandy were closing in on the Wallace Olds.

"You got me out of that one just in time," the dreamer said. "We were just about to the end of the road!"

From that day on we never ate mush or oatmeal or Cream of Wheat, we ate a lot of different-flavored mobiles!

A last cup of coffee and they were off to work.

I've never been one who enjoyed housework; I generally run out of dishes before I wash any, if you get my drift. But at our island camp it was another story. There weren't any walls or grimy windows confining the mind, no neighborhood kids roaring up and down the street trying to lay a film of rubber over the blacktop, no blaring stereo from the apartment above, no ringing telephones. It seemed that my hands almost subconsciously found work, whether scrubbing up breakfast dishes or greasing leather boots, stitching a torn shirt or hanging the sleeping bags out to air. It didn't matter where I chose to do some little task either, for in every direction there was a flawless view, and no window needed opening to let in the breeze.

The Bennett Range, stark granite mountains, rose from behind the camp and the north shore of the King River, rolling out of sight three thousand feet above us less than a mile away, to continue upward to rugged peaks a thousand feet higher. South, across the river, rolling ridges splotched with forest and exposed bedrock rose gradually to become the mountains we'd climbed through. Two great valleys leading back to snowy peaks were the routes to the Chilkoot and White passes. To the left—east—a void indicated where Lake Bennett lay, to the west was the forest, with the serene King River issuing from it in a wide bend.

A lot of things ran through my mind, not unlike in any other time, but with one marked exception. Thoughts drifted in and out like falling leaves—they weren't squalling and screaming for attention only to be admitted to a dozen waiting rooms where my mind raced feverishly between them, trying to give each some consideration.

I marveled at the government—that is, how we four had guided our mutual course by consensus; touched on current events (the light breeze that kept the mosquitos at bay); reviewed my personal priorities (making bannock bread that rose and pudding that pudded); and considered the future, that any time now we would float logs to camp and construct our raft across the river from our island. Our gross product was forty-odd logs. Our cost? We were running short on grub. Before long the canoe came round the bend; it was evening.

"Beans and bacon, baked potatoes and corn, bannock, and pudding for dessert!" I called out as my partners pulled up our canoe.

"The logs are on the banks ready to be floated down," Paul said with elation. So went the day.

That evening around the fire, my work done, I mentioned something we all knew—we were getting low on grub.

"I've got a temporary solution," Bob offered, "that could provide for a little fun, too. Every day they feed the tourists at the station. Why not become tourists? We could wrap binoculars and cameras around our necks and canoe over to the station staying out of sight.

When the trains come in they'll be blocking the view from the station to the lake and we can walk nonchalantly up to the coaches, climb on, and get off with the tourists on the other side, walk in, and eat."

I liked it right away, and Paul was smiling devilishly, but Jer looked skeptical.

"Fine for you guys," he retorted, "but that red-headed battle ax would recognize me for sure."

"I've got that figured out," Bob continued. "There are three dining rooms, right? One wing each for Skagway and Whitehorse passengers, and the small one in the middle for the train crew. She won't recognize Keith and me. Would the girls rat on us?"

"No, that's for sure," said Jer. "They don't like her much either."

"Anyway, when we see which dining room she's in, Keith and I will take that one, you guys go in the other. Eat your fill and bring home what you can!"

At midday we hung up our suspendered trousers and matching hickory work shirts and primped up in our Sunday best—something clean. For all we knew it was Sunday anyway. I even wore my glasses!

As we climbed into the canoe I looked sternly at Jerry.

"Careful now, we can't have you falling out and messing up your good duds."

"Come on Jer, sit here," Paul said condescendingly as if he was helping someone's grandmother. Jerry was just coming to grips with the canoe, something new for him. He'd nearly tipped it over twice before finally succeeding beautifully the day before.

"Ah, you guys are no good, that's what I think," he said good-naturedly. "Just wait, I'll squire this rig around as easily as my pickup before we're done."

We paddled down the King in fine spirits. Like stalking hunters, we skirted the Bennett shoreline. We crossed the Lindemann River and pulled the canoe ashore, out of sight and two hundred yards from the station. We could see the train coming down the lake and moved closer, stealing in behind some alder bushes. When we heard the train's brakes we strode confidently to the cars.

"Here goes nothing," Jerry mumbled, shaking his head, and we boarded.

The second train, from Skagway, was pulling in too, and we waited until the passengers from both were mingling in front of the dining room lines. Bob and I spotted the hostess and joined the throng that smiled past her into the dining hall. So far so good.

There were ten at our table, two middle-aged couples and a family of four. Bob and I were guarded but friendly, keeping our comments to the meal and Bennett, pretending we'd never been here before. The meal was identical to the one we'd had on our way to Skagway and we wasted little time digging in. Everything would have been fine if one of the women hadn't kept trying to draw us into conversation. Finally she asked, "I don't remember seeing you boys on the train, which way are you going?"

Jesus! I hadn't thought of that, which dining room are we in? And I had to answer *now*—I mean who doesn't know which direction they're going on a train?

"Whitehorse."

"Skagway."

We both answered simultaneously! Now we were in the stew. The whole table stopped eating to stare at us, the two charlatans! Something had to be said, and when I looked to Bob he quickly looked down at his plate, the rat. I could see he was laughing, too, so it was up to me. I decided to fess up, hoping for understanding. I told our whole story about heading down the Yukon and coming over the pass, and Bob filled in the missing parts. We even mentioned Jerry and Paul in the other dining room. They loved it, and before we knew it we had eight accomplices in our dining room caper. They all climbed into the act, asking for additional platters of meat and spuds, even going so far as to "borrow" food from the neighboring tables! It was all I could do to slip the goods into my garbage sack without laughing out loud. I had a lap full of food, and the twinkly-eyed grandmother to my left kept slipping me platters under the table!

The seemingly famished condition of our table quickly came to the attention of the waitresses who were at first unbelieving. Stacks of empty platters in front of Bob and me, coupled with our inability to keep straight faces, focused their attention on us, and then Colleen recognized Bob and instantly knew the set up.

"Where's Jerry?" she whispered, bringing more apple pie. "Mary might recognize him."

"In the other dining room," I answered, "with Paul."

"Good," she replied. "We'll try to keep her in here."

I nodded and watched her spread the word among the girls in a conspiracy of whispers and smiles.

When the meal was finished we walked out with our new friends as a crowding, covering escort. The map pockets in the backs of our jackets held sacks of meat and potatoes, and we carried the jackets across our arms, covering our apple pies!

We bid good-bye to our friends and made our way to the canoe. Jerry and Paul were waiting there, having made good their escape. They too had a load of food.

"It was tight," Jer said, beaming as we climbed into the canoe. "Mary looked in once and might have recognized me, but somebody called her back."

Bob explained our getting caught and the girls' complicity, to roars of laughter. All in all it was a successful operation, but we agreed once was enough!

The logs came down in a two-day run, two men rolling them into the river and working them through the two hundred yards of rapids, where about half of them jammed, and two men retrieving them a half mile downriver in front of the camp and herding the logs into the slack water behind our little island. Working in the rapids, where many of our logs hung up on protruding boulders, was tricky business, in fact downright risky, working your way out into the waist-deep foam to pry the logs loose. The water was cold and quick to sap away energy. A stout pole was essential, your third leg in crossing and your pry pole for unjamming logs. Falling wouldn't have been any fun at all, but there was some consolation in knowing you only had to protect your head and possibly hold your breath for two hundred yards, until you were spit out in the calm water where the canoe was tied. The camp end of the run was a cinch. We could spot the logs at the turn above camp and wade out to intercept them. In the end we had forty-six logs either in the boom behind the island or grounded on its tip.

Other than deciding to have a cook, our group was blissfully free of regimen. We made decisions by consensus, as they needed to be made. Inevitably, the two most obstinate of the four of us ended up deadlocked over an issue—in this case the design of the raft—and that stubbornness became a bigger issue than the original problem. Jerry and Bob were inclined to sit it out and wait for a plan to work on; it didn't matter one way or the other to them. They voiced reasonable opinions, but it was the deadlock between Paul and me that needed resolving. I wanted the logs to be placed crosswise then linked together as Schwatka had done with his raft in the eighties. Paul wanted to run them lengthwise. We argued until we were both purple in the face. It was ridiculous, but dammit, I knew my idea was better. Paul was equally sure of his plan. All seemed lost.

The solution, however, was simple and set an important precedent. Jerry suggested we draw straws! Because we didn't have any straws we used matchsticks. In the future, whenever there was an even division in opinion among us, lady luck was the arbiter. I lost this time, and be damned if we didn't have a good raft anyway!

The raft took shape on the bank across the river from camp. It was a lucky stroke, because the bank wasn't too high for horsing the logs out of the water one at a time, nor was the water too shallow for tipping each half back into the river. We slung a line from camp to the "raft yard" and pulled the logs across one at a time. Then Paul and I grunted the raft logs into place on our building platform, a cantilever made of slick logs balanced out over the river. Four thirty-seven footers and eighteen eighteen-footers made up each half. At thirty-seven by eleven feet, each half was just small enough to fit through the lock at Marsh Lake. Bob, at camp, selected the logs so that large and small ones would be distributed in each half equally and sent them across, while Jerry—poor Jerry—was in the woods with his ax telling logging stories to himself while he hewed eight ten-inch by ten-inch by eleven-foot beams, each from a solid tree. Four of the beams would span each half, holding the raft logs together.

It was a good division of labor. Jerry's axemanship was so much better than anyone else's that it was crazy for him to be doing anything else till the ax work was done, and we'd all agreed Bob should be able to move about freely to take pictures, because we wanted a record of everything we did.

We cut notches for the beams, four rows of them across each half. They were carefully measured and "squared with the world," because the beams, or crosspieces, would have to meet the crosspieces from the other half in order for a good splice to be effective. When the crosspieces were set in their notches and we were content, our hand auger was hauled out. With it we would auger a hole $1\frac{7}{8}$ inches in diameter down through each crosspiece and the log under it, and drive a dry wood pin in the hole. When the raft was in the water the pin would soak up and expand, making a tight, strong joint.

There's an art to turning a hand auger, a knack that comes after drilling a lot of holes. Momentum—that's the key. You have to keep up your momentum, you have to keep your body and shoulders moving as a giant flywheel while your hands crisscross adroitly and quickly, going from short end to long end of the steel bar handle as the auger chews its way down below you. It's a wrenching, muscle-jamming experience if you slip, for the auger stops, and you have to exert yourself even more to get it back into motion. When it's moving smoothly you are an oscillating strap of spring steel, your every muscle working in concert from the gripping flats of your feet to your hooked last finger joints and the twitching muscles of your cheeks. We came to know it as the torture crank, and worked it in rotation, one man dancing with the auger and two resting. Jerry was now chopping away on the more than two hundred pins that would be pounded into the augered holes.

Then one day we were looking at a raft. The halves had been effortlessly tipped into the river and joined together with stout beams pinned into place along the crosspieces that, unbelievably, matched! It was floating easily and seemed huge at 37 by 22 feet. We built a frame of green pine for the tent and decked part of the raft with poles, but, the more heavy green wood we added, the closer the top of the raft got to the water line.

"It'll never do," Jerry remarked. "The decking and framing have to be done with lumber. We can float two tons on it, but if it's all green wood we're sunk before we start."

He was right, there was no getting around it.

"The hell with it," Paul said. "Let's pile our gear on, float down to Lake Bennett, and pole around the end of the lake to the Lindemann River, across from the station. We know we're going to sail down the lake, and that's where we want to start. We need food anyway."

We broke camp and piled our gear on the bit of a deck we had, donned our rubber boots, and pushed out into the King River and sinking disappointment. Only the tops of the biggest logs were above the river!

Bob started laughing. I didn't see anything funny and glared at him. All our work was under water. But I slowly came around as did Jer and Paul. The joke was on us! Then everybody laughed.

"Look at it this way," I said. "Now we know for sure we have to get lumber!" I guess as shakedown cruises go, ours was successful, because we learned what improvements had to be made and, though it was close, we didn't sink.

Late that day we poled our raft into a secluded cove, a miniature bay scooped from the stone, just right for our raft. We dubbed it Buccaneer Cove, for it was a dandy place to refit and prepare for our "ocean" voyage down Lake Bennett. We were hidden from the station, with the Lindemann River between it and us. Mind you, we had nothing to hide, but on the basis of our experience, the fewer encounters we had with Bennett officialdom, the better.

A stiff breeze was coming up the lake, and no clouds were in sight, so we slept helter-skelter on mossy shelves in the stone. No bugs, no rain, only the deep night sky.

We finished unloading the raft the next day, stripping all the framing off. At that point we were ready to begin anew, so Bob and I headed for the station, just as the trains were coming in. We wanted to accomplish two things: to arrange to have some food shipped to us, and to find out if we could make some arrangement for scrap lumber.

While Bob sought out the White Pass railroad foreman, I looked for the conductor. I spotted him, in his neat uniform, talking to some tourists. He was the same friendly conductor we'd had. As I stepped up he recognized me.

"Hi! I see you made it across the pass. How's the raft building coming?" he asked.

"Just about finished," I replied, stretching things a little, "but we're running out of food. Is there a way I can get grub out here?"

"Sure, give me a list, and I'll take it in to Bobby Watson in Carcross. He runs the general store; he'll fill your order."

I quickly addressed the envelope with our list and money inside and handed it to him.

"You'll have it tomorrow," he said, waving as he went in for lunch. "I'll bring it out with me."

Just as the conductor stepped into the dining room, Bob came out.

"I saw the foreman; he said he'd talk to us after lunch. I talked to Mary, too."

"What for?" I asked.

"She can't be all bad," Bob answered. "Besides, I wanted to know if we could eat here once and a while. She was real nice and said we could for two-fifty a head. That's not bad." He paused, then, sheepishly, "Actually I was talking to Colleen and Suzelle, telling them we had moved over to the cove. Mary walked up, and I had to say something!"

That sounded more like it, but it also looked like we might have somehow slipped off her "dirt" list!

In fact, we hit a grand slam that day. The foreman listened to our tale of woe, turned down our offer to work in return for scrap lumber, and showed us the dump, saying we could have anything we found in it, in addition to bits and pieces he pointed out around the yard. We were back in business and wasted little time carrying the good news to Jerry and Paul.

We returned for our first load of scrap lumber the same day, filling our canoe. The next day we were more thorough and straightened up the yard a bit in appreciation. We had lunch at the station and picked up our food order from the conductor. Mary was even nice to Jerry!

"I can't figure it out," he said as we returned to camp. "I don't think she remembers the big blow in the trailer, and I'm not going to remind her!"

Pieces of plywood became our tent floor, raised a foot and a half above the logs. We hoped that would be high enough to keep waves out! The lightest lumber went into bunks, heavier lumber was for decking and walkways along the side of the raft. As with the raft itself, the tent frame and decking were built to come easily apart at the middle, and our four stout splices were carefully left easily accessible for removal and reassembly. The tent was raised over its frame (it would have to be removed when the raft was split), which was low enough to get under the railroad bridge at Carcross once we lowered the ridge pole. All in all, it was pretty much like putting together one of those Chinese puzzles where a fistful of multifaceted blocks of wood ends up a smooth round ball if you know how to put it together. We weren't quite sure what it would look like, but we ended up with a raft!

It was gratifying to see we were floating high, even after we moved in, each of us to call a corner of the tent his. We lived two to a side, our bunks running the length of the walls. Chance (through a deck of cards) paired Jerry and I on one side foot to foot, Paul and Bob on the other.

After moving onto the raft, our work took a more leisurely turn. Most of the hard work was finished, and it seemed that only odds and ends needed tending to. A kitchen consisting of a counter and shelves was built onto the rear deck next to the tent. Sturdy sweep mounts and two sweeps, and great oars hewn each from a single solid tree eighteen feet long, were added.

We had visitors. After the thaw in hostilities between us and Mary, we saw more of the Bennett people. In the evenings we would cross the Lindemann by canoe, answering calls such as "Oh, boys, come and get us!" And every evening we would have a little more done on our raft to show off. It pleased me no end to see our raft looked over so admiringly and enviously.

The last act in the building of our raft was the raising of the mast, a thirty-six-foot spruce spar stepped forward of the tent and guyed to each corner of the raft. Our parachute sail was lashed and furled to an eight-foot yard that we could hoist up and down the mast. When set, we planned to control the sail by its shroud lines on both sides. The final touch, the placing of our Alaska flag at the masthead, was accomplished to the cheers of our Bennett friends, invited to witness the finale. Now we were really ready. But the wind wasn't.

The wind continued to blow from the north and for three days we fidgeted around, making headboards for bunks, bedside shelves, an improved walkway. From the bottom of my duffel I pulled out sheets and blankets, cackling all the while I made my bed at my partners' envy, but the wind stayed contrary long enough for White Pass linen to find its way to the other bunks!

We decided to have a going-away party and invited all the Bennett folks from the foreman and Mary to the flunkies. It was quite an affair, though refreshment was skimpy. It was the first time Mary or the foreman saw the raft, and they liked it. About fifteen people sat inside the tent at one time. Every time another came aboard, brought across by one of us in our faithful ferry, the canoe, Jerry would casually step to the deck to see how far we sank! We were floating high, at least out of the water, so all looked good.

I found myself later in the evening sitting in the corner of my bunk talking to Suzelle.

"We'll miss you guys, you know," she said. "Who will we steal pies from the kitchen for now?"

"You could mail them to us!" Bob called from across the tent.

"Yah, and we'll send you a beer from Whitehorse," Jerry said.

"Better yet, we'll drink a beer for you in Carcross!" Paul added.

"You know, I have half a mind to quit and go with you. Could I ride as far as Carcross?" Suzelle asked.

That was a new one for me; what to do about somebody who wanted to come along.

"That's not a good idea," I answered. "We don't know what will happen to this thing once it's underway, especially if one of the storms we've heard about hits. It might just break up. I think I'd just as soon worry only about me until we find out what this thing is like. Besides, where would you stay?"

Three voices each saying "here" brought to my attention the fact that my partners were listening to my conversation, interested in how I answered Suzelle's question. In my eyes we were a crew of four.

"Keith, come here, I want to show you something." It was Paul, he'd slipped out on deck. I excused myself and joined him. He was grinning from ear to ear and pointed at our flag. The wind had shifted. A faint offshore breeze from the south had our flag flicking its tail down the lake.

"Let's cast off," he whispered, "real quiet like. We can take everyone back in the canoe before we get too far."

So it was that a dozen people, a floating party, slipped quietly from Buccaneer Cove to be borne into Lake Bennett by the current of the Lindemann river and a soft breeze.

3

Trials on the Yukon:
Pole Trolls and Tempests

A crashing in my head, like a book slamming shut on short dream episodes, brought me from fitful sleep to sharp awareness. Waves were hitting the raft, mostly against my corner, as they had been all night. Another big one, I thought.

Two days out of Bennett and somewhere on the west shore of the lake, we were weathering a minor storm on a lee shore, unable to clear a point of land jutting into the lake. Inky darkness was all around, the sounds of wind and water augmented by the groaning of rubbing wood and creaking timbers, the raft bending as the waves rolled beneath us to shore. A two- by twelve-foot plank wedged down between the raft logs ground its way into the lake bottom eight feet below us and kept us from washing up on the beach. It had started as a centerboard to increase our sailing angle to the wind, and now served as a makeshift anchor. Two lines ashore kept us from swinging to the beach.

I was warm in my bed, but I rose to tour the deck anyway, and what I saw gave me confidence. The raft was being "pounded" by three-foot waves that seemed spent by the time they hit us. All the same, I reflected, the sounds and feelings of the ocean were alien and sorely out of context with our immediate past. Satisfied with the tautness of the lines to shore and that our centerboard-anchor was holding, I was shivering in the cold night wind and hurried back to bed. It was cold. I'd left the covers turned back when I went on deck. I'd remember to close them up next time.

Shortly after our cast-off from Bennett, we had canoed our guests

63

to shore and made our farewells. We were finally waterborne and as Paul so aptly put it when all of us were alone on board, "We may be seventy-five years late, but we'll get there yet!"

"Seventy-four years and two months," Bob corrected. And so it was. On May 29, 1898 word reached the Stampeders at Bennett that the lakes were opening; the ice on the lower ones had already succumbed to the sun's growing strength, releasing its grip on the shores. Before two days had passed, the seven thousand "boats" built at the head of Lake Bennett (or to be more accurate, the seven thousand "contraptions"), whose one common thread was that they were all intended to carry their inhabitants to the Klondike, were underway. What a sight to imagine—a lake splotched with grand scows under sail and oar, sleek double-enders, packing crate boats and rowboats, canoes and prefab rigs carried painfully through the passes, two- and three-log rafts with blankets for sails, all manned by the 40,000 hopefuls from everywhere, all caught in the fever of being first to the gold. Such a great race! Never before and never since has there been one like it.

Our first night on Bennett turned out to be anticlimactic. The wind quit, and, just as our spirits were rising, the sail drooped down. There was nothing to do but shrug our shoulders and go to bed, our raft tied down along the railroad embankment within sight of the station.

The next day we got our wind, steady and strong. Up went the sail and our raft slid from the shore heading north. We even made enough headway for a wake to appear behind us! Throughout the day the wind increased in stages until nightfall, when whitecaps began to appear and a point of land barred our way. Rather than sail into a strengthening storm on a reach we weren't sure we could attain to clear the point of land, we elected to play it safe and went ashore to wait the dawn. We'd come twelve miles and had fifteen to go on Lake Bennett.

The day dawned blustery and gray, but no matter, we agreed in a general pow-wow over breakfast to give it a go, to put our money where our mouths were, so to speak. A bellyful of sourdough hot cakes and steaming coffee made the morning look better, even though the wind was growling along at twenty miles an hour or so, whipping the lake's surface into whitecaps. The wind had, however, veered slightly to the east, placing the point we had failed to weather within our reach.

The canoe was lashed across the stern securely to break the waves, and two long lifelines were played out from the trailing corners of the raft. If one of us fell overboard there would be no stopping the raft in rough weather and the canoe would be a chancy rescue boat at best. We placed life jackets about the raft at vantage points for either grabbing or throwing and each of us packed a single bag to exit with, should the unforeseen require it. We agree we would have to put down more centerboards and half an hour of beachcombing provided us with two more long, stout planks. They would be slipped down through the gaps between the logs and either extended or drawn up according to the depth of the water. At least we felt prepared when we cast off.

The short distance to the point along the weather beach was more easily traversed than anticipated; the two additional centerboard planks markedly reduced our drift. A few stabs with poles were enough to keep us from running aground. Steadily we drew away from the beach, easily passing the point on our way out to the lake. We plowed resolutely to the center of Lake Bennett; it was easy. Then we turned tail and drove before the wind.

The storm we'd apprehensively sailed into turned out to be fields of gentle-natured three-foot waves, some sporting tiny curls! The roar of the wind was lost without the forest and the shore. The chasing waves that we feared would wash our decks were dispatched with a shrug by our gently rocking raft and lost under its tail. The deck remained dry. Whoops of laughter rebounded around the deck, long due congratulations were passed out and received. We had hardly finished marveling at our functional raft before Bob was yelling into the wind astern, "I want bigger waves!"

13:32 — Abreast of the island, about five degrees west of north, or S.E. Made a mile and a half in 47 minutes on a 37° reach. We can get more—how much, I'm not sure. Speed 2 mph.

Around and around the deck we strutted, stowing this and re-tying that, but mostly being proud and happy.

13:58 — Wind is abating, strung the sail another 10 feet higher. She's a good raft, handled our small storm of up to 4 foot, maybe 5 foot waves,

> with the wind about 20 mph. She bends as expected in the waves but
> our splices and pins are holding well. HO! HO! The sun is out, it's a
> beautiful day.

She bucked and yawed in a begrudging way, a bit of water splashing here and there, but she was a Ferrari to us, bursting down the lake at a dazzling two miles an hour.

We trimmed the raft by adjusting the placement and depth of the centerboards; fine tuning was accomplished by shifting the set of the sail, sometimes ever so slightly, with the parachute shroud lines which were gathered and tied to two long ropes (or sheets as the sailors say) that ran astern to each corner of the raft. There, on deck at the door of the tent, one man could easily sail the raft once it was underway. He had only to raise, lower, or change the positions of the centerboards or take in or play out the sheets. We took turns, bravely sailing back and forth across the lake, our lifelines trailing behind us.

> 19:05 — Around the corner, within sight of the Carcross railroad
> bridge. We made the last 7 miles in 3 hours of easy sailing, should be in
> Carcross within the hour.

We were. Securely tied, I looked back up the lake, a view I'd seen less than a month before, yet what I saw now was different by a world.

Well, Carcross hadn't changed. Matthew Watson's general store was buttoned up till Monday, activity at the railroad depot had likewise ceased, and the cocktail lounge at the old Caribou Hotel, a gold rush holdover, was predictably lively. Its clientele of perhaps a dozen the last time I'd visited had swollen to at least twenty, all on account of it being Saturday night, and they all seemed bent on competing with the jukebox and each other in a hubbub of noise! We joined right in, three at a time, each of us took a turn watching the raft and our belongings, and it was pretty late when the last "rafter" hit the sack!

It was a busy stop, Carcross. Motion was in us and time flew, though not unpleasantly. First thing in the morning we checked in with Carcross's lone representative of the Royal Canadian Mounted Police, constable Jim Card. The nearest Canadian customs office was in Whitehorse, forty-odd miles away by road; we hoped the Mountie could officially admit us into Canada. Secondly, we wanted the Mounted Police to know our plans in case some emergency required them to either contact us or search for us. The constable returned to the raft with us and swiftly concluded his official business to the satisfaction of all. As the Mountie was leaving, an affable gent stepped aboard, and introduced himself as Ralph Bolivar.

"Jesus Christ, I didn't know what to make of you guys when I saw you coming down the lake last night," Ralph said. "I figured you was an iceberg!"

"An iceberg?" I laughed.

"Yes, I couldn't think of nothing else you could be except an iceberg left over from the spring."

"When did you figure out we were a raft?" Paul questioned.

"Not until you lowered your sail," he said, with a twinkle in his eye. "Your logs is almost underwater and I couldn't see 'em. Couldn't you guys find some greener ones? Then nobody would know you was afloat, they'd be so far under."

That turned us all inside out. Bolivar hadn't waited ten minutes to give us the dickens for using green logs! If his tools—he was a carpenter—were as sharp as his wit, he could accomplish anything! He hailed from Nova Scotia originally, but had spent the last thirty years or so as a happy bachelor in Carcross.

Jerry and Ralph got along famously, both being master story-tellers and excellent on the witty comeback, so just after Bob stole out to record Carcross with his camera, Paul and I left to pay a visit to chief Dan Johnson and his wife, Vicky. We left as Ralph was telling Jerry a story about how he got hit in the face with a frog in the old days while seal hunting with dynamite.

The Johnsons were happy to see us and, over a cup of coffee, we related our journey to them. Dan introduced us to his father, the stately gentleman I'd nodded to on the way in, and explained that his dad had been a packer on the Chilkoot during the rush, when a teenager. For the rest of the evening we listened to the old man's tales. They were beautiful, long, and detailed. He spoke with the mind and thoughts dating from a time when the story, passed and learned by word of mouth, was the only way to preserve knowledge—a time before television and radio, before there were newspapers and books in his land, even before the time words in his language had written symbols. He told us of prospecting with Tagish Charlie, his uncle, and one of the original discoverers of gold in the Klondike, of beaver trapping with him, and he spoke in a sonorous voice, slowly and peacefully, with an accent I'd never heard but knew instantly—the pidgin English of the Indian who had learned English only as a second language. His native tongue was now a dying language. It was late when Paul and I returned to the raft.

First order of business in the morning was moving the raft under the railroad bridge. We wanted to be done with it, so when the time came we could be on our way with little fanfare. There was a second reason. Our raft was a novel attraction. From early morning and the arrival of local kids and camera-packing tourists until the late, late hours and the departure of the last tipsy local, we played hosts to the curious. That was great until you wanted to go to bed, change clothes, read, or just be alone.

We lowered the mast, laying it alongside the walkway, and removed the tent ridge pole, dropping the tent to the top of our bedposts, then walked the raft down to the bridge. Alas, we had erred. We needed to cut off at least three inches of our interior framing to slip the raft under the low bridge's steel beams.

"Couldn't we lower the raft slowly under the bridge until each high point of the tent frame touched the bridge girders, then grab hold of the girder and force the raft down in the water and under the girder rather than hack up our tent frame?" I asked.

"It's worth a try," Paul answered. Jerry and Bob were in agreement. It could save us tearing out and rebuilding our interior framing.

It was a struggle, but it worked. We were under the bridge in twenty minutes.

Just below the bridge, at mid-channel, a weathered old piling provided us an ideal anchorage. We tied to it and regained a margin of solitude. Henceforth, we journeyed to and from the shore in our canoe.

Our raft remained tied to the piling four more days. Paul finally rendezvoused with Kora Bailey, a long-time friend of the Crews family, and her fourteen-year-old nephew, Kurt. She had been Paul's baby-sitter—mine, too, on occasion—though she couldn't be more than three or four years older than I. Kora had come to Carcross to attend a wedding at the Bennett Church which was built during the gold rush. She planned to travel there by train, her nephew in tow.

The couple to be married, even more surprisingly, turned out to be our acquaintance of the Chilkoot trail, Skip Burns the guide, and his fiancée, Cheri!

Kora had worked in Juneau with Skip. The North is a small world, really, and the wedding, she told us, would be the first for the Bennett Church. It seemed the congregation it had housed during the gold rush had left with the ice, gold being stronger than God at the time!

Since the wedding wasn't until August 2, five days away, Bob and I elected to go to Whitehorse and develop our film to date. We were all curious to see what we had. Paul and Kora would drive down to Atlin, and Kurt, who took an instant liking to Jerry, would stay with him and watch the raft.

Whitehorse was hectic. Bob and I hitched in and stayed with people we met through the two Swedish girls Paul and Jerry had talked to on the train. We spent three days in the darkroom at the Whitehorse Star, and at the end were satisfied with our results.

We hitchhiked to Carcross on August 1 to find Paul, Jerry, Kurt, and Kora planning a caper! They had decided to attend the wedding together, and rather than travel as paying customers on the passenger train, they planned to hop the night freight!

It seemed like a great scheme, but Bob and I were itching to go north, not south, on our raft, not the train. Our visit to Whitehorse had been one of those "wheels-spinning-but-no-progress" sort of affairs. We would press on.

On the basis of our sailing in Lake Bennett, it seemed we could meet Jerry and Paul either at Tagish, twenty-five miles down the lakes, or at the Marsh Lake dam, twenty miles beyond Tagish. We would have to sail six miles almost due east, through Nares Lake and the first three miles of Tagish Lake, then across Windy Arm and continue east for another five miles before Tagish Lake turned north. Then it was all north to Tagish and the bridge crossing the narrows between Marsh and Tagish Lakes, north still to the dam at the end of Marsh Lake. True, the locals warned us about Windy Arm and about entering the east–west segment of Tagish Lake from the south. They warned us of its terrible storms and the great bay across from its mouth, Sucker's Cove, where unfortunates washed up, but they had also warned us of Bennett's storms, which we thought we had handled rather well.

It was settled. With little more ado we drifted the raft below the highway bridge, raised the mast and popped the sail, as Paul untied us. We had a light breeze headed our way. Jerry called after us from the bridge. "We'll be looking for you at Tagish!" and with a wave of his hand was off toward Carcross and the night freight with Paul.

Led by the faint current and directed by the slightest breeze, hardly enough to ripple the mirror reflections of the mountain and forest in the surface of Nares Lake, Bob and I poetically sailed into the sunset.

"Why us?" Bob asked later as we lounged on the rear deck, soaking in the beauty around us. I shrugged my shoulders and smiled, there was nothing to say. The sense of joy and well-being that was tickling me from the inside out couldn't be put into words. We were moving steadily, intuitively toward the neck between Nares and Tagish Lakes, perhaps a quarter-mile long and a mile away. Carcross was dropping from sight three miles behind us, yet the sail hung limp and Nares Lake was glass.

Each took his turn sallying about in the canoe, ruffling the lake's surface in the evening light. I ventured ahead of the raft into the channel. All was calm, one of those times when you don't make any noise at all if you can help it so as not to disturb any of the goings on in nature that you might see or be party to if unobserved. To carry it even one step farther, I lay down in the bottom of the canoe, ostensibly to gaze at the sky and rim of hills and mountains that protruded over the gunnels, while I drifted toward some unseen destiny. Actually, I took a snooze and slipped ever so slowly into the channel out of sight of the raft.

I don't know how long my nap lasted, but it was blissful. I woke and looked up, it didn't seem darker. Then I sat up. I'd drifted to within fifty yards of the beach, still in the narrow neck between the lakes, and there on the shore stood a big ole grizzly bear, staring at me in my tin canoe!

It didn't know what to make of me; no signs of alarm drifted my way, and since both of us sensed we were safe, we were content to enjoy our proximity in observation of the other. As I drifted along, the bear ambled parallel to me, not forgetting to nose here and there under stumps and brush for whatever grub he might find.

We'd been moving along together for ten minutes or so when I heard the soft hum of an outboard motor coming up Tagish Lake toward the channel I was drifting in. Damn, I thought, it'll be here any minute and it's sure to scare the bear. About that time the bear heard the boat and cocked its head to one side, seemingly gauging the boat's arrival by the increasing noise of the motor. When he had the situation figured he took a couple more steps, then tripped into the willows without so much as a nod of good-bye. There he halted, about twenty feet from the beach, and waited. He was well camouflaged but visible to me. I'd seen him enter the woods.

Just then the boat came around the corner, moving rapidly past me. It was a cabin cruiser with an open top; two men stood behind the windshield against which two rifles leaned; a third man drove. I waved, they waved, and the boat was off into Nares Lake, leaving me bobbing in its wake.

The bear watched it all, then, when the boat was gone, returned to comb the beach as if nothing had happened. Anyone who says animals are all dumb is really wrong!

In order to keep up with the bear, now ignoring me, I would have to paddle. Bringing the paddle out provided the all too familiar clatter that aluminum boats are renowned for and my bruin friend slipped into the bushes for good.

I returned to the raft which Bob was casually skippering into the narrows, and related my experience. What a capper for a marvelous day!

Then we made a fateful decision. Before venturing into Tagish Lake, we decided to add sturdier sweep yokes to our sweep mounts forward and aft, and tied up for the night where we were in the channel, maybe a hundred yards from Tagish Lake. We could see no sense in sailing through the dark hours, even with a favorable breeze. The wind would blow the same way tomorrow. After supper we canoed across the channel to the bruin's stomping grounds, cut some forked alders, returned to the raft, and fashioned four sturdy yokes— two for spares—and turned in.

Gray, drizzly skies greeted me when I rose to rustle breakfast. Even the painstakingly prepared sourdoughs and bacon had little effect on our spirits. We needed to sail east for ten miles, but the wind we saw in our flag at the masthead was blowing north. It was an ideal wind for eighty percent of our lake sailing but would be disastrous to us now. No matter how close we sailed to the wind we would inevitably end up on the north shore and eventually Sucker's Cove, across from the mouth of Windy Arm.

We talked little; there was nothing to say. We had waited for the wind before; we could wait again.

By 5:30 in the afternoon we had succeeded in utilizing a short lull in the wind to drift out of the channel to the south shore of Tagish Lake, all told about two hundred yards. Impatient to be moving, we tried something new.

3 August

19:00 — We're half a mile from where we began at 17:30. I started out with the ¾-inch manila line looped around my shoulders, pulling the raft along the south shore. Bob, on the raft, kept it out from the shore with a pole until shallow water halted the backbreaking work. Following that, we both took to poling the raft. With improvised walkways along each side and good poles, poling had promise.

Time for a coffee break.

4 August. After breakfast.

Our coffee break ended up night's shelter. Wind is still blowing hard from the east. Shortly, we commence our tedious poling against the wind.

When the lake became deep enough for the raft to float close to shore, I returned to the beach and plodded along the waterline tied to the raft like a donkey at the end of the heavy manila line. It was Bob's plight to pole and pull the length of the raft, back and forth, back and forth, in perpetual monotony, both helping to move the raft forward and keeping it from swinging toward shore and grounding in shallow water.

Daydreaming is great for the individual sunk in a monotonous task, because counting progress is hopeless. A point of land that stays in the distance forever, once achieved, will be replaced by another as the goal.

15:05 — Wind changed for 2 minutes, then back. Sail up, sail down, about 600 feet of progress. We'll have to revert to pole and pull.

15:20 — Wind changed, up sail. . . .

15:50 — Wind backed around from the east, lowered sail, aggravating, believe me. Back to pole and pull.

18:00 — Sail up, sail down. I feel like a jack-in-the-box. Commence

73

poling again. Altogether we've gained so far on Tagish Lake *maybe* 1500 feet by sail.

By nightfall I had gone through the first stanza of every song I knew and was disappointed to find out I knew the first stanzas to a lot of songs but none of the rest of them. I'd done it in silence, though; singing or talking was a waste of energy.

20:20 — Poled for 2½ hours, time for a break. We're within 1600 feet of the point, continuing wind from the east to pole against. Enough for today.

The morning of August 5 was going to be different, we decided, clear and sunny with a west wind. If not, we would at least begin the day with a hearty treat of bacon and eggs.

Bob made the first move in the morning, I woke as he moved through the tent door at my head onto the deck.

"What's the word?" I asked. My words traveled through the tent walls unhindered. No answer, but the dull hue inside the tent told me the word was "overcast."

"What's the wind doing?" I asked. Still no reply. Well, no wind was better than a contrary one.

"Bacon and eggs?" I asked meekly.

"Yep."

09:30 — Poling since 8:15. My nerves are getting a little stretched. This pole/pull bullshit has got to stop. We're half a mile from the second point and at the moment hung fast on a rock somewhere about the center of the raft. What a day—already. The Pole Troll who lives in the bottom of the lake and tries to hang on to your pole long enough for you to fall in the lake tortured me all morning. Finally the damn pole broke and I keeled over backward into the water. After changing, I, of course, stepped on a loose log, pushing it down just far enough to fill my boot up with water. Put on another dry sock. Not 10 minutes later both boots were full of water and mud from slogging along the shore with the rope. The "sand" here is stinking, sloppy goo.

One man on the raft, one on the shore worked best, but we would change, usually out of boredom or for company, when the lake was shallow enough for us both to pole. Then we could walk back and forth the length of the raft, each on one side, chatting about whatever came to mind.

So it was that we "P and P'd" (poled and pulled) our way along

Tagish Lake against an east wind at about three-eighths of a mile an hour, sometimes smiling and marveling at our progress, other times gloomy and depressed, wondering how we'd get anywhere near the Yukon proper if we had to P and P the whole fifty miles to it.

Windy Arm, the jaws of the devil to hear Carcross folks speak of it, hadn't had much space in my thoughts as we P and P'd toward it. Windy Arm reaches like a handle into an upside-down pick head, the east-west portion of Tagish Lake. That handle is a narrow, twelve-mile-long notch with three-thousand-foot shoulders plunging to its shores, a three-sided tunnel for the wind to roar through from the heart of the rugged, stormbound Coast Mountains. How and when we would cross its mile-and-a-half-wide mouth we would deal with when we got there.

So it was then, as we rounded our last prominent point before reaching the arm's west shore, still three-quarters of a mile distant, that Windy Arm burst into my head with little formality, dashing out so many frivolous thoughts.

Bob and I were both poling the raft along, unconcerned by local events. Come hell or high water we would keep moving our three-eights of a mile an hour. I poled on the lake side of the raft, Bob on the shore side. As we rounded the promontory, my pole was plunging rapidly deeper and deeper into the water before lodging on the bottom.

"How's the water on your side?" I asked, curiously.

"Getting deeper," he answered. "Same over there?"

By then I was back on the bow, ready to begin my march to the stern, jousting the bottom with my fifteen-foot pole.

"Hang on," I replied, swinging my pole into the lake. "No bottom," I answered, feeling uneasy. Our flag was standing straight out from the beach.

"No bottom!" Bob called in moments.

"We'd better sweep in!" I said to him, thinking how lucky we were to have sturdy new sweep yokes. The wind was already moving us away from land and the farther we drifted from the protecting hills, the stronger it got.

Everything should have gone just right, according to plan. The raft was supposed to draw back to the shore like clockwork, powered by our big sweeps, Bob and I providing the muscle. But our first turn at the sweeps proved otherwise.

"Harder!" I yelled to Bob. We were losing ground, ever distancing ourselves from the shore. I bent my back to the task, pulling the big sweep through the water. I was pulling for all I was worth, yet we were barely holding our own. If we couldn't get back to shore, we'd end up on the north shore, perhaps in Sucker's Cove. We would either be battered apart on the windward shore, driven high aground, or, at best, have another half a dozen miles of hopeless P and P before reaching Perthe's Point and the continuation of Tagish Lake.

A passed-over stanza in Robert Service's poem *The Trail of Ninety Eight* crashed into my head like a gong:

Thuswise, we voyaged Lake Bennett, Tagish, then Windy Arm,
Sinister, savage and baleful, boding us hate and harm.
Many a scow was shattered there on that iron shore;
Many a heart was broken straining at sweep and oar.

"No go!" Bob yelled, over the groaning of our alder yokes turning in their log mounts. "Maybe we can reach shore with a line!"

Bob knotted our longest lines together, and by the time he handed me the end I had the canoe in the water and was ready to go. We were really losing now, the tent and superstructure acting like sails. I paddled like a madman for the shore, the line tied to the thwart. My heart began jumping as I closed the stony beach, I just knew the line would come taut before I got there.

"Fifty feet," Bob called.

It would be close, but I could see bottom.

"Line!" he yelled.

With one hand on the canoe I jumped for shore, splashing into a foot of water, pulling the canoe after me till the line was tight. Then I held onto the canoe, our rope tied to its stern, me glued to its bow.

"I got it," I yelled, when I was sure I could hold it. Then I dragged the canoe and line ashore, foot by foot, until I could secure the line to a tree. By walking the line from its center down the beach, I pulled the raft in. We tied to the point that had almost been our undoing and ate lunch.

"Which goes to show," Bob said, over a bowl of beans, "we thought we had it bad, but it can always get worse!"

For the rest of our journey by P and P, we kept a line ashore, either tied to something substantial or with a body pulling it.

By seven that evening, we had P and P'd our way to the shore of Windy Arm. The wind was coming down the arm steadily, but it was hardly strong enough to kick up the odd whitecap. Yet, even without whitecaps the waves were beaten into spray on Bove Island, a substantial bedrock battlement in the middle of the arm. Bove Island had its own miniature forest, but it was lopsided. The trees were full and thick on its lee side; stunted, sparse and wizened to the south. What a miserable place to be a tree, I thought, forever and a lifetime humiliated before the wind. Its shores were rocky, on the windward side long and barren. In the distance, to the north of Bove Island, lay Sucker's Cove.

We stopped for a bite to eat, checked our maps, and did some figuring. Our best reach on Lake Bennett had been thirty-seven degrees, a figure both Bob and I felt could be improved on with more centerboards to slow our drift and by tightening our spinnaker like a parachute into a tauter, more efficient square sail that would allow us to point up closer to the wind.

"Now if we're sure of improving our cross-wind sailing but still figure on a thirty-seven-degree reach to be safe, how far up Windy Arm do we have to P and P in order to sail across above Bove Island?" Bob asked, both of us pondering the map held flat on Paul's bunk by a pair of slippers, a hammer, and the cribbage board.

I put the protractor on the map and slid it up Windy Arm along the shore till thirty-seven degrees just cleared the island, then scaled the distance.

"Figuring the wind to come straight down Windy Arm," I answered, "we have to move up the beach four-fifths of a mile to our starting point."

It was a beautiful evening, leftover waves from the dying wind lapping the shore, so we elected to get the P and P out of the way for good.

The beach was rocky and perfect for trudging along and provided my diversion. Sometimes I would be clattering along a washed pebble beach in the back of some small cove, other times climbing over and around craggy promontories above the quiet lake.

We moved right along, having ironed out quite a few of the wrinkles in lining our raft along the lake. We slowly built up the raft's momentum to a bit less than half a mile an hour, then kept it that way by steady work.

"Do you think we can get enough centerboards down to really affect the drift?" I called to Bob. I was standing on a crag above the water, keeping the raft moving toward me by pulling in the line hand over hand. When I had enough slack rope piled up I would jump down the back side of the crag with it to the beach beyond, swing the line clear of the rocks, and resume my trudging.

The raft was nearly below me. Its lone occupant with his long pole that rose and dipped, rose and dipped, was beginning to take on the shadowy cloaks of evening.

"Sure we'll improve," Bob responded. "Besides, I've been thinking. If we lower the tent to the level of the beds, we'll reduce our drag considerably. Remember when we almost lost it today? Well, we really didn't start drifting fast till the wind hit the tent."

"That reminds me of something, too," I said, stopping. "The wind was blowing northeast where we almost lost it, yet when we came to Windy Arm, it was blowing almost north. It's my guess that the wind along the east side of the arm turned eastward when it hit the main lake, causing the discrepancy. It should be the same on the west side, and, if that's the case, we only have to sail maybe three-quarters of the way across before the wind we hit will be turning our way."

"I'll have to think about that," Bob said, as I jumped out of sight with the coil of rope, playing it out as I went.

We made our four-fifths of a mile in record time; one hour. It was nearly nine o'clock at night, but conditions were so ideal we decided to P and P another four-fifths of a mile just to be on the safe side.

I returned to the shore with my constant companion, the tail end of our hefty manila line. I had a life jacket for padding against the cut of the rope on my neck and perched it on my shoulder. I tied a loop in the rope and laid it around my body like a bandolier. Leaning into it, I began slowly sidestepping down the beach into the darkness. The only sounds were the rustle of stones underfoot and the methodical splash of Bob's pole on the shadowy log jam that followed me.

By 11:30 we'd made the extra part of a mile. It was a good thing we had. While checking my figures I found that a thirty-seven-degree course from our present position would bring us up on Bove Island. We needed forty-seven degrees to clear it.

I slipped my log book into its place on my shelf and slid between the sheets. It was an optimistic entry; Windy Arm had been nothing but peaceful for us.

23:55 — Windy Arm isn't always mean and nasty. Tonight it yawned a few times and dropped into a calm sleep. The last glimmer of sunset far to the north and the few stars that peeked through the blanket of clouds seemed to soothe it.

   Tomorrow we sail, 37° with a true south wind to hit the point of Bove Island, 47° to clear it completely. We'll go for it.

The last thing I remember was snuffing my candle. It hadn't so much as flickered until I leaned up to blow it out, disturbing the air.

"Whop, whop . . . WHOP!" I was ripped from my sleep, and lay there for an instant, gathering my bearings. The raft was rocking and creaking. I heard waves crashing. The tent was being battered by the wind; its flapping had wakened me.

"You awake?" I whispered to Bob.

"Yah, that was a loud one," he whispered back.

"It sure was," I said. "It scared the hell out of me." I must have been right at the deepest possible part of sleep. Now I was wide awake and listened carefully. Waves crashing? Must be on the windward side of the point we were tied behind. Rocking and creaking? Must be the spent corners of the waves tailing around the point. The tent flapping subsided to a rustle.

"You sure the line's tied good?" Bob asked.

"Yah," I answered. I was no longer so alarmed. We were protected behind a point of rocky shore that loomed over the raft a good ten feet and extended beyond us fifteen or twenty feet into the lake.

"Yah, I'm sure," I repeated. "But it looks like a windy day tomorrow."

"Good-night." Bob replied. It was anything but that.

I started awake again, although not from so sound a slumber, to the flapping of the tent, a sharp all-pervading sound that couldn't be ignored, it was all around. I felt like a mouse in a kettle drum. I listened for a while and again it didn't seem as bad as it did when I woke, though the raft was rocking more noticeably and I could hear waves splashing against us.

I dropped into the lightest of sleeps, but was again shocked awake. This time it didn't subside. The tent rippled and flapped in terrifying reports, like cannon fire. Waves were crashing against my side of the tent and I could for the first time hear a whining—the wind in the shrouds.

I hurried into my trousers and threw on a jacket. An hour before, I might have thought the raft was secure, but now I wasn't sure of anything. I wasn't alone, either, in disposition or course of action. Bob was right behind me as I untied the tent door. The flap tore from my hand to whip madly the instant I released the knot.

The northern corner of the sky, over the arm of Tagish Lake that we hoped to be sailing along after crossing Windy Arm, was nowhere to be seen. There were no stars, nothing luminous but the phosphorescent glow of breaking water that was all around us, even protected as we were by the promontory. The wind that was strong enough to batter our tent mercilessly was incredible at the masthead, standing above our sheltering rocky point. Our flag, utterly flutterless and rigid, stood straight north. Of the four guy lines that stayed the mast, two were as tight as bow strings, and had stretched, to boot. The mast leaned north five feet from center at the top. The other two guy lines jumped about, uselessly slack. Any effort to take up on the forward guy lines would be ridiculous under the circumstances.

The lake side of the raft was awash, waves breaking against our canvas tent. It couldn't stand much of that so Bob and I hurriedly gathered all our centerboards and pulled up pieces of deck to build a breakwater. We nailed our bulwark to the outside of the tent, yelling to each other in the dim of the storm.

The raft's logs were holding together well, though not without considerable groaning and wracking as waves rolled over and under them.

Next we tightened the tent lines, ensuring against its being torn away from the incessant tugging of the wind.

Lastly, another line was strung out and tied ashore, our first checked and resecured. As I stood on the shore I had strong thoughts about carrying my sleeping bag over and finishing the night on solid ground, but I returned to the raft, determined to tough it out.

Back on board, I looked around the kitchen but couldn't tell much about what was missing. For starters, the dish towel and wash rag were gone; we would know more in the morning. I was soaked from the waist down and shivering in the wind. In my haste to get dressed I had forgotten to put socks on. Just as well, though—at least they would be dry in the morning. I looked where I'd hung them, on the ridge pole. It extended beyond the tent over the deck and served as a clothesline. Damn! My socks were gone too!

Sleep came once more with the warmth of my bed, only to be interrupted one more time. I could hear spray hitting the tent. The waves slamming the bulwark not a foot from my bed were breaking above the level of my head. I shivered into my wet clothes, trying to do so without touching them, and toured the deck, flashlight in hand. Bob hollered, asking if I needed help. I answered in the negative, our breakwater was doing its job well, it just wasn't high enough. I nailed another board onto it, extending its height to four feet at the corner where the waves were breaking highest.

Needless to say, I woke up in the gray stormy morning somewhat less than rested, with a feeling of helplessness before the absolute force of the storm.

Windy Arm was a psychological ice cap, freezing every speck of moist optimism that Bob and I had. Its center was a cauldron of storm-smashed waves; plumes of spray all but obliterated the barren, rocky beaches of Bove Island. Crashing foam had inundated the two small islands to the east, just the upper part of one was visible. It shook the hell out of me. If we'd decided to sail the night before, we could have been caught in the storm.

The storm continued through the day, so Bob and I climbed one of the hills behind the raft to check my theory about the bending wind currents. From the top of a knoll six hundred feet above the lake we could see the course of the wind clearly etched on the lake's surface. Sure enough, the wind followed the land contours straight down Windy Arm and arced both east and west on reaching the main lake. The center of the wind bore straight across Bove Island into the far shore and Sucker's Cove. When we sailed, if we could make it three-quarters of the way across without hitting Bove Island, the turning wind would be our ally and pass us into the continuing lake.

I spent the rest of the day reading, going on deck to check the weather, and writing in my log.

17:00 — Sitting through the storm is highly aggravating. If we didn't need to reach 47° we would go. But the reach is a must or we've lost 2 days of P and P and will still have to P and P out of Sucker's Cove.

It wasn't till late afternoon that it was really evident that the wind was abating. We readied everything for quick departure, just in case.

20:45 — The wind has abated some from its 30–50/mph. Now it's come down to about 20.

Half an hour later we cast off. The whitecaps had disappeared from the waves, even at the center of Windy Arm, and the wind had dropped even further to a respectable ten miles an hour. We were bent on casting off as efficiently as we could, but nevertheless we slipped down the lake a good thousand feet before settling into our reach and bearing away at an angle across Windy Arm. Wherever the raft logs were exposed, stubs of planks and boards, scraps of plywood, even an old door found on the beach, protruded to indicate our centerboard maze.

I marked our course and time carefully, thinking, if we couldn't clear Bove Island, to sail to its lee; but to no avail, we had to commit ourselves in the first fifteen minutes and we did. We would either clear the island or be marooned on it.

"Won't know for sure till I can get some idea of how far we are from the island," I said to Bob forty-five minutes into our crossing. "But so far, I think we're making about forty-five degrees at a mile an hour." Smiles broke out; if all held we had it made. Bob had her trimmed up magnificently, we were pointing about eighty degrees away from the wind and losing about forty degrees or so to slip. Nothing to do but wait.

"I hear a boat!" Bob said, cocking his head. The faint hum of an outboard engine could be heard. Sure enough, we could see a dot with a white bow wave coming around Bove Island. It was making for us. The boat soon pulled alongside, a sturdy freighter canoe piloted by a tall, rugged Indian. His cargo? None other than Jerry Wallace!

"Ho there, whatever your name is," he called in mock formality. "Permission to come aboard."

"Jesus, am I glad to see you!" I said. "Whatever brings you out here in the middle of the night?"

"My friend here, and a case of beer!"

We tied the boat in the lee of the raft and continued on our way. We recounted our tale of woe, while Jerry informed us that the wedding had been great and that Paul and he had become worried after we hadn't shown up at Tagish. The storm really set them to wondering, so Jerry came out. Paul, with Kora and Kurt, said he'd meet us down at the foot of Marsh Lake. We each had a beer and thanked Jerry's friend who, on noticing the stiffening wind and our now rocking raft, departed without formality for Carcross.

The three of us stood around the deck in our rain gear, good protection against the wind. We were half way past Bove Island, rocking in the growing waves that were now crashing over the windward side of the raft; the wind was back up to about twenty miles an hour and we were moving right out.

Bob and I were ecstatic. Success was all but won; Bove Island was three-eighths of a mile below us. We were plowing along steadily, minute by minute, achieving our goal, the shelter and curving wind of the east shore.

"Check the lean in the mast," Jerry commented.

I barely heard him, but turned to look up. I had been watching the waves breaking on Bove Island, sending spray far over the rocks. We had whitecaps now, though nothing in terms of the previous night. I was thinking I would have liked to have been on the island last night just to see the storm's violence. Then I noticed the mast. It wasn't just leaning, it was falling! We all realized it at once.

Bob, standing by one of the sheets, immediately untied it and was on his way to the other in a flash. Jerry and I raced forward. We'd been caught unawares. The mast was falling on the tent, being driven by the sail.

Jerry and I reached the mast simultaneously. It was leaning back on the tent frame and would soon smash our canvas home.

"Sail's loose!" Bob called.

"Stand by!" I yelled. Jerry and I were both swathed in clinging parachute silk, trying to work the halyard loose so we could lower the yard. We had to get the sail out of the way to restep the mast.

"I can't get the halyard loose. It's pinched against the tent frame!" I yelled to Jerry.

He quickly put his strength into lifting the mast, gaining me a gap of inches.

"Hurry," he snapped, "I can't hold it long!"

It was long enough, though, for I managed to free the halyard.

"For Christ's sake, hurry," Bob yelled.

With the halyard free, Jerry and I unceremoniously jerked the sail down, bringing the yard down with it, flapping and billowing to the deck.

Bob came forward and we inspected the damage for an instant, with a view of how to effect immediate repairs. The bare mast leaned against the tent; we were pointed for Bove Island, lined up true with the wind by our centerboards aft.

The strain had broken the log that one of the forward stays was tied to, just at the first crosspiece.

"Tie it anywhere," Jerry said to Bob and returned to the mast. I joined him and we stood the mast up again with the assistance of the wind. It was quickly done.

"Trim the sail the instant it goes up," I called to Bob as Jer and I began to hoist the sail, but I was talking to myself. Bob was already aft, gathering the sheets, ready to set the angle that would put us back on our reach.

As the sail went past my face on its way up the mast, I found myself staring right at the center of Bove Island, its rocky, spume-sprayed beach, and for the first time I could hear the waves breaking.

"Tighten the edges!" Bob screamed. I jumped to it, Jerry doing the same on the other side of the raft.

We apprehensively watched Bob draw the bow around as we gained headway, until we were parallel to Bove Island. We were only two hundred yards off the beach, but with every minute we moved along it, we came closer to the island's end.

That was as close as we got. We picked up the curving wind current and cleared the point of the island by the same two hundred yards.

In the next hour we sailed out of Windy Arm and into the inkiest black night yet. About midnight, somewhere in the narrows off Perthe's Point, we agreed only one man was needed on deck. The wind had all but died, fluttering one direction for a while, then another. We decided to take turns being helmsman in two-hour shifts with the next man on call, sleeping in his clothes, ready in an instant to lend a hand. The third man could be sure of two hours real sleep unless there was an emergency.

Bob volunteered to take the first shift and I would be on call, so with little fanfare Jerry and I raised the tent and turned in.

"Huh?" I answered with a start.

"Are you ready to sail?" Bob said softly through the tent wall.

"Be right out," I replied just as softly, hoping not to wake Jerry. It was light, the tent glowing white all around. Bob had sailed all night.

As I slid on my last boot, Bob passed me on his way to bed. I hurried on deck, to stare right into the forest! One sweep of my eyes was enough to calm me. The sail was nearly limp, the flag fawning about the mast. We were on shore, or within seconds of being on shore, fifteen feet away, yet only a slight whisper of the water meeting the land was to be heard.

"Jer, old buddy, can you lend a hand?" I called, not really being able to suppress a chuckle, a hand to P and P, not sail.

Thump, crash, bump, Jerry was on deck.

"What's the trouble?"

"Well, Bob has left us in a bit of a fix!" We could hear him laughing.

Jerry and I P and P'd about a quarter mile to the last and final turn in the lake. It was a sunny, beautiful morning. From that point, easily gained, we caught the wind out of Taku Arm and turned our backs on the Coast Range and its tempests. Tagish Lake, at least its seven remaining miles, ran north, away from the mountains. We rocked our way down the lake without care, the wind at our backs.

When Bob woke, I was proud to tell him we'd made forty-nine degrees on our reach across Windy Arm.

The wind held all day and by early afternoon we were sailing into the five-mile stretch of river that separates Tagish and Marsh Lakes. We would have to lower our mast to clear the bridge, a rickety old piling affair built during World War II to span the lower end of the river, but we were sailing so well we elected to use both wind and current until the last minute, then furl the sail and drop the mast, securing it alongside. When that was finished, we swang out the long sweeps and clawed our way to shore, tying up above the bridge in a still eddy that seemed to be placed there for our convenience.

A fistful of people stood on the riverbank staring down on our unorthodox craft; they looked like Rembrandt's Potato Eaters leering down on us. Then they flocked aboard and began asking questions.

Answering questions about our raft, which we were all proud of, was a lot of fun at first but they never seemed to stop; the people seemed to come to the raft in shifts, and we had work to do. We were intent on departing Tagish as soon as possible. Our immediate problem was the bridge. The spans between the pilings all looked about the same size, big enough for the raft, but, to be sure, we climbed onto the bridge and measured them. Our curious questioners followed.

The bridge was rickety beyond belief. It seemed only about one in three pilings was solid; the rest were rotted through.

"Damn good thing we didn't hit it," Jerry said, shaking his head. "We probably would have tipped it over!" As you would have it, the spans were about 19 feet 6 inches, our raft was 22 feet wide! It was just plain disgusting.

Tagish, the once-thriving community where all Klondike hopefuls checked in with the Northwest Mounted Police, showed no signs of its illustrious past. In fact, but for the campground, a single home, and what looked like a hot dog stand with the moniker TAGISH ANNE'S over its door, as far as I could see, Tagish had withered to a worn-out bridge.

We entered the tiny shop, our entourage left outside in suspense, pondering the problem of too big a raft and too small a hole. It was a kitchen without the rest of the house, white enamel stoves tended by a jolly giant of a woman, undoubtedly Tagish Anne. The aroma was irresistible. We succumbed, bought three pies, and commenced eating and spilling out our story to our attentive hostess, who, enjoying the palaver, threw in a couple extra pies just to keep us talking. About halfway through our first pies, a wee stick of a man came in and Tagish Anne promptly introduced him as her husband; she easily made up three of him!

We invited them down to visit the raft, but Tagish Anne demurred. Jerry knew why.

"Aw, you don't have to worry about it holding you up," he smiled, "we had twelve people on it one time and it didn't sink!" Anne went. Night was coming again, but we showed Mr. and Mrs. Tagish Anne around the raft before taking on the bridge.

We agreed we either had to saw off part of the bridge or saw off part of our raft in order to get between the piles, and elected on the raft as the solution that would get us into the least trouble. So we sawed off two logs on one side, rolling them under the raft so as not to lose their flotation, and slipped between the pilings with inches to spare on either side.

Our entourage, now standing like ghosts on the bridge above us, was enlisted for mast raising. By tying the raft to the bridge, the mast could easily be pulled up from above. When we threw the lines to the onlookers they caught on quickly, turning from skeptical critics to enthusiastic supporters. We were done in a flash, thanked all, and drifted down a hundred yards to another convenient, solitary piling in midstream, where we tied for the night, out of reach of the prying and curious.

Marsh Lake turned out to be a five-day idyll. Clear sunny days of swimming and relaxing, warm nights and Jerry's first northern lights, light breezes whose only fault was blowing us north until late in the night, leaving us becalmed, the sail hanging limp. Then, just like clockwork, the breeze would switch and send us back the way we came. The first night we went to bed secure, trusting to the fates to take us where they would. In the morning we found ourselves hung up by our centerboards on the shore, nearly where we'd started the day before! At that carefree rate we could be forever running up and down the lake like a yo-yo, so on our first breaths of the north breeze we angled our way to shore, content to take our four- or five-mile progress for the day.

Our last day on Marsh Lake, Sunday, was unique to say the least. Many Whitehorse people have cottages along its shores and spend their weekends there. They came out in all kinds of boats to visit us. At one time our raft, harnessed to the wind, was dragging seven boats along, lashed to both sides, sometimes three deep! The Yukoners were great fun and good company. We shared our coffee, piping hot, with them; they shared their beer, nice and cold, with us.

At the foot of Marsh Lake a lone figure stood on the shore flailing his arms at us like a hapless semaphore. It was Paul, on schedule, just where he said he'd be. Kora and Kurt were with him, and all three piled aboard for the two-mile journey to the highway bridge, the dam, and the lock whose measurements we had so carefully built the raft to fit. Spirits ran high; all the lakes except one were behind us, and we would soon be tasting our first real river, the twenty-five-mile stretch that led to Miles Canyon, on the outskirts of Whitehorse. But first, the lock.

The four of us furled the sail, and with our two passengers, swept out into the current. The current was weak, but strengthened gradually, so that when we saw the highway bridge, with the dam a quarter mile below it, we were moving right along, faster than we had ever traveled, and we didn't fully realize the implications.

We planned to tie-up above the highway bridge and lower the mast, then float under and drift down to the lock, where we would split the raft and take each half through.

It was a new feeling, floating along in the river's current. After lying prone before the wind's capriciousness for so long, we were finally drifting steadily toward the sea, and as long as we stayed in the river we would continue to do so. As we neared the highway bridge, the dam visible and audible a quarter mile below it, I felt strange. I'd crossed the bridge many times in my life, but now I was crossing it at another angle and on another plane; in fact, from another world.

"Let's tie her up," Jerry called. Nobody was eager to—the drifting was a joy—but Paul and Bob climbed in the canoe and headed to shore with a small line which they tied to a tree. They remained on the shore to watch us swing in. To our horror, the line came taut and quickly snapped, not slowing the raft's progress for a millisecond. We were only a hundred yards from the highway bridge.

In a time so short I doubt it could be measured, nerves and muscles and thoughts slammed into high gear. Bob and Paul were in the canoe and powering toward the raft. "Get to the other end," Jerry advised Kurt and Kora.

I grabbed the stern sweep and aimed the raft so that when the mast hit, it would topple off behind us. Jerry was on the other sweep working feverishly toward the same goal. We weren't far enough around, but I left the sweep and grabbed an ax, yelling to Jerry as I jumped to the guy lines, "I'm going to chop her free!"

"Roger," he boomed back. We were under the bridge; fully six feet of the mast would hit it.

"Clear!" I yelled, and without waiting for an answer, chopped one guy line then leaped to the other as the mast hit the bridge with a loud crack. The second guy line snapped from the edge of my ax like a spring, and the mast, now free, slammed into the river.

We were dismasted: Lines, mast, sail, and yardarm floated behind us, making it impossible to maneuver ashore with the sweeps.

Jerry and I were hastily pulling the rigging aboard when Paul and Bob arrived.

"More line, our biggest!" Bob exclaimed. Paul was poised on the stern of the canoe, ready to speed to shore.

Bob grabbed our nylon line, I spliced it to our three-quarter-inch manila, and they were off. Jerry had finished pulling in our mast and rigging and we both bent our backs to the sweeps, trying to close the shore.

We were halfway to the dam when Paul and Bob reached land. Jerry and I had managed to sweep the raft in about forty feet; we were still more than a hundred feet off the beach.

"That's got it," Paul hollered. He'd tied the line to a sturdy birch.

Jerry and I relaxed as the line came taut, it had been a nerve-wracking few minutes, but it seemed we'd pulled it out. A big eddy was ahead of us when the line slowed us, we would swing into it and out of the strong current that bore off to the dam.

To our absolute horror, the raft didn't slow down and the line parted. Just as relaxation had been replaced by anxiety, anxiety now gave way to fear. And I knew it had been my knot that gave.

A hoarse cry to *"sweep!"* croaked past my lips as I grabbed the sweep, a plea to use every last bit of everything we had. There would be no more chances. It was apparent we were going to skirt the protective eddy and rush into the dam where our raft would be jammed and slammed and ripped into so much matchwood by the river. I barely looked up when I saw the canoe alongside, my mind was planning how to get Kora and Kurt into the dam's bracing when we hit. My welfare had been pre-empted by their presence. At the moment the collision became absolutely inevitable I would race forward and somehow get them to safety at any cost, and that moment was nauseatingly close.

"We're going to hit!" Jerry yelled. It was time. I raced forward. Kora and Kurt were standing behind Jerry, out of the way. The din of roaring water was all around—the dam a minute away. Our total attention was focused on it, choosing our best chance for survival. In moments we would know exactly where we were going to hit; our fate would be decided in seconds. We would have to lift or pull, somehow get Kurt and Kora into the framework above the water.

I felt the raft lurch, and then, to my amazement, it began

swinging to shore! I glanced over my shoulder for an instant; the line was taut! Paul and Bob had made a last supreme effort to tie us up and succeeded. We slipped into the edge of the eddy and the raft moved quietly to shore.

I started to shake. I don't know how many calories a few minutes like that uses up, but I had to sit down. Jerry was already seated. We all looked a bit peaked; little was said until we normalized.

That was the last time anyone sailed with us. From that day on, when the raft pulled out we alone were aboard.

We were on our way again in the morning, though the close call of the previous evening was branded in my mind. We removed the splices that held our raft together and took it through the lock, one half at a time. All in all, the operation went smoothly; five hours later our raft was once more shipshape, though with a mast shorter by some six feet.

Twenty-five miles of true river separated us from Miles Canyon when we cast off below the lock/dam at Marsh Lake. Kora and Kurt would drive to Whitehorse to watch our journey through the canyon.

We let the raft go wherever it willed, just to see what would happen. Where would it ride in the current? Would it stay in the river's center, or slide along the shore? How easily could we maneuver it with the sweeps? How accurately? Could the raft run into obstacles with impunity? We had many things to learn and we had to learn them ourselves—few people lived who could advise us.

We managed the twenty-five-mile piece of river all right, sort of. The only mishap was one broken sweep that resulted in a delay of a few hours while we hewed another sturdier one, another hairy tie-up attempt that resulted in a swamped canoe and wet clothes for Paul, and a mile run through the brush for me as I tried to keep up with Jerry and Bob on the fast-moving raft. Luckily, we were wise enough to begin our tie-up attempt far enough above the mouth of Miles Canyon to give us ample time to try another if the first should fail. Even so, we used up four miles of river before we managed to stop the raft. We were finally tied perhaps half a mile above Miles Canyon, and now had to face what had originally been thought of as our first serious obstacle.

In a quiet interlude, the raft slips across Nares Lake.

Dawn and sunrise vigil at the sweep. In the high latitudes, summer days are long and nights are a fleeting succession of sunset, twilight, and sunrise. Often the rafters drifted around the clock.

The raft's tent, crowded but cozy, was home for the crew for two summers. The author (left) and Jerry wait for a contrary wind to die before casting off from Galena.

Paul on his one-man raft. He regretfully left the others late the second August and floated one hundred miles to the airport at Bethel, to join the professional skiing circuit.

Deck turns to floor and galley becomes kitchen as Bob (top) and Jerry transform the raft into a cabin where the three will wait for the Yukon to freeze before continuing their journey on skis.

The finished cabin by starlight.

In winter, the frozen Yukon becomes "Main Street" for the Eskimo citizens of Marshall (population 175).

Reaching Marshall in January, the skiiers joined in "Slavi," the Russian Orthodox celebration of Christmas. Following their star (background) from house to house, the villagers reenact the wise men's journey in this week-long festival.

Buffeting headwinds from far out over the Bering Sea pushed chill factors as low as minus 100 degrees. Sometimes beard, mustache, and face mask froze solidly together.

What Jack London called "the white silence" enveloped each man in the trio's harrowing struggle across the barren Yukon Delta.

In late February the trio skied onto the vast, frozen Bering Sea where a plane would pick them up. "Reaching the sea turned out to be an anti-climax," mused the author. "We all wanted to keep going!"

Wipeout, Whitehorse, and Plans for a June Reunion

The exploration and settling of North America could be capsulized in a list of the few places where nature pared off the unwise or careless. These regions of hardship, the western deserts and the Donner Passes, seem to grow more hostile or difficult with time. Their reputations do not diminish; they magnify.

Miles Canyon was one of those places, as mythical as it was real. In Lieutenant Schwatka's words in 1883, the Grand Canyon of the Yukon was a ". . . diminutive Fingal's cave . . resembling a deep black thoroughfare paved with the whitest marble."

To Jack London, during the gold rush, ". . . it was a box, a trap. Once in it, the only way out was through. On either side arose perpendicular walls of rock. The river narrowed to a fraction of its width and roared through this gloomy passage in a madness of motion that heaped the water in the center into a ridge fully eight feet higher than at the rocky sides. This ridge, in turn, was crested with stiff, upstanding waves that curled over, yet remained each in its unvarying place. The canyon was well feared, for it had collected its toll of dead from the passing gold seekers."

The river surged through a narrow cleft in a vast sheet of volcanic basalt, columns of basalt having been bashed out in a fault something like twenty-five or thirty yards wide and a mile long by the necked-down river. Water tore through the canyon in a sustained rage. Halfway down the gorge, the walls bulged for a great whirlpool that Indians believed doomed all caught in its suction, never to reappear. After passing the eye of the storm of hell, the walls narrowed again,

continuing to the canyon's end and a brief respite before the Squaw and Whitehorse rapids. Here, the river tumbled over stone steps, rearing in great waves, making the three-mile passage from the top of Miles to the end of the Whitehorse the most turbulent piece of river on the Yukon.

It was certainly not an impossible stretch of river to navigate for the experienced (some say the first man to take a fully laden boat through was a trader in 1894 with a load of booze for the miners at Forty Mile), but for clerks and farmers of the Stampede, it was a bit much. In the first few days of the arrival of the flotilla from Bennett, some ten people drowned and 150 boats were wrecked attempting to shoot through. Yet all was not grim for those who could laugh at themselves. Two Swedes in 1895 made the longest passage of Miles Canyon, a passage generally only minutes long. They spent six hours circling the whirlpool before finally swinging free. A solitary Englishman calmly rode through the canyon and Squaw and Whitehorse rapids without realizing he was in danger.

Inspector Steel of the Northwest Mounted Police, on arriving at Miles Canyon in 1898 during the rush, decreed only experienced river men would pilot boats through—the qualifications of the pilots to be decided by the men in red, and a steep fine levied on violators. This action undoubtedly saved countless lives and outfits. For the most part, goods were transported around the canyon on a wooden-railed tram built by the enterprising Norman MacAulay who charged three cents a pound. The boats were run through, empty, by the river men.

So I harked back and romanticized as I stood with my three partners above the entrance to Miles Canyon, three quarters of a century after the rush. MacAulay's tramway was a shadow of ant-riddled, crumbling wood, and Squaw and Whitehorse rapids were no more, smothered by a monolith of the twentieth century's finest, the North Canada Power Commission's hydroelectric dam and its reservoir, Lake Schwatka. The reservoir backed up to Miles Canyon lowering the river's fall through it. The canyon was no longer ridged in foam, the whirlpool was gone, yet the three miles that commenced with the canyon's jaws still loomed as our greatest obstacle. We could no longer calculate our chances through the Squaw and Whitehorse rapids. We couldn't portage our gear and let the raft go, manned or unmanned as the risk prescribed, to be retrieved later. We had no alternative but to portage everything we had with us, raft included, around the dam.

Though tamed, the canyon was formidable for our large raft. Still the water turned it into a near ninety-degree right-hand turn. The river was high and fast, in the canyon perhaps eight to ten miles an hour. Our short experience with the raft in the river above the canyon was enough to impress on us its unwieldy character and the force of its momentum. If we hit the canyon anywhere in our course through its narrow confines, something would give. The catch was to figure out where to place ourselves in the current above the canyon in order to be sure of riding the river through the sharp right turn and into the defile without hitting the walls. That part hadn't changed at all.

We inched into the current three-quarters of a mile above Miles Canyon. Paul, pulling on the forward sweep, bobbed in and out of view from behind the tent as I watched the river ahead. Jerry kept pace on the rear sweep, Bob and I stood on the rear deck with him, stout poles in hand. We would use them to fend off the canyon walls if necessary.

Once in the current there was little to do but wait. There wasn't much talk, other than the outwardly casual banter between Jer and Paul as they kept the raft lined straight in the current. Bob busied himself with his cameras. I walked the deck checking to see that life jackets were at hand. Each of us had a little something to occupy himself with to kill time.

"There she is," Paul called as the mouth of the canyon came into view. We had only to traverse a great eddy where the river stacked and milled before pouring into the canyon. We drifted along the right of the swirl, destined but still uncommitted.

We waited. Our eyes were glued ahead, looking for some clue to our course in the water rushing into the canyon. As we closed, it came. If anything, we needed to move to the right and began sweeping that way.

Oh God, I thought, we are moving right, but not fast enough.

I slid my hands along the pole I clutched, settling my grip on the smooth spot I'd already chosen a dozen times. Paul was pulling hard forward. Jerry's sweep bowed under his strength.

"How're we doing?" Jerry puffed in midstroke.

"I don't know. . . ," was Bob's reply.

We passed the right edge of the canyon mouth, the raft locked in a fierce duel with the river, both now beyond our pitiful influence. The raft with its tremendous momentum was being carried across the canyon, gripped in an inexorable crosscurrent that tried to ram us down into the canyon. We were counting on that current, and with every second it failed us, we neared the far canyon wall. Ponderously, we began our turn into the canyon; too late. I ran forward, bracing my pole against the wall to fend us off. It was a ridiculously ineffectual gesture, and immediately forced me backward like so much straw. Nothing could stay us, not for a millisecond. As I jumped for the free side of the raft, Paul looked pitifully vulnerable against the rock face.

"We're going to . . ."

The words were lost in a terrible splintering crash. The mast waved, then toppled back on the tent, the deck wracked and twisted beneath my feet. The raft hesitated, then slowly began to cartwheel along the stone wall in a grinding tearing rasp of wood against stone.

"*Paul!*" I called, rushing to the catwalk along the canyon wall.

He was all right. I could just see his head beyond the tent, then I looked around quickly, prepared to exit. I would swim the canyon before being trapped in our wreckage.

Logs were bobbing away from the raft like the slowly spreading fingers of a hand, some attached to stubs of broken stringers and cross pieces, some short, some long. One corner of the tent drooped into the river; there was no raft under it. The collision had transformed us from a rectangle to some sort of parallelogram.

I yelled to Jerry. "Front corner's smashed. Is she holding where you are?"

"Still together here." Jerry answered me from the stern sweep, then yelled forward, "Can you sweep, Paul?"

"A little," he yelled.

"Hold her in till I come around!" Jerry yelled. We were already halfway through our first cartwheel, there was certainly no sense in cartwheeling along the canyon side until our parallelogram was round.

We were hard hit, but still afloat with a somewhat manageable raft.

Jerry arrested our cartwheeling just as we paralleled the canyon and hit with a glancing blow that jarred us again soundly, but sheared no logs from the as yet undamaged side. We scraped along the wall for a few moments before Jerry began pulling the now downriver end of the raft away from the wall. Paul's sweep was hardly usable, its mount partially unsupported, the raft having broken apart just up to it. His deck slanted into the river, yet he carefully swept away from the wall. The imminent danger passed; we were under control, ever so steadily pulling away from the wall.

Bob and I went to work on emergency repairs, bringing in the wayward logs we could reach and jury rigging the mast.

We were barely finished when we sped into the placid waters of Lake Schwatka. As we limped into the shore, Paul's sweep finally played out.

The inside of the tent was a shambles. Floorboards were wracked out of place, nothing was square, bunks had fallen down, the corner under Bob's bunk was under water. Most items stored on the floor were wet, most of everything else was on the floor. It was a mess. There would be no sense in putting our house in order—we still had to somehow manage the dam.

Though we'd made it through Miles Canyon, faces were very long. An eighth of the raft had been sheared off and broken up. We had struck out in the canyon department.

A lane led along the lake shore, passing docks and float plane landings on its way into Whitehorse. We heard a car; it was Kora and Kurt. Kurt volunteered to watch the raft that evening, and the four of us piled into Kora's car with our dirty clothes and headed for Whitehorse. First order of business: a cold beer.

We regained heart, and by Friday morning had made arrangements for the transport of our raft around the dam. Alan Innes-Taylor, whose aid was indispensable, enlisted the help of General Enterprises, a large contracting firm that would provide the crane and operator, and White Pass Petroleum Division, that loaned us one of its familiar green-and-yellow tractor-trailer rigs, a big Kenworth with a flatbed trailer. The plan, once the raft was split in half as for the Marsh Lake lock, was to load the damaged half onto the trailer, then load the good half with the tent framing on top of that. It was all the old crane with its five-ton capacity could do to wheeze and lurch each half out of the water. There were some nervous moments, but the operator's soft touch prevailed and all went well. Jerry and I climbed in the cab with the driver for the slow ride through downtown Whitehorse to the riverfront, where the steamers, from the turn of the century until the early fifties, had been winched out before freezeup and launched after breakup. The steamers, *Casca* and *Whitehorse*, still squatted there on their blocks, waiting for a spring that would never come. We would rebuild our raft in their shadows.

We backed the raft down to the water's edge. The crane was in place; it should have been easy. The first half of the raft rose, swung, then, with a crash and splintering of wood, fell to the ground, a jumble of logs and lumber.

Bob started laughing, Paul followed, then Jerry and I. There was nothing else to do. It was terribly funny, such irony. We had used up all our depression after Miles Canyon, yet that was only one eighth of our trouble. The crane operator was the last to join in the laughter; he'd somehow felt responsible. It couldn't be helped, we explained, our raft was made to float on water, not fly through the air! The already busted up second half was laid unceremoniously on our "junk pile."

An onlooker sped to town with the last of our spare funds for beer, and we finished the day in style.

We really hustled getting the raft back together. The last thing we wanted was all of Whitehorse laughing at us. We pieced it together, this time running the logs crosswise and the stringers lengthwise, because our longest logs had snapped at the middle. We raised the tent frame a full foot above the water, improved the decks and walkways, and staggered six thirty-foot dry logs lengthwise under the raft, pinning them there for strength. Our losses were pride and time, but we now had a raft that drew two feet of water instead of little more than a foot.

When we pulled out of Whitehorse, we not only had a new, rebuilt raft, but some new friends as well—people to thank, people to say good-bye to. We'd slept on floors, chesterfields, spare beds; and we'd shared meals and evenings with the people of Whitehorse. Though we did the work, they were as much a part of our rebuilding as we were: Old-timers, newcomers, optimists and pessimists, young and old helped us in whatever ways they could. In that regard, the finest quality of the northern frontier has changed little.

On August 24, nine days after entering Miles Canyon, we drifted away from Whitehorse. Our summer would soon be closing down on us. Some 460 miles of river lay between Whitehorse and Dawson to the north, not to mention thirty-five-mile-long Lake Laberge, which would finish off our sailing. Five Finger Rapids lay ahead of us, twenty miles below Carmacks, the only community on the Yukon between Whitehorse and Dawson save for the Burian family at Stewart, eighty miles from Dawson. Dawson was our goal. With luck, we would arrive before freezeup, store our raft, and continue the following year.

As Whitehorse slipped behind us and the sounds of its life were lost, I finally, finally felt we were on our way. We'd surely slip under the bridge at Carmacks, with the river low—the natural obstacles we would meet as they came.

26 August 1972

We're under sail once again, on immortal Lake Laberge, our 20-mile journey from Whitehorse a piece of cake. The mercury hangs at 40°, snow on the mountains, dew everywhere and my fingers are cold. Hot cereal for breakfast. Hopefully we make it OK, but tying up every evening may not be so easy. There aren't a lot of sheltered coves on the lower lake, just plenty of high, stone bluffs.

By mid-afternoon the wind had stiffened considerably, and though we were making good time, our raft wasn't as fine a sailer with the logs running crosswise rather than lengthwise. The helm took constant manning, and we had no centerboards down; there were no more convenient slots for them.

By mid-afternoon, our lack of centerboards had become critical. We were being blown by gale winds toward stone bluffs on the east shore, unable to sail with any angle to the wind. We weren't far from the "X" on our chart where the steamer Thistle sank.

20:00 — Tent's down, sea anchor is out, emergency gear ready. Five to 7 foot waves are carrying us into the shore due east of Richtofen Island. There is a cove, our last chance; I hope we hit it. The raft seems to be taking everything all right, but against the shore? Writing on our rocking deck isn't easy. . . .

21:00 — Made it! Whew! Blow, you mother, blow! You can't get us in here!

As if in acknowledgement, the wind began to slacken.

The next morning we built centerboard racks along the sides of the raft.

Lake Laberge had its fun with us. When it stormed, we ventured out carefully, always within reach of some protected bay, bight, or cove, or else we waited. When the lake was calm, we P and P'd along the eastern shore's jumble of stone. When the weather was ideal, we sailed. We had the wind turn on us, once one-hundred eighty degrees in ten minutes. More than once we had to sail back into the heaven we'd just departed.

We watched the whimsical weather like hawks. The flag at the masthead was everyone's constant companion, its minutest shift or change in flutter noted. Southerly winds were our only real friends. North winds and west winds we couldn't sail out against, but used to return the raft to our east shore.

Our third night on Laberge was memorable. The wind utterly died before we made shore. We waited calmly through the sunset, hoping for a breath of wind to carry us the quarter mile in. Night closed around us, absolute in its stillness. Before the last hues of sunset were gone, the stars stole across the sky and soon they covered it completely, right down to the edges of the earth. Falling stars streaked and faded in the near sky, in the far sky clusters could be divided with the eye. The dim stars missing from the constellations on most nights shone clearly.

We sat long on the deck, without stirring, mute, as in a spell. Then, as if by mutual arrangement, Jerry and Bob made ready to sweep the raft ashore. Paul and I pulled away in the canoe tied to the raft midships with our long line. We hit the end of the line with a jerk and began our toil.

The moon loomed into sight and, as the stars had humbled the sun, the moon now eclipsed the stars. It was so huge it seemed to come through the trees on shore rather than from beyond them. We stopped paddling, the creaking of the sweeps on the raft ceased, as the moon rose, silent and splendid, above the forest.

The sky seemed clothed with a blanket of soft, pure frost, removing any harshness from the moon's brilliance, and lending the night a warmth meant only for the soul. We were mesmerized.

"Holy Jesus . . ."

The moonbeam fell to the lake, we were on its path.

I looked back to the raft.

"You're all lit up!" I called.

"You're riding the moonbeam," Jerry replied.

We followed the silver beam to its end in the dark shadow cast by the bluff. The edge of the shadow was so abrupt and distinct I felt I was paddling into a black fog.

"Can you see us?" I called back.

"No," Bob answered. "It's eerie; you've completely disappeared."

We beached the canoe and pulled the raft in, hand over hand. We didn't build a fire on the beach; it wasn't that sort of a night. It was more for solitariness, for deep thought, for stretching out to the stars rather than drawing into the fire.

All went well for us the next day; a fine southerly carried us to lower Laberge. Homing on a speck of white that turned out to be an old steamboat marker, we sailed into the river and quickly furled the sail for the last time. Our headway through the water slowed and stopped but our movement was sustained as the current gradually took over.

"Time check," Jerry called, leaning over the map, pencil in hand. We would carefully mark our course and position, ticking off the miles we traveled each day.

I glanced into the tent at the clock over my bunk and answered, "One-thirty."

"Here we go, fellas!" Bob said, and Lake Laberge disappeared as we rounded the first bend.

We were on the "Thirty Mile," its end—you guessed it—thirty miles farther on, at our junction with the Teslin River. The Thirty Mile is the eternal child of the Yukon, clear and swift, boulder strewn and impetuous. It twists and turns through a confining earthen canyon, to Hootalinqua, "The place where two rivers meet" in the Indian tongue.

At first we kept the raft lined up, floating downriver backward from how we had sailed, the big rear deck facing ahead, downstream. We were elated not to have to claw for every mile at the mercy of the wind. The river would do the work. In the little bit of river we'd run, we knew enough to have learned to keep the raft straight, and to try to keep from hitting things, notably the shore. For a while I worked the sweep at the rear of the raft alone, and found it easy for one man to keep the raft lined up, facing downstream. But if I tried to change our position in the river, to move the raft either to the left or to the right, we only pivoted. That took two men, both sweeps.

We rounded a number of bends with flying colors, though sometimes the river turned a bit sharper or faster than we did, and we found ourselves watching sticks still in the main current pass us by, until we swept back into the faster current and were on our way again.

Our first test on the Thirty Mile would be U.S. Bend, carefully marked on the river boat chart Alan Innes-Taylor had given us, including an additional tidbit, an "X" with a note, "Steamer Domville wrecked, 1899."

14:47 — Around U.S. Bend. There's a big U and then an S turn. We made it. The Thirty Mile would be a cinch for small craft, canoes, motorboats, and such. Rocks could be easily avoided, minor rapids maneuvered in or around. Obstructions hidden under the surface could be passed over or avoided easily at the very last moment. We are in a whole different ball game. With our unwieldy raft and its momentum, infinite care must be taken to avoid any contact with immovable objects. Just the existence of something we could hit, no matter how unlikely, causes concern. We just can't paddle or motor anywhere we want. The parts the steamers took care to avoid are clearly marked on our steamer chart, though we quickly found out the chart is not at all to scale, so we often wonder when the obstacle to avoid is approaching! Anyhow, the boats drew as much as 4 feet, we draw 2, that little bit is in our favor.

We passed Twelve Mile Rock, saw others. We would have to be alert to correct our course quickly to avoid them. We watched for any disturbance in the river ahead indicating boulders just under the surface.

17:20 — Our first hang-up. We spent 25 minutes aground on a lump of moss along the right bank. Odd, just a freak chance, but it happened.

We began to work at keeping away from the shore as a matter of course.

Six hours after sailing into the Thirty Mile we slipped round its last bend and into a still bay. At the back of the bay a handful of cabins sat in a grassy opening in the forest—Hootalinqua Station. We tied there.

It was dusk, under an overcast sky, but there was time yet to look around. Four buildings stood, five if you count a marvelous three-holer behind the last cabin. The largest structure, a building made of massive, hand-hewn logs, was identified by a sign as the Northwest Mounted Police post. It was empty; hadn't been inhabited for some time, probably since the steamers shut down, and it was open to the elements, with the sky showing through its roof. One corner of the building, by the looks of the wires running in and out, had been the telegraph office. Two nearby cabins were likewise open to the elements and had probably been residences. The smallest cabin and the only one habitable was used by the Yukon Water Resources survey crews and other passersby, as indicated by a tattered spiral notepad on the table that served as an informal register. The cabin was stocked with an ax, saw, food, and matches, just enough to qualify as a true godsend.

Darkness fell over us before we finished exploring, and we turned in. Paul had slipped off earlier to try his luck with a fishing pole, and it paid off—we had grayling for breakfast.

We were up and around before breakfast, the dew was heavy, the air chill. Another look around Hootalinqua revealed nothing new save the log foundations of more buildings hidden in the grass. Trails crossed the area, one leading to the graveyard, another along the overgrown telegraph line. It was hard to tell what, if anything, once stood in the now encroaching brush.

Bob was busy with his camera, Paul was off again with his fishing pole, and, in our search for remains, Jerry and I found a thicket of black currants. We'd already spied raspberries around the old buildings, so we picked a bowl full of each to go with breakfast. Yum, yum! The raspberries and grayling, including two more Paul caught, disappeared right away. The tart currants were made into a kind of jam later on. We didn't have gelatin, so we poured most of the juice off and with sugar and a bit of water added, it made a pretty fine fruit juice! The "jam," actually the mash that was left over, wasn't exactly in the class with what moms make, but it fit the bill. Besides, we were out of regular jam.

We were on our way by half past nine, our curiosities more whetted than appeased. In its heyday, Hootalinqua Station had been one of many thriving communities along the Yukon.

These towns were most often found at the mouth of an important tributary. The discovery of the rich Klondike goldfields precipitated the tidal wave of the Stampeders. But, like the tide, they sought not just one beach, and the farthest creeks and valleys of the vast Yukon watershed were flocked to, felt pick and shovel, made and broke bodies and hearts.

During that fevered time, when gold was shipped to mints by the tons, great fleets of steamers flying the pennants of their trading companies—British–Yukon Navigation Company, Alaska Commercial Company, North American Trade and Transportation Company, and others—vied for the lucrative trade in anything from gum boots and nails, steam boilers and printing presses, to oysters and champagne and little-old-lady tourists. Dawson absorbed the great bulk of the trade. Dawson was the beginning, the proof, that the North would support civilization. With Dawson's arrival, the prospects of another rich or even richer discovery were born.

Communities like Hootalinqua were trade and communication hubs, like pumps on a pipeline, supporting the whole operation, the whole movement. Their existences were ensured as long as people needed the river. When the steamers stopped running, Hootalinqua died.

The brisk, damp morning and the telltale dabs of color here and there on the leaves reminded us we had a long way to go before the ice started running sometime in mid-October. We had 380 miles yet to drift.

We didn't think twice about our course as we pulled out from Hootalinqua. In fact, by pulling in where we did, we were committed to drifting through the channel to the left of Shipyard Island, where the steamer *Evelyn* lay rotting in the bushes, then sweeping into the heart of the Yukon, where the Teslin River entered, nearly doubling its size.

As soon as we saw our channel, we realized there was a right side and a wrong side to passing Shipyard Island and we were definitely on the wrong side. Telltale ripples indicated a shoal crossing from the island to the left bank.

Oh, God, let it be deep enough, I thought. The shoal was around us now and we began to scrape along the bottom. I expected us to stop but we continued, the raft rattling and shaking as we drove farther and farther onto the gravel reef. We looked around at each other, then at the deck jolting under us.

"We're still moving," Jerry said in amazement. Though our momentum had slowed, we were nearly halfway across the shoal.

"Quick!" Bob said. "Let's get off and push."

We jumped overboard, the water was just knee deep. Our efforts helped some, but even so, our momentum was slacking as we bulled our way onto the bar and ground to a halt, nosed into a ledge of gravel the raft had pushed before it like a bulldozer. The stern, still afloat in the shallow trough, was swinging to the right in the current.

"Watch your legs!" Paul yelled.

But we were all already clear. Getting pinned between the raft and the bar under a foot and a half of water wouldn't be a bit funny. The grating ceased, the raft stopped. The water gurgled around our grounded whale.

We tied our long line to the raft, and threw the rest in the canoe, paying it out as we paddled upriver to the point of Shipyard Island. We would try to pull the raft back off the bar, against the current. Jerry found a tail holt as we rigged the block and tackle, then the four of us leaned into the line, hopes high. The four-block purchase gave us a lot of power. Plenty of power, we thought, until the 1600-pound test line stretched tighter and tighter, thinner and thinner, and the raft didn't so much as budge.

"Hold," Jerry said, sweat beading his brow. "She'll never go."

It was true. We canoed back to the raft for a bowl of hot beans and another try.

"It's deepest this way," Bob called.

He was wading back and forth perhaps sixty feet away, sounding the bar below the raft. The water was above his knees.

"I think if we get this far, we'll be all right."

We didn't budge the raft at all until we attacked it with pry poles, and that's how we finally worked the raft free. Each of us jammed a stout pole under the raft, then squatted down till his backside and worse were dunked in the cold water in order to get a shoulder behind his pole, then took turns calling the two words that will forever remind me of the Yukon. "Ready," to set feet, shoulder, grip, and mind, then "Heave!" when we surged in unison with all we had, for only with four manpower could we move the raft. Real progress, the kind that brought twisted smiles and animal determination, was six inches or so per go. We levered one corner at a time, first prying the raft sideways to the current to get the full advantage of its force on the raft's greatest length, then we went back and forth from end to end, prying first one corner then the other toward our goal, keeping the length of the raft facing the current. It was three in the afternoon before we floated free. Sixty feet is a long way, a few tough inches at a time.

The Yukon, with the Teslin added to it, began to take on the shape of a good-sized river. It ran in the bottom of a not-too-confining valley perhaps three miles wide, and was now at least two hundred yards across. The river crossed and recrossed its valley, and when we slid along its edges, we had stately bluffs or high cliffs of stone for a bank.

When we saw islands ahead, we studied the river's surface for hints of its intent. The fast current showed more signs than slower water; it rolled and boiled, was more disturbed. We would follow it with our eyes far ahead and guess which side of an island it took, then help it by sweeping the raft that way. Some we guessed correctly, some we figured wrong. Then we watched the main current arc away, down the other side of the island, while we took a detour. Most of the time it didn't matter, and we returned to the main current or the other half of a current split by the island. We only ground to a stop once, and it took just ten minutes to free ourselves.

We stayed out on the river, trying to ride the heart of the main current. If we stayed in it, it didn't matter which side of an island we passed on, there was plenty of water under us. For miles the river ran true, without islands or sharp bends, and we had time to ourselves.

The sweep at the mast, our sailing bow, became the rear sweep, its tiny deck the rear deck, just right for one man and himself. The large (by comparison) forward deck became just "the deck," its sweep the forward sweep.

We organized the running of the raft into two-hour shifts, two men on duty at a time. We took turns working with each other. The man at the forward sweep had the ultimate say in deciding a course, the man on the rear sweep was responsible for keeping the raft parallel to the shore.

Important decisions were usually made mutually by the duty crew, the off-duty crew wasn't involved, though kibitzing wasn't unknown. Shifts started each day with cast off, the crew not working at mealtime cooked, the next crew washed up. When you weren't on duty, you had plenty of time to sew or read or snooze or think—time for yourself.

The Yukon is dynamic, always changing. Its force cuts into its banks, makes bars and rivers disappear, and carves new channels in the valley floor. The material it moves is deposited somewhere downstream, choking off old channels, forming new bars, new islands. What an irony that the rich ground in the valley bottom with the best sunlight along the river's banks for growing trees should have doom locked in its blessing, like the Aztec maidens who were given every honor precisely because they would be sacrificed to the gods. So the tall straight spruce along the "cutbanks" leaned, tipped, then bowed far out over the water as their support eroded away, and they became sweepers, before finally losing to the river.

We avoided the sweepers like the plague, like shallows, like canyon walls. They could sweep everything—tent, bunks, mast, the whole works—off the raft if we hit them. We always kept an ax handy as a last resort.

It was too dark and, consequently, risky for us to travel the river after eight, especially on cloudy evenings, so sometime around six we began edging closer to shore and looking ahead for a good place to tie for the night. After seven, the first likely spot was taken.

The two off-duty men made up the "kamikaze crew," as it became known, and canoed to shore with the tail end of the long line loosely tied to the thwart. As soon as the canoe touched shore, the bowman grabbed the line and ran down the beach parallel to the still-moving raft, looking for a substantial tree to take as many wraps around as he could before the moving raft drew the line taut. The line would stretch like a rubber band, becoming taut as a bowstring as the raft slowed, then swung into shore. It was always a tricky chore for the bowman, crashing through the snagging brush, rope everywhere, circling the trunk of a tree. To tangle a foot in the rope coil, or to get a finger or arm between line and tree meant instant amputation.

The stern man would offer assistance if he could get the canoe ashore and reach the "scene" before the fireworks were over.

Our third day out of Hootalinqua was fair beyond expectation. We drifted fifty-three miles with just one minor grounding. The weather was cheerful and sunny; we didn't even work too hard getting ungrounded. We swept out of the current three miles above Carmacks and rode the slack water under the highway bridge without having to lower our mast. We were most careful in our tie-up, dreading the thought of careening along the waterfront and "owning" a handful of smashed boats we couldn't pay for!

Pay for the boats, ha! When we tied up at Carmacks we had enough money for two beers with a bit of change. We were still out of jam and now out of sugar to make it with. We were out of salt, and craving a change from beans and bacon with a half inch of furry mold on it, craving something fresh and green. We needed gas for our

Coleman stove and maybe, just maybe, a heater stove and some mail were waiting at the post office.

Carmacks, on the left bank of the Yukon, was named after G.W. Carmacks, the Californian who was in on the discovery of gold in the Klondike in 1896. He'd lived in the region before striking it rich; they say he found the coal that had been mined across the river before the mine closed down.

A road kept Carmacks alive. The gravel highway led on to Dawson, then beyond it, past the asbestos mine at Clinton Creek in the Forty Mile, and it had a fork to Mayo and the mines at Faro and another to Ross River and the Cyprus-Anvil Mine. The big ore rigs, the modern equivalents of the steamboat, moved round the clock between Whitehorse and the mines, orange trucks for Cassiar asbestos; green and yellow, White Pass. We could hear them from the raft, gearing down as they came into town. Sometimes the drivers stopped for grub or a cup of coffee, to stretch their legs, check tires. When they pulled their eighteen-wheelers out we listened to them rise through the gears, far away and lonely, as they gained the open road.

It was Saturday, and wouldn't you know it, Labor Day weekend—no post office till Tuesday. Flat broke, we decided to look for odd jobs.

Work of some kind or another was always in progress at a North Country roadhouse. Half of them were kept open with baling wire and rubber hose, and surely some heavy work could be found to give us enough money to buy our few necessities. Accordingly, first thing in the morning Jerry and I went to the biggest roadhouse, figuring the bigger it is, the more work there should be to do.

We walked into the restaurant. Working men were drinking coffee, two sat at a table over plates of sausage and eggs. Jerry's eyes rolled toward me. While we weren't exactly starving after a big sourdough breakfast, the aroma of sausage and eggs was awful appealing.

"Can I help you?" the waitress asked.

"We'd like to talk to the manager," I said. She looked at us kinda' funny, then stepped into the kitchen.

"Maybe we shoulda' changed," I whispered to Jerry.

"Oh hell, we put on clean clothes in Whitehorse," he answered. "Besides these are working clothes."

107

Just then another woman came out, a big, good-looking blonde. She wore an official smile.

"We came in last night," I explained. "We're broke and were wondering if you had any odd jobs we could do?"

She asked us if we came on the big raft. We said we had. She left and returned with her husband, a healthy, happy fellow in his mid-thirties. We explained our situation, leaning a bit heavy on the part about being low on grub.

"What can you do?" he asked, sizing us up.

"Just about anything," I replied, feeling expansive.

He beckoned us to follow and we went out behind the roadhouse where everything that might have some future use was deposited.

"I'll bring out a couple of hammers. Pull the nails out of this pile of scrap lumber and I'll see if I can think of anything else. How does two-fifty an hour sound?"

We weren't really in a position to negotiate, and Jer and I were soon jabbering away at each other as we pulled nails. We stacked the lumber according to its dimensions while saving all the rusty nails in a can.

It took us two hours, and when we went to turn in our hammers we left behind neat stacks of lumber and a can of nails.

"You know," he said, looking at the pile, "I could use a hand moving a couple of heavy freezers out of the basement. I'll get my pickup and find a dolly."

"Let's have a look at them first," Jerry said, and we followed him into the roadhouse basement. Jerry and I hefted the freezers, they didn't seem all that heavy, so we just grabbed them one at a time and moved them by hand. About that time he started thinking pretty hard about finding us more to do.

"You guys want to pour a concrete floor?" he asked.

"Where?" I answered, and he took us around front to a log building. Half the concrete floor was already in, the other half, about fifteen by thirty feet, was yet to be done. He had enough cement to mix concrete for half the unfinished area, he told us. It needed to be graded and leveled and, because it was for a garage, a drain that would be in the last unfinished quarter had to be allowed for and the floor sloped to meet the future drain. Bob and I could design and stake it easily enough. We needed to find from Paul, our construction ace, if we could do the concrete work.

"We'll let you know in an hour," I told him.

We brought Paul and Bob up to take a look. Paul found the "boss" and went through all the logistics and came back smiling.

"Hey, guys, no sweat."

We held a little pow wow. It was time to put in our bid. He was a nice guy and had found some work for us, so we asked for fifty dollars, more than enough for our needs, with a dinner for four at the roadhouse thrown in. He readily agreed.

Next morning we hit it bright and early and, I think, took the boss a bit by storm. We prepared the floor, designed it to drain, laid the forms, hauled the gravel in his pickup from out on the road, brought water in a fifty-gallon drum, also in his pickup, mixed the concrete both in a wheelbarrow and a small, too slow one-half-yard mixer, and poured it; then Paul applied the finishing touches, carefully troweling the floor glassy smooth. It was a beauty and it took just five hours, start to finish.

"How much do you guys want to finish the last section?" he asked, having a hard time hiding his eagerness.

"You don't have enough concrete," Paul replied.

"I'll find some somewhere," he responded quickly.

"Ah, just a minute, we gotta talk it over," Jerry answered, and we huddled out of earshot. "Anybody want to do it? We've got another day," he asked.

"Are you kidding?" Paul answered. "We're on vacation."

"How about I tell him three hundred dollars?" I asked. All agreed.

He smiled when he heard our price, and shook his head. Our work was finished.

That night we ordered the biggest steaks on the menu, milk, ice cream, pie—you name it—and literally waddled back to the raft. On our way, Jerry said with a gleam in his eye, "He thought he got a good deal at fifty dollars, but we sure made up for it at dinner!"

Later that evening, Bob worked out a deal with a helicopter pilot just finishing his season flying firefighters for Yukon Forestry Branch: one of our famous—mostly among us—sourdough hot cake breakfasts in exchange for a ride in his machine when the raft went through the Five Finger Rapids, twenty-one miles downstream. Bob wanted to take pictures of the raft and the pilot wanted to see it, so the deal was struck.

We planned to leave Carmacks as soon as we could after visiting the post office and buying our grub the next day. We would drift to within a mile or so of the Five Fingers, then tie for the night and proceed the next morning after hiking down and looking the rapids over.

The post office on Tuesday was a complete strike out; no mail, no stove, nothing. We purchased our supplies, ten pounds of beef, sugar, salt, eggs, spuds, and onions, salad fixin's, and a can of white gas. We left word with the RCMP that we expected to arrive in Dawson by October 1. We had plenty of food, etc., and privately hoped we would make it earlier.

We had 258 miles to go. We'd drifted an average of between four-and-a-half and five miles per hour from Laberge to Carmacks, 202 miles. The river looked good, on the maps at least, with few islands or bars from Five Finger and Rink Rapids, six miles below the fingers, nearly to Minto, where it widened and was splattered with islands and shoals. Our riverboat chart showed the "Minto Flats" to be a maze with the channel neatly threading it. But below the title, Minto Flats, there was an ominous note on the old chart, "subject to changes." That "subject to changes" section seemed to stretch all the way to Fort Selkirk and the mouth of the Pelly, a distance of about eighty miles. We planned to stop at the abandoned Fort Selkirk at the mouth of the confluence of the Pelly. It's 108 miles from Fort Selkirk to Stewart, at the mouth of the Stewart River, from Stewart only 70 miles into Dawson. If we had time when we neared the goldfields, we wanted to stop and hike up some of the creeks and look around.

Finished with Carmacks, we pulled out and drifted easily to a cautious tie-up three-quarters of a mile above Five Finger Rapids.

We cut through the woods that evening to the rapids and on inspection confirmed everything we'd heard, read, and been told— take the right channel. It was nearly a straight shot and deep; the other "fingers" or channels through the stone that had been breached eons before were rough and convoluted. The right channel, plenty wide for us, was the one the steamers had used. Shooting down through was easy enough for them, but coming up they needed the assistance of an endless cable and a steam winch anchored in the stone above the rapids. They just hooked on. Getting into the proper channel looked easy, a matter of hugging the right bank closely, then simply riding the current on through. It would be a quick passage because the water

110

was swift, breaking into coamers as it left the confine. It would be all over in half a minute.

The next morning we built spare yokes and an extra sweep, just in case, and were finishing up as the helicopter arrived. Bob took to the air, the three of us to the water on the raft, and down we went, slick as a whistle, plunging merrily through the coamers into calm water.

On the first island below the rapids Bob stood, deposited there by his magic carpet. We toyed with the idea of passing him by, waving amiably then canoeing back to get him later. But canoeing upstream then racing to catch the raft would be no easy task, so we fetched him back.

"I had a look at Rink Rapids," he told us. "Seems to be rapids nearly all the way across, but along the right side smooth water runs straight through." So it was.

15:35 — Dinner's cookin'—a good feed it should be, too.

It's a relief to be through all our rapids. Even with the island-bar archipelagoes ahead of us, I see no real difficulty. As the river gets wider, there are bound to be islands. At the same time it picks up a lot of volume so that now many channels have enough water for us. Plus we're a lot better at reading the current. The receding water level tends to hold us into the main current too.

Check the food—not long now.

Bob and I start our shift 45 minutes from now. We've seen lots of big birds—eagles, ravens, and even sea gulls. The gulls were flying along the river north to south in formation, looking like a flight of bombers in their steady head-on formation. In their winter feathers, they hardly resemble the dirty gray birds one associates with summer. Their feathers shone a warm, clean white.

We passed Yukon Crossing where, before World War II took history to task, leaving highways and air corridors as its legacy, the Dawson trail carried winter commerce along the Yukon.

Facing downstream, a river has a left and right bank, whether you're headed east or south, north or west—makes no difference. Turn around, face upstream and stretch your arms out wide, point to both shores. Your right arm points to the left bank, your left to the right bank. That's just the way it is.

From Yukon Crossing, we were over the hump, more than halfway between Whitehorse and Dawson; but for the archipelago of the Minto Flats, it looked to be clear sailing, and with luck the flats would be handily navigated.

We entered them later that day, apprehensively, and while there were many islands and bars, the mainstream was true for us. We stayed in it, tying exultantly at the location of Minto that evening.

Unlike other river communities that dried up for lack of gold or in the final chapter when the steamers were laid up, this one was abandoned mysteriously in 1953. Locked in winter, with little coming or going, Minto saw a string of unsolved murders. Knowing the murderer to be one of its citizens emptied the town as if the plague had struck. Now accessible from the Klondike Highway by a narrow dirt track, and used as a camping ground, Minto was a handful of cleanly picked log shells.

We pulled out early next morning, our tentative plan to finish with Minto Flats, cruise deftly through twenty-four miles of maze, surge past the last island, and swing calmly to shore in front of Fort Selkirk. Tentative, I say, because the Yukon was clogged with islands right up to its junction with the Pelly, and also because we could always expect anything to happen at any time. It was the only way to keep optimistic, as in our mile-by-mile, point-to-point P and P, a world behind us on Tagish Lake.

Fortune seemed with us as we successfully threaded our way through the islands. We passed the Rock Palisades, high columnar basalt cliffs close on our left, and were careful to stay away from the myriad channels to our right that fell over shallow bars and through narrow chutes into Hell's Gate Slough. We held left until finally we rode the minor channel. Most of the river was beyond the islands to the right, and we rejoined it at the mouth of Hell's Gate Slough. It was always like that. We tried to hang on to the good going, but it wasn't easy.

I lay on my bunk during my two-hour break, Bob and I having crewed together. The day was gray, cool, and ominous. Being on deck was a job requiring endless decisions. I'd be on deck again soon enough, and was content to have my shift behind me and still be moving. Sleeping bag over me, warm and toasty with book in hand, I was on the quarter deck of H.M.S. *Lydia* in the South Seas with a young Hornblower who was very much in love and didn't quite know what to do.

The inside of the tent was a different world. It was warm, light, and out of the wind. The deck conversation, though every word of it could be heard clearly, ended at the canvas, a psychological sound barrier.

Only when I registered a certain degree of concern, anxiety, or novelty in the deck talk could I be dragged back to reality. We were somewhere in the Ingersoll Islands. Jerry was on the front deck; Paul was at the rear.

"What do you think, Jer," Paul called forward, "go right?"

"I don't know, Paul," Jerry answered. "Looks like left to me."

That conversation had played countless times since we'd been on the river, that record had been worn scratchy by every combination of the four of us. I went back to the South Seas.

"Better wait a bit till we're sure," Jerry added.

That wasn't new, either.

"We'd better go right, current's turning right," Paul said. "We're on the right of the break."

"Hard to tell," Jerry said, "but I think it's going left."

More silence.

I was all ears now, and not a little amused. I looked to Bob lying on his bunk, knocking with my eyes on the psychological door that divided all our rooms, the quarters of the tent. He, too, was listening, book face-down on his bag.

Planning far enough ahead to be sure of every island wasn't always possible; sometimes they came too quickly. Then we would close until we were sure which way the current went, then help it, sweeping as the circumstances required. To sweep hard left for twenty minutes only to find out as you drew close to your island that you were going right anyhow made for wasted work.

"We're on the break, go left!" Jerry called urgently. Immediately his sweep went into action.

"Go right . . . right," Paul called, and he too was quickly sweeping.

Bob and I were laughing now.

"Make up your minds!" Bob called.

The sweeps stopped.

"Too late for that," Jerry replied calmly. "Take a look."

Bob and I stepped on deck, just as we began to thump. We were crosswise, being skewered on the rocky point of a gravel bar that split the current.

It was too funny for words, we all broke out laughing on that big river. Bob and I'd got rubbed a bit for hanging up for twenty-five minutes on our shift, now this!

As usual, our first attempt to get off, the one where you don't get wet, failed. Two and a half cold hours later, we were free. Paul and I went right to work, after a bite to eat and some hot tea, repinning our long logs under the raft, as they'd sheared their pins. Bob and Jerry manned the sweeps.

We were in a minor part of the river and soon surrounded by islands and bars. Every time I looked up from my work, we seemed to be in a channel barely wide enough, let alone deep enough, to navigate. But we kept moving. Trying to regain the main river, I felt like some poor motorist who'd missed his exit on a Los Angeles freeway. We finally spilled out, after another minor sticking and unsticking episode, into the confluence of Yukon and Pelly—Fort Selkirk in sight across about a mile of calm water. Just in the middle of it we grounded for the fourth time that day. That's where we spent the night, aground, in a black drizzle. It was a bum night; first thing in the morning we would have to go back into the river, anything but a pleasant thought.

Breakfast too was a dour affair, ominously quiet, even with bacon and eggs, prepared as a morale booster along with our trusty "oatmobile." There wouldn't be anything pleasant to talk about until we were moving again. I made myself think of something different as I prepared for the plunge.

We'd seen two sheep on the bluffs across the mouth of the Pelly the night before, just as we thought we had it made, before grounding out. Whether they were basking in the warmth of what little sun reflected from the rock or were camped there for protection I didn't know. Even on that gray evening, their white coats were splendid. Earlier the same day we'd seen two sleek black bears wobbling along the shore, their heavy coats rippling over the layers of fat beneath. The pieces of autumn were certainly slipping into their places. We'd heard the commotion of geese on the low, bare, exposed top of a shoal, two hundred yards away. Shortly after first light they formed up noisily and took to the sky, continuing their southern journey.

Oh, the water was cold as I stepped over the side. In dejected silence we worked the raft into deeper water till we floated free. Spirits warmed again as we drifted with the current into Fort Selkirk.

In mid-summer 1843, Robert Campbell of the Hudson's Bay Company, two Indians, two French Canadians, and a fellow European by the name of Hoole, all piled into a great birch-bark canoe expertly built by Hoole on the banks of the upper Pelly River. Campbell had instructions from Sir Thomas Simpson, the farsighted director of the company's north and south divisions, to follow the Pelly to its mouth, to its junction with the great river the Indians spoke of west of the mountains.

A tall, tough thirty-five-year-old Scot, Campbell had been the first white man to cross the great divide west of the Mackenzie River in 1840 to the headwaters of a river that flowed west. He named it for Sir John Henry Pelly, home governor of the Hudson's Bay Company in London.

Campbell, on the very western tip of the company's reach, followed the Pelly to its junction with an even greater river and returned, confirming the suspected for Simpson.

Simpson wondered whether it led to the Quikpak of the Russians, far to the west on Norton Sound, or into Cook's River on the south-central coast of Alaska. Campbell's name for the new river, the Lewes, was not to survive.

For the next five years Campbell was busy building the chain of posts needed to extend supply lines to the fort he would establish at the Pelly's mouth. Finally returning to the confluence in 1848, he built his fort, named for the fifth earl of Selkirk.

Fort Selkirk, with so much promise, could only have been painful for Campbell. Barely enough supplies dribbled in to keep him and his men alive, let alone to establish a good trade stock. Without an adequate stock, he could send few furs back. Finally, with his first adequate supplies in hand in 1852, he looked forward to the fur trading success that he had earned. But, for Campbell, when it rained, it poured.

The Chilkat Indians on the coast sat astride the passes to the headwaters of Campbell's Lewes River, resolutely preventing the entry of white traders to the interior. Instead, the wily Chilkats carried white trade goods along the river themselves to the "Sticks," or woodland Indians, driving their own hard bargains for furs, which they then traded to the white seamen on the coast. Not at all pleased at learning Campbell was in their territory, a large war party crossed the passes to the great lakes at the head of the river and rafted down to the fort. The confrontation with the Hudson's Bay Company men, who were greatly outnumbered, was bloodless though heated—Campbell was burned out, lock, stock, barrel, and fort.

Campbell headed down the Lewes, a route he'd explored the year before, proving Fort Selkirk and a newer fort, on a great river with the Indian name "Yukon" (meaning great waterway), were in fact on the same river. Campbell was bent on reopening Fort Selkirk but to his despair it was not to be. Fort Yukon, though much farther north, was more easily supplied from the Mackenzie than Fort Selkirk. At that, fully seven years passed between the shipping of trade goods from England and the arrival of the furs they had purchased.

The reopening of Fort Selkirk, on the left bank of the Yukon across from the ashes of Campbell's Post, was left up to Arthur Harper, one of the first miner–prospectors to reach the Yukon, in 1873. By 1889 he was married to an Indian wife and more interested in selling supplies to the increasing number of miners in the country than tramping the hills himself. He built his trading post at the mouth of the Pelly watershed. It was a natural, and his supplies came upriver from the mouth by steamboat.

The gold rush passed Fort Selkirk by. Probably its greatest single influx in population was the Yukon Field Force that wintered there in 1898–99. Made up of contingents from the Royal Canadian Rifles, Dragoons, and Artillery, they were hastening to Dawson to keep the Yanks in line and to protect their territory.

But as long as the Yukon was the route, Fort Selkirk would survive. In 1938, even the Hudson's Bay Company returned at long last to the fort, but its visit was short. In 1950, the Hudson's Bay Company post closed as Fort Selkirk emptied, its inhabitants drawn to the new trade route, the dirt road that had reached the Pelly, forty miles from the Yukon.

We roamed the remains of Fort Selkirk, its thirty-odd buildings and cabins stretched a quarter mile along the river bank, under a soft September sun. The soft light and color in the leaves lent a fitting atmosphere to the theme of man's impermanence, though signs of him were all about: a rusting Model A Ford; a schoolhouse complete with texts, chalkboard, and desks with inkwells; empty homes that had known a woman's touch; tiny cabins with one bunk, one table, one chair, one window, and one door. A single cabin looked inhabited, but no one was there. Sod roofs rotted through and fell in first, a dry roof with roofing paper, such as was over the trading post, lasted longer. From around the old homes we gathered enough wild rhubarb to stew for dessert.

Standing alone, as if time hadn't touched it, was the Anglican Church, with rich fir paneling and as yet unbroken stained-glass windows. It was spotless, uncanny. I couldn't bring myself to enter without slipping off my rubber boots.

We canoed across to look for Campbell's fort, but found no traces of it. Perhaps it had been washed into the river.

Evening came on in fog; from the town our mast stood like a tower above the clouds.

We were three days at Selkirk.

Our first side trip—the thirty-two mile run to the Selwyn on a now brown-green river swelled by a third with the Pelly water— couldn't have been better. We were at the break, where one day's warmth and splendor were the gift of summer, the next day's gray chill the warning of the season closing on us.

That evening, tied at the mouth of the Selwyn, we cut the cards to see which three would be hiking. We'd seen a lot of bears and agreed our food supply was for us alone. One of us would stay on the raft to ensure it stayed that way.

> In bed, writing by candlelight. The mellow burnt-amber hues the candles generate are soft, pleasing, easy on the eyes. We've all gone to candles at night; that way nobody has to get out of bed and turn off the lantern!

Our lantern hung from the ridge pole just far enough inside the tent door that, after ducking and entering, you could easily stand up without hitting it—if you remembered. Jerry ran into it with his nose, Bob and I at eye level, Paul—poor Paul—it hung just exactly to his hairline. He rarely saw it before the clang. Our logic for leaving it in such an awkward place was that any idiot could learn to move around or under obvious obstructions. None of us were idiots, so there should be no excuse for hitting the lantern with our heads. Obviously there was no reason to move it. The clang of the lantern was worth a dozen Bill Cosbys—it was a built-in humor valve.

I glanced around the tent, prying cautiously into the three other worlds beside mine that existed there. Paul, across from me, was steeped in shadow, eyes closed, either asleep or deep in thought. He had securely fastened the tent flaps, making the door airtight with clothespins. Otherwise any breeze or draught would howl over him on its way out the "window" Bob had made in the tent wall above his head.

From Bob's end came the twang of dental floss. Sleeping bag to his waist, he had his journal and pencil face-down on the bag before him. Bob's candle flickered slightly, the blobs of recyclable chewing gum carefully parked on the railing above his shelf casting moving shadows on the tent wall.

Jerry was harder to spot behind the pile of clothes that inevitably ended up in the no-man's land at the foot of our bunks. Our clothes rack was heaped high with everything that could hang—clothes, towels, long underwear, spare trousers—we hardly ever saw the pegs, they were so buried. Jerry, too, was sitting up, reading through a collection of Russian short stories. Quietly I slid down into my bed, extending my feet under the pile of clothes, then I kicked them over toward the tent wall, making foot room for myself.

"Here, here, let's have none of that," Jerry said, without so much as moving a hair.

I said nothing, snuffed my candle, and drew the covers around my shoulders tightly. It was part of our own continuing game with each other. When we both stretched out, our legs overlapped. There wasn't room for two sets of feet and a pile of clothes, so the first one "there" got the best spot and invariably did what I did. Then we would maneuver all night for the one comfortable position. Very rarely would either of us bother to move the clothes. It was the game; whose clothes they were didn't matter.

"Good-night, Jer," I said innocently, gloating over having won the first round.

"Hrrr, mumblemumblemumble."

I lay in a cloud of utter peace, so basic, so complete, so pure. Sleep could take me whenever it wanted. Good-night, geese I hear flying overhead. I hope you, too, find a nice spot to sleep tonight before continuing your long journey.

At Selwyn Station, we found a half dozen things to note, including a fancy two-room log house with a porch, no less, and newspapers of 1931 vintage on the walls. But it was hidden back in the alder like a bird's nest in a marsh.

Wipeout, Whitehorse, and Plans for a June Reunion

Our hike up along the Selwyn itself—a beautiful clear, cold stream (especially when wading across it up to mid-thigh)—was less than fruitful. The double-rutted path leading back on its right bank petered out after a short distance in an old forest fire burn. Crossing forest fire burns—if you choose to try and stay on top of the jagged tree stumps—is kind of like being a tightwire artist. Backing and forthing and jumping from log to log, balancing on each one. Trying to move in a straight line is an endless trial of climbing over, stooping under, clambering around. Either way it isn't much fun. You hardly ever get a chance to string three good paces out in line without some obstacle to change your stride. For four miles we pushed back, Bob, Jerry, and I, across the burn, through alder, fording the Selwyn three times, and climbing high to pass along the shoulder of a short mini-canyon. Beyond the canyon we found no trace of the road, though we did find some signs of woodcutting in old stumps in spots the fire hadn't reached. It was raining hard, so we headed back to the raft, passing a large old campsite that apparently had belonged to a fire-fighting crew.

That night while we slept, we caught a salmon in a bit of net hung off the end of the raft. I didn't know what was going on; Paul was on deck in his underwear in the dark trying to beat that poor fish over the head. It was flip-flopping all over the deck!

As we pulled out of Selwyn, Paul spotted a sow black bear and three cubs walking along the foot of the high cliff across the river. We were soundless, and, though the old mama couldn't see us, she must have picked up our scent, for before we drifted within 150 yards, she scampered her brood up a defile in the cliff like a bunch of mountain goats till they reached a patch of brush and disappeared.

Our confining valley had narrowed; we were being borne through what was just about as close to a canyon as it could get without being one. Always on one side of the river, rugged stone faces climbed steeply up five hundred to a thousand feet above us and on to peaks out of our vision. Any semblance of forest, other than a thin line of brush and tree, was reserved for the alluvium of the streams that entered from the mountains, and for the narrow valley floor even with the river, less than a mile wide. In places, the valley necked down till it pinched the river, other times one side of the river or the other was green to a depth of a quarter mile or so back to the walls. I

119

was forever looking around, my sense of movement very real in this ever-close rocky embrace. None of us spent much time in the tent.

At one point we heard a lone wolf call, distant but clear in our giant sound chamber, coming from the forest at the mouth of an unnamed creek. I answered, howling back, and received a reply. We howled back and forth a few more times till I grew tired of it. He must have seen through my howl or got tired of it at the same time, because when I quit, so did he.

We were only four hours drifting the seventeen miles to Britannia Creek.

In the morning, Paul, Jerry, and I set out on a nice cat road, heading inland from the Yukon. There had been some placer mining along Britannia; the cat road ran through a small cabin that had been bulldozed over. The trail wound on, away from the stream and up the valley flank, through a glittering, autumn-yellowed birch forest. We topped timberline, then we stopped on a knoll, about ten miles from the Yukon, two thousand feet below us. It seemed like we'd sneaked up there from out of a hole in the earth; rolling hills led off as far as we could see. Crimson poured down them, like a thin syrup. Some of the hills showed rugged peaks, but the higher ones were snow clad. The road stretched on, over the next far hill, without revealing a clue. The expanse was awesome; it sure made me feel small. Behind us lay the notch of the river, beyond it more peaks and summits, ad infinitum.

After a bit we turned back and strode down, down into the golden forest toward our raft.

A two-hour drift to Ballarat Creek the next day seemed longer, maybe because we had to wait till the fog lifted before pulling out. Eerie mists were coming earlier in the evening, and taking longer to melt away in the morning.

Ballarat was a down-under name carried from the Australian goldfields of the nineteenth century, named perhaps by a miner who'd been there, perhaps in honor of a rich memory, or in hope of its revival. We found a cabin and an overgrown road heading inland, and the next morning I was left behind, alone on the raft in the sun. Ah, glorious solitude. I was scratching away in my log when Paul returned with a bad blister.

I'm going up to the cabin at Ballarat again and write and contemplate. It's old, tidy, and still usable. Yesterday I visited it and sat inside just thinking. I experienced a feeling of acceptance and understanding that seemed far beyond the temporal.

Shortly after Paul's return, our only waterborne visitors, in fact the only people we'd seen on the river since leaving Whitehorse, stopped at the raft. Bedamned if it wasn't Skip Burns and his new wife, Cheri, making Skip's last river trip of the year with eight youthful charges! After an appropriate time I left, gold pan and log book in hand. It was privacy I craved that day.

I panned Ballarat's gravels for a bit while I listened to the bubbling of the water over ankle-deep rapids, felt the brittleness of the air on my cheeks, followed the sunbeams into waterholes looking for little fishes, and watched for that glint in the pan's crease. In time I returned to the cabin and slipped into its peaceful seclusion.

Before leaving, as the forest shadows grew long, I added to my earlier entry.

> The beauty of what I've seen and lived this year has a strong, warm hold on me. While we need to get to Dawson soon, I'm dragging my feet. I don't really want to get to Dawson; I don't want this to end. A week or so from now, we'll be faced with Nixon, television, hours, dates, expectancies, justifications, the tick-tock and roar of our American world. I don't look forward to it at all.

Bob and Jerry clattered down the rocky bank to the raft in long mechanical strides just on cue—the beans were hot and waiting. They'd followed the road back to the Yankee Girl Gold Mine, a jumbled mixture of standing, partly standing, and falling-down offices, shops and cabins, old machinery and parts. After mapping the remains and taking many pictures, they returned.

My hopes of idling along to Dawson, stopping and exploring as the mood struck, were shot to hell by what we beheld at first light the next day. Gray clouds hung low over the river; the fog was thick. It was snowing and the wind splattered the soggy snowdrops all over us. At the bottom of the clouds, less than a thousand feet above us, the snow lay in a thick blanket over the crimson bushes. The water temperature, which had stayed so long in the fifties, had slipped six degrees in two days, to forty-five degrees. We were underway again by early afternoon and decided to press right up to the edge of darkness before tie-up.

As evening came, we neared a flock of perhaps three hundred cranes, camped on the point of a gravel bar ahead. As we approached, some discussion went through the flock concerning our approach. We were stone still, to the point of not even moving our eyes, and succeeded in getting to within a hundred feet of the flock. They looked tired and weary, their heads under their wings, some maybe already asleep. A few, maybe sentries, watched us closely, murmuring among themselves. I was sure any false move would send them all aloft.

At our closest point, some grew anxious, and I was sure they were going, but, surprisingly, some very soft, calming words eased their tension and we passed without the alarm being sounded.

A quarter of a mile below the cranes we spied another great flock overhead, flying south, constantly changing leaders, altering their great "V." Heavy clouds blocked their route and they began to mill about in deliberation. The cranes we'd passed joined the discussion from the gravel bar and soon the milling ceased as the airborne flock began to descend. Not en masse, but in an orderly, downward, winding line that reminded me of a genie returning to its bottle in a wisp of smoke.

Our late run that evening, though it brought us to within three miles of the White River's mouth, caused some difficulty. No easy place to arrest the raft afforded itself; darkness finally forced us to try.

Bob and I, manning the kamikaze crew, watched our first stanchion, a stout tree, be torn from the bank by the fast-moving raft. Our second stanchion, after a running and paddling race to overtake the raft and line, failed when the line became taut and snapped. Our third try with the now-spliced line finally succeeded in stopping the raft.

Next morning we had ice in the coffee pot. We didn't need water buckets, we floated in one. There was little dallying; Jerry and Paul shoved off at 7:50.

"Jer," I asked later, "where were your feet last night?"

"Christ, you could have been two feet taller and never touched them," he answered. "If I could have got them under my armpits I would have. Boy, I was cold. You could read a newspaper through this goddamn sleeping bag. I think they call it a down bag because some sick chicken flew past it."

122

09:40 — On deck with gloves on. Cold wind from the north. I'm wearing wool long johns, a wool pullover, a wool shirt, heavy trousers, wool socks, leather boots, heavy wool coat. On top of this I've got on my rain pants and coat, wool cap and leather gloves, and my nose is still running like a faucet. It's a clear day, though, and we haven't hit any bars yet!

We passed the mouth of the White, its wide valley stretching westward. The White, with its glacial origins in Alaska's Wrangell Mountains, is the roughest, wildest major tributary of the Yukon, its current swift and turbulent enough to keep the heavy glacial silt suspended. Hence its name. Below the mouth of the White, this gray, murky mass mixes into the Yukon, distinctly changing its character. No more green, only gray.

Our raft logs disappeared in it, though only inches below the surface. It seemed we were rafting with only a deck; it took some getting used to.

We still had mountainous shoulders, but they were miles apart from the White's mouth on. The river spread to more than a mile wide in places, and was bar and island studded. The channel roamed back and forth across the plain in great arcs and bends.

Two hours on, we passed the mouth of the Stewart River, seventy miles from Dawson, the last major Yukon tributary in Canada. The Stewart, far bigger than the Thirty Mile we'd floated from Lake Laberge, was absorbed with little fanfare by the Yukon, now one of the great rivers of the world.

Just below the tributary's mouth, we passed the community of Stewart, one-time supply depot and transfer point for Stewart River steamers. We saw a neat white house and a store, along with a number of other cabins, and an optimistic sign, CABINS FOR RENT. The only year-round river residents we'd seen, excluding those at Carmacks, seemed industrious.

We were being buffeted hard by the wind and were having a tough time holding in the main channel. We didn't dare leave it, and watched Stewart fall behind. I wondered if they saw us.

An hour below Stewart, it happened—we ground to a halt. We were lucky; half an hour in the water prying and grunting freed us. But two hours later we were forced out of the current by the wind, now whipping across the river. A narrow channel, hardly as wide as the raft, loomed ahead. The wind drove us toward it, sweep as we might. We switched allegiances quickly to the new channel—we had no choice. After some smart maneuvering into it, we grew more hopeful. Our chute just might carry us into a good-sized channel running along the bluffs. But our hopes were dashed when we turned a bend and faced the proverbial dead end. Our channel fanned out on a gravel shoal and babbled playfully over it to the channel we'd hoped to reach, 250 feet away.

It wasn't really a laughing matter. We pried the raft as far as we could, about thirty feet, before it would budge no more. We were thoroughly chilled and depressed. We were stuck hard in a foot of water, yet we hadn't even got to the tough part. Most of the shoal was only four to six inches below the surface.

Discussion that evening was hopeless. Alternatives were suggested. Should we hike out or canoe to Dawson leaving our gear cached? No, we would float into Dawson, even if it meant dismantling our raft and moving it log by log over the bar.

> 20:10 — I sure don't feel much like writing. We're aground. This is probably our last comfortable night aboard. Tomorrow we start tearing our home apart. Will our efforts to reach deep water succeed? It's anybody's guess. We could sure use a couple days of Indian summer to change spirits. Good-night, home, I hope you survive.

The weather next morning didn't help matters at all: 28 degrees Fahrenheit, fifteen-mile-an-hour wind, blowing snow, and, worst of all, the river temperature had reached 41 degrees on its downward dive.

We canoed everything movable ashore, and even in the canoe we scraped bottom. We unceremoniously dropped the mast; the tent frame came off in one piece. It wouldn't even float away, and we left it stuck on the bar. Then we were ready to try moving the bare log raft.

Lighting a big fire ashore when we could no longer stand the cold, we once more grabbed our poles and entered the river. An hour was all we could take, by then the incredibly icy chill that had numbed our legs senseless in minutes was reaching into our trunks. The alarm bells of exposure sounded. It was time for the fire.

As my feet warmed, feeling returned. My feet burned all over, it seemed a thousand pins jabbed into them where tiny rocks and pebbles had washed into my tennis shoes and been ground into my senseless feet. It was fully two hours before I regained even the temperament to discuss continuing. Still my feet ached; they didn't feel as if they were completely hooked on.

We kept drinking coffee and eating beans, then gradually faced our "problem." We had successfully pried the raft toward shore where Paul had found a narrow channel, just deep enough for the raft. The distance was perhaps 150 feet to the channel, but we had yet to go over the hump, less than six inches of water. We could reach the raft from the island with our block and tackle. As a last resort, before tearing the raft into small sections, we would try it. Anything was better than getting back in the water. Jerry, Bob, and I manned the rigging. Paul, with his hip boots—the lucky dog—pried on the raft.

Getting my feet to work right seemed to sap what energy I'd regained, but I could see Jerry and Bob were similarly handicapped and slow of movement. On our first try we moved the raft, though not easily. We were at least warm. On the second set our tail holt pulled out and the three of us collapsed, like three drunks at a keyhole when the door is jerked open. We laughed at ourselves, and the laughter was like a beautiful sunrise. We would win.

Two hours later, with our raft free, we began reloading. The tent frame was floated down and horsed on sideways—we didn't care how the hell it faced. We pitched the tent on it, piled our junk aboard, and moved back in. I made one very short entry in my log before falling asleep, exhausted.

> Next year, full wetsuits, feet and all. It'll be a long time before I forget the aching cold in my body.

Once again we set out early. The wind had eased to a breeze, though a cold one; there was ice in the water bucket. Now we used a bucket to settle the silt out of the river water before drinking it!

Were we ever gun-shy! Even though the islands and bars thinned out and we had control again, without a stiff wind working against us, we were very nervous. We rode only the center of the biggest current. Gradually we regained confidence.

> 09:35 — Sliding through this country only 75 years or so after the wave of people who "civilized" it with their mining communities is interesting, an anomaly.
> In a way, it's wilder now, though we witness marks of man's prior occupancy. About a half hour ago we passed the remains of Ogilvie, a

settlement on an island across from the mouth of the Sixty-Mile River. But the miners and prospectors are gone now, with their towns. Nor have we seen one Indian family on the Yukon; in fact, not a single Indian. They've moved to population centers, abandoning their subsistence way of life. The land should be going back to nature, a nature for the first time in eons without man. That, though, can't happen—man's *presence* has passed over the land and remains indelibly. The emptiness and peace is but a lull before first the United States and later Canada are driven here by their unexplainable obsession with using things up.

On we drifted.

14:18 — Just passed 21 Mile Rock. We know it's 21 Mile Rock because some people in a freighter canoe are painting "21 Mile Rock to Dawson" on it!

14:22 — Oh, God, we're thumping . . . but we're over!

Ten miles above Dawson we began working our way to the right shore; if there was one tie-up we wanted to be sure of, it was this one. Then we rounded a bend and saw the unmistakable scar on a hill in the shape of a stretched moose hide.

Dawson, the City of Gold. We'd made it, even if we were seventy-five years late!

We tied the raft well above town and walked in. We were broke, but how many people hit Dawson with full pockets, eh?

On the outside, Dawson was a dusty, dreary ghost town. There seemed to be more boarded-up windows and leaning, false-fronted shells of buildings than anything else; even the boardwalks had swaybacks and buckles in them.

But inside there was warmth, old-style. At the Eldorado Hotel the proprietress overheard my telephone call to Anchorage to start two cars moving this way to pick us up and bring some money. Fran offered to front us enough credit, on our word, to stay afloat.

In the next three days we ate a lot of bacon and eggs, drifted the raft down to the old Klondike Mine Railway just above Dawson, across the Klondike, where "Lousetown" had been. It was now a jumble of alder and brush with dumps of old bottles all around, but in Dawson's heyday a bridge crossed the Klondike linking Lousetown's boardwalks and shacks to Dawson proper. Lousetown was Dawson's Oshiwara, its Reperbann, the home of the pleasure girls. Our raft would rest in good company!

Wipeout, Whitehorse, and Plans for a June Reunion

We pulled the raft apart, piece by piece, log by log, and stacked it in the woods, above the high-water line. Each piece was numbered and coded, our raft ended up a very big Chinese puzzle, to be solved the following spring. We did a lot of walking back and forth from Lousetown to Dawson, staying clear of the old gal at Black Mike's Inn who told us she didn't want any "hippies" cutting through her property. When she wasn't looking, we did it anyway.

We got two rooms in town as night temperatures were dropping to near zero, but we found it very hard to sleep. Even with the windows wide open, it was too warm. The walls were claustrophobic. Civilization would take some getting used to.

On September 21, Charlie and Becky showed up with Mom's car and Bob's VW, though Paul, in a hurry to make the ski circuit, had already left, hitchhiking.

Next day we were on our way, Charlie with a load of gear headed back over the Sixty Mile Road to Anchorage alone. Jerry, Bob, and I took a leisurely route by way of Whitehorse with Becky. Just down the road from Dawson I made my last entry for the year in my log.

Riding in the back of the VW, I'm watching as the trees, leaves, creeks, smells, and sounds speed by, all kept away from me by the steel body of the car. I feel like an animal in a cage being taken to a zoo.

Little need be said of our winter, other than we were resolved to return and continue our journey. Jerry headed for logging country, Paul to the pro-skiing circuit, Bob and I to Anchorage. Bob took an office job, and I found work bartending in a ski area forty miles south of the city.

Somehow we had to find a way to continue the next year.

5

The Rafters Rejoin and Meet the Can-Can Queens

There's something about a June day, one of those perfect ones that kiss your every endeavor with a bright outlook. It was like that when we cast off from Dawson the following June.

"Hot damn, boys! Here we go!" Bob exclaimed.

I was almost shaking with excitement, my eyes stretching to see around the first bend, my mind racing along the course that lay ahead of us. It was all new country, every bit of it.

Fourteen hundred miles of Yukon River wound from Dawson to the Bering Sea. We would cross the border into Alaska leaving Canada behind, face 280 miles of maze in the 15,000-square-mile Yukon Flats, drift above the Arctic Circle touching the land of the midnight sun before dropping back to float through the heart of Alaska. We would face the Rampart Rapids, and we would visit Ruby where my granddad and his brother had lived and mined. Somewhere along the line we would decide whether to raft to the mouth or stop, build a cabin from the raft, and ski out onto the Bering Sea after freeze-up on a hard-frozen, white Yukon.

There's nothing like the first day of an adventure, when everything is yet to come, but the feeling lasted only as long as I didn't turn my gaze to Dawson, slipping past my shoulder. When I did, I hesitated, I wanted to hang onto Dawson. I didn't just see its false fronts and facades, I looked down its dusty streets into its heart. I turned away.

"Let's sweep her out," Paul called. I leaned into the sweep; it felt good.

129

It seemed an eon ago when we quit Dawson's ominous autumn streets, bent on returning, but without the faintest clue how we could do it. Not only had we each lost a season's work, we'd spent everything we had.

That winter was our longest and most difficult grounding. We had to get support for our expedition. Bob and I approached *Alaska Magazine*, hoping to trade them a story with pictures for backing.

"I'd like to help you," Dick Montague told us in *Alaska Magazine's* Anchorage office early in November. "It's a great story, but we just don't have the funds for an expedition like yours."

"You have any idea where we can go?" I asked, trying to hide my despair.

"Well," he answered, "it's a natural for *National Geographic*. Let's run it by them. If nothing else, they'll develop your pictures for free just to have a look."

That's what happened. We laughed about it, Bob and I; the fact that *National Geographic* was interested enough to develop our film swelled us up a bit. I mean, how many ordinary guys all of a sudden have *National Geographic* interested in them? The trouble was, we weren't sure how interested, and time was ticking away.

The "*Geographic* Connection" was still floating around unmade at Christmas, so Bob and I scraped together what we could, enough to fly to Washington, D.C., and enter our cause in person.

We were a week at *Geographic's* headquarters, selling our expedition office by office, editor by editor. After every successful interview and grilling, Bob and I figured we were in for sure, only to find out we had only earned access to another level.

I think if anything helped us in our complicated climb through the *Geographic*, it was a straight old "lay it on the table" Alaskan approach, coupled with a realization that the people who put this magazine out are human like everybody else. That's a bit hard to see right away; Explorers' Hall alone, at ground level, is so impressive, so intimidating, that if that's as far as we'd gotten, I wouldn't have felt half bad, like the Cowardly Lion and the Scarecrow in the Emerald City. We hung in there and got the final go-ahead on the ninth floor. They would let Bob and me tackle the job of photographing and writing a story for them. When we left Washington it was with our tickets proudly tucked into *National Geographic* travel folders.

Bob and I began ferrying gear back to Dawson in late April,

hoping in the process to stay in Dawson long enough to take pictures of the breakup of the ice. We set up a sort of headquarters at Black Mike's Inn, a one-time mining camp a mile out of Dawson at the Klondike River. Our room was in the old bunkhouse. The old gal that didn't like us much the preceding fall turned out to be a gem, as long as she was sure we weren't hippies or some other such detestable characters! Apparently Bob and I passed the test; in fact, Black Mike's Inn, run by Myrtle and Laurie, sort of adopted us. I can think of a lot worse plights, too. We got good cooking and home-style treatment.

I think what endeared us to them was that we drove out the road and stared at the river ice all day, every day, for ten days, waiting for it to move. When it finally did go out, on May 14, we were asleep in our rooms. They really liked that.

We picked up Jerry in Whitehorse on our way back to Alaska for our remaining gear. Fresh from the logging camps, he was raring to go.

Family friend Jim Crittenden joined Bob, Jerry, and me on the return journey to Dawson to drive the van back to Anchorage.

At Pelly Crossing, the three of us unpacked the canoe, planning to drift the 250 miles down to Dawson, picking up a half a dozen big, long dry logs, and a new mast at least forty feet tall. Bob continued on to Dawson. He wanted to take pictures at some official ball. He was sure getting good mileage out of that picture-taking business!

Our canoe trip was delightful and uneventful but for some sunburn, a bit of rain, finding shipwrecked Pierre stranded on the tip of an island thirty miles from anywhere, and almost losing Jimmy as he rode our five-log raft into a treacherous log jam, while Jerry and I raced to his aid in the canoe. He made the transfer from raft to jam on the fly an instant before our logs were flipped under the jam so fast a canoe paddle lying loosely on top of the ten by forty foot raft had no chance to float free. It popped out casually when, after hours of treacherous work, we tore the jam apart far enough to free our logs.

Pierre, a young French Canadian, and his partner had started out on the Yukon at Carmacks, but they'd had some sort of falling out and split up their outfit. Pierre built a small raft and continued alone until he lost out to a cutbank and sweepers on the island where we found him. He'd lost everything except his sleeping bag, his pipe and tobacco, and had barely made it himself. We found him flapping his arms at us like a goose in molt trying to fly. He hadn't even started a fire, but was sucking away on his pipe. He was a good sort, though, and fit right in. He became cook. We'd have taken him on to Dawson, but we stopped at Stewart and the Burians offered to take him down by riverboat.

Rudy and Yvonne Burian were great folks, their home in Stewart a tidy, one-family community complete with store, museum, cabins to rent, and the stately old home we'd seen from the raft. They welcomed us warmly, as Alan Innes-Taylor said they would. Yvonne had grown up in the town of Stewart River, where her father had been the steamboat agent. She married Rudy when he came there to work, first at odd jobs, later for the Inland Water Survey of Canada.

"There were two taverns here at Stewart when I was a kid," Yvonne told us. "We had a telegraph office and police quarters, though the Mounties came up from Dawson only in the summer. There were lots of people living along the creeks, and Stewart was a thriving community."

As with many other river settlements, Stewart was bypassed by the eventual road between Whitehorse and Dawson. "Steamboats couldn't compete with the trucks," Rudy explained, "and people began drifting away. The gold miners' expenses went up so high they couldn't make it any more."

How long the Burians themselves will remain in Stewart depends on the vagaries of the Yukon. Several years ago the river changed course and is now washing their island away. "We've had to move the house once already," Yvonne said. "We put it on rollers and dragged it along with our tractor. But I don't know what we'll do if the river keeps coming. The house can't take another move, and, in any case, there's only so much island remaining!"

Jerry, Jimmy, and I arrived in Dawson on June 17 with our logs and mast. Paul had arrived the day before, Bob was ready; it was time to rebuild our raft.

Dawson. Drear, windy, and cold it had been the fall before, and forlorn. Late fall in the North isn't a flattering time. Even so, a tiny beat of the old heart was there, a reminder of ancient good times, a glimmer in a derelict's eye. . . .

By 1896, twenty some years after the first bunch of prospectors came into the Yukon watershed, gold had been found in enough quantity to support two bona-fide mining communities on the Yukon: Fortymile, at the mouth of the Fortymile River, and Circle City, 230 miles downriver from Fortymile, in Alaska. Working out of those communities were the prospectors looking for new discoveries. One of them was Robert Henderson, a die-hard prospector if there ever was one.

In July 1896, Henderson was returning up the Yukon with supplies from Fortymile to a creek he'd been working just north over the divide from the Indian River. He guessed his creek was a tributary to a clear, fast river, the Thronduick, whose name was said to derive from the Indian, meaning hammer water, after the stakes hammered into its bottom to form fish traps for catching salmon. Henderson figured he could get up to his diggings quicker by going up the Thronduick, and he was pretty sure he could recognize his creek, "Gold Bottom," from below.

At the mouth of the Thronduick, Henderson ran into George Washington Carmack, who was camped there with his Indian wife, Kate, their daughter, dubbed Graphie Gracie by the miners, and his Indian in-laws, Skookum Jim and Tagish Charlie. They were preparing to catch salmon and maybe cut a saw log or two to float down and sell to the sawmill at Fortymile if the urge took them. No hurry.

Now, in 1896, if a fellow was left with ten cents worth of gold in every gold panful of creek gravel he washed, he was making good money; the creek was worth working. Henderson figured he had more than that on Gold Bottom. He told "Siwash" George Carmack this, and invited him to stake on Gold Bottom, a customary courtesy in those early days when there was room for all.

If he'd left it at that, the future might have been different for Bob Henderson. But Henderson had a flaw, as we all do. His was to cost him the first option on the hottest tip of the century. Henderson didn't like George's Indian relations and in no uncertain terms told Carmack that he didn't want them staking on his stream, though it would be all right for the white man. Carmack didn't take too kindly to Henderson's offer, and figured the hell with Henderson and his Gold Bottom; he, Skookum Jim, and Tagish Charlie would find their own creek.

But Carmack was curious about Henderson's Gold Bottom, and sometime in August he took time out to wander up to the head of Rabbit Creek with Skookum Jim and Tagish Charlie and to cross over to Gold Bottom to see how Henderson was making out.

They saw colors in Rabbit Creek on their way up, and when they found Henderson, they mentioned it to him. But Henderson was too worried about what Indians were doing over on his creek to be civil. He refused to sell the Indians tobacco, yet he offered some to Carmack. Carmack and his friends left shortly, Henderson suggesting Carmack prospect Rabbit Creek on the way back and let him know what he found.

On the way back down Rabbit Creek, Carmack's industrious partners found the gold that changed the North, and from then on Siwash George Carmack forgot his romantic life, his Indian companions, his existence of the wind.

Carmack filed his discovery claims at Fortymile as was customary, with One Below and One Above for his Indian partners, all the while spreading the word about his new strike. At first he wasn't taken seriously. Siwash George wasn't his only nickname—some knew him as Lying George Carmack. But when they saw his gold, different in character than any found so far in the nearby diggings, there was a rush to stake on his creek. Carmack sent no word to Bob Henderson.

By the end of August, Rabbit Creek, renamed Bonanza, had been staked from top to bottom, some twenty miles, and by the end of September the richest placer creek in the world, Eldordo, a gurgling little tributary to Bonanza, was likewise claimed up. Robert Henderson got the word from prospectors too late to locate on Bonanza or Eldorado. The ten-cent pans that would have provided him with bacon and beans and another season looking for the big one were no longer in demand.

Not only miners rushed for the Klondike. Joe Ladue, a twenty-year-old man on the Yukon, one-time partner to Arthur Harper, Jack McQuesten, and Al Mayo, picked up his town of Ogilvie—sawmill and lumber, lock, stock, and barrel—and moved it down the mouth of the Klondike to establish a new town. He named it Dawson, after the Canadian geologist who had mapped parts of the upper Yukon. Ladue's small cabin was Dawson's first structure, and it doubled as a bar. Ladue lost no time banging up new buildings.

Now, mind you, this whole operation—the gathering of miners from local creeks, the emptying of Fortymile, the building of Dawson—was done basically on speculation. George had found surface gold, others staking had likewise found surface gold, but the true richness of the strike wouldn't be known until someone sank a shaft down to bedrock and found the pay streak. That can be a tough operation and a lot of stakers, not really interested in the work part of the deal, began swapping and trading, buying and selling on pure speculation. Claims changed hands for bags of flour, sides of bacon, boat fare "outside" (*i.e.*, the part of the world that wasn't the North). Every claim from One to Forty on Eldorado was worth at least half a million at sixteen dollars an ounce, some a lot more than that, yet men were winning and losing them for pocket change.

The hard workers of the men on Bonanza reached bedrock in early winter, confirming riches beyond even the wildest speculation.

I can understand getting excited over gold. Once a person has seen very much of it, he more than likely would get to thinking that there just had to be a lot of it waiting for him in some creek, unfound. Consider the possibilities those guys had in the Klondike—a thousand dollar gold pan then (it wasn't unheard of), could bring thirty thousand dollars today. Think about that, scooping up an overgrown frying pan full of gravel, washing the gravel off till the gold was in the pan's bottom. Thirty thousand dollars for, say, ten minutes of work. That's crazy! Exactly. Dick Lowe, working a small fraction between two claims, cleaned up $46,000 in eight hours, at today's prices, at least $1 million for a day's work. There was so much gold in Dawson that winter that salt sold for its weight in gold, rancid flour for three dollars a pound. You could get into a card game for a dollar but you might have to cough up a thousand for the third raise. Twenty dollar bills sold for twenty-five dollars.

When the town of Circle got word in January that confirmed the Klondike strike, Bill McPhee stepped from behind the bar in his Pioneer Saloon and said, "Have at her, boys, I'm off to the Klondike!" Dogs worth twenty-five dollars sold for as much as a thousand dollars to haul the Circle miners and camp followers up the frozen river to Dawson.

It was true, the big strike everybody worked for had really materialized. No more ten-cent pans, selected pans now brought as much as eight hundred dollars.

So it was in June of 1897 that the steamers *Alice* and *Portus B. Weare* took their loads of miners down the Yukon to the sea where they shipped out for Seattle and San Francisco, for a "blow," taking with them the gold that would shock the world.

"A ton of gold—Klondike!" the papers cried. The rush began. Every man just knew he would be the first to the gold. All through the winter of 1897–98 they toiled, killing themselves to be the first to the goldfields that had already been staked.

When this mob began arriving, early in the fall of 1897, Dawson's brilliant days began. These folks brought the goods: cigars, kittens, newspapers, pianos, champagne, and oysters. They were the bodies that made Dawson City the star of the North, who turned its shabby prospectors' wall tents into homes and buildings of every description for the dancehall girls, gamblers, milliners, doctors, priests, and tobacconists. Dawson became a city; west of the Mississippi it was second only to San Francisco. Many of its merchants grew rich without setting foot on a claim.

Charlie, Oscar, and Julius Tryck drifted into Dawson with their partners in a handmade scow in 1900. By then, large conglomerates listed on the New York Stock Exchange were buying Bonanza Creek claims.

Word of a new strike had passed through Dawson, news of gold in the beach sands of Nome. Just like that it was over. The brilliance, the glitter, the intangible essence, headed downriver for the new strike.

My grandfather's party worked the winter of 1900–1901 in the Klondike. After the 1901 breakup, they, too, were on their way downriver to Nome.

Dawson has had every reason to die in the last seventy-five years, first losing its glory, then by slow stages its gold—even its government left. But it hasn't died. Once you've bestowed a medal on someone, no matter what happens you can't take it away. There is still a Dawson, a town of six hundred souls, a Dawson that doesn't relate very well to anywhere else. It's still at the end of a long road, its prices are still ridiculously out of line, and, most important, there is in the summer an air of abandon, of whimsy and youth.

Arizona Charlie's Palace Grand Theater is open again, beautifully restored, a young acting troupe on its stage. Not far away Diamond Tooth Gertie's Dance Hall and Casino, the only legalized gambling house in all of Canada, is open and doing business with a flourish of ruffles, pink skirts, and luscious thighs, high-kicking to the tunes of a ragtime piano.

Old fogies dodder along the boardwalks, Winnebagos raise dust. The creeks and streams still fall through their valleys, the millions of yards of washed rock tailings testify to the gold that was. And they're still mining it, in a new rush with its floating price.

In the Midnight Sun Restaurant we met Pete Brady, who at age eighty-three runs a small placer mine on nearby Hunker Creek. Using sluice boxes, he washes gold-bearing gravel dug from the creek bed; the heavy metal collects in riffles, or barriers, in the bottom of the box.

"Came here in 1908 from old Ireland, I came," Pete recalled, with a touch of brogue after all these years. "Me brother and me, we mined the creeks and had the bear by the tail quite a few times." He shook his head sadly. "But the bear got away, aye, got away—too hard to hold."

I asked if he had ever made it down into Alaska. "Aye," Pete answered. "Met up with two prospectors here, 1915 it was. Tim and Mike Buckley, their names were. We rowed all the way down the river to Ruby, close to eight hundred miles. There was gold in Ruby, too, don't you see." I mentioned that Ruby was where my grandfather and his brother had mined, at a place called Long Creek.

"Long Creek!" Pete exclaimed. "I was there for two years myself. And what would their names be?"

"Oscar and Charlie Tryck," I replied.

"Ha!" said Pete. "A couple of Swedes. I knew of 'em, I did. Fine lads, people said, and done quite well. As for me, I had six hundred dollars going into Ruby and come out two years later with one ounce of gold. One ounce. Sixteen dollars!"

All things being equal, we elected to get our raft back together and move down in front of Dawson where we spent a leisurely week on the finishing touches. It was a good move. Dawson is unquestionably one of those kinds of places we four fit into, no sense having to walk four miles to the action! We went more than once to the Palace Grand and its three tiers of boxes where the miners had drunk champagne and thrown gold nuggets on the stage. *The Fate of the Poor Miner's Daughter* was playing, a good old-fashioned melodrama you could hiss and boo at, with lots of pretty girls. We took in Diamond Tooth Gertie's, in the old Arctic Brotherhood Hall, with its three floorshows a night, featuring a high-kicking can-can line and a knock-out modern edition of Diamond Tooth Gertie herself. The Sourdough Saloon was alive with young people, as was the Eldorado.

We weren't in any hurry to leave Dawson, that's for sure. Especially after the evenings that started with four boisterous souls headed for Dawson's bright lights and ended with me shagging it home alone. Bob's friend, Robyn, drove up from Whitehorse to be with him, and Jerry and Paul outshone the local men in the eyes of two of Diamond Tooth Gertie's alluring high-kickers, soft-spoken Sue and ten-thousand-volt Shanly.

They can say what they want about the wild excitement of the gold rush boomtowns, but there's little doubt in my mind that they would have been just so many clumps of somber cabins if it hadn't been for the women.

Just when we could delay our start no longer, the bug bit me. I realized I had a real soft spot for Donna, a sparkling blond dancer whose blush melted me.

I don't know how many of you get into that sort of a jam, but I sure could have stayed in Dawson longer. We had a marvelous going-away party on the raft, everyone came; more than thirty people crowded aboard, and we didn't even sink.

Our "moms" at Black Mike's, Myrtle and Laurie, gave us a Yukon Flag to fly with our Alaska Flag. Black Mike himself, the centenarian who came in 1900 and stayed, gave me a horn to announce our coming downriver. It was hard to leave, but we did. We even had a bit of Dawson with us, some of our decking was scavenged from old sections of boardwalk donated by the city.

I looked downriver. We were off on the Yukon again, with our deck under us, summer around us, the future before us, our bunks and the sweeps and our bacon and beans and yes, our new wetsuits.

Our mast stood tall—four stories above the deck—and a rope ladder led to the crow's nest. At 40 by 25 feet we were larger, and our one layer of logs drew just eighteen inches. Along one tent side, covered storage shelves held our food and tools. Inside the tent it was the same, four bunks and a pile of junk. Our outdoor kitchen was more spacious, all our decks bigger and nicer. We were home. Dawson slipped from sight.

Our first stop would be the ghost town of Fortymile, named for its distance from Mayo and Harper's long disappeared pre-gold rush trading post "Fort Reliance," eleven miles below Dawson. We wanted to be there on July 1, Canada's Dominion Day, for an unveiling ceremony. The first centennial of the Royal Canadian Mounted

Police would be celebrated with the dedication of a Cairn at the site of Fort Cudahy, the first outpost on the Yukon, established in 1894 about half a mile downriver from the mining town of Fortymile. And the girls from Gertie's would be there!

Once again we were folded deep down in the Yukon's stony valley. The forest was alive, the birds singing, the leaves a thousand shades of green. The air was warm and smelled of the life the warmth brought. We drifted through the wee hours, the high summer sun barely setting, the night but a dimming in a long amber twilight.

It was easy running: The Yukon was high and swift, swelled with snow melt. We didn't see one gravel bar. The return to the soft hiss of silt rubbing our logs, the forlorn creak of the sweeps, the kaleidoscopic panorama of stone and forest, island and cloud, river and sky was exquisite, banishing sleep in a night that never came.

1 July 1973

03:45 — Fortymile. Had 'er tied at 3 sharp, 52 miles in 9 hours, 5.7 miles an hour and no hang-ups. Even tied without needing the canoe and kamikaze crew. Just stroked into shore and stepped off with the line! The girls from Gertie's in Dawson are coming to the ceremony with our friend, constable Russ Morrison.

Oh, we looked around Fortymile, mapped its buildings and took pictures, but our thoughts and discussions centered on the girls. I mean, the river is old buildings and a thousand other incredible experiences, but it isn't women. That's the rub. I spent the winter in Anchorage, saw Washington, D.C., visited New York. All that time I was around girls; they were everywhere. But I end up at the end of the proverbial road to Dawson, ready to step beyond, and there a high-kicking college girl from Ontario stops my heart.

Well, I got a good shock when Donna came to the ceremony with another guy. It wasn't a happy fellow who volunteered to watch the raft while the others went up to Clinton Creek and a steak fry with their girls. I hoped Donna would come down to the raft.

Well, she didn't, but I went back to Dawson.

Bob and Robyn stayed with the raft while Paul, Jerry, and I hiked up the road to the Clinton Creek Mine, hopped in Robyn's car, and roared back for a last visit to that den of iniquity, Diamond Tooth Gertie's!

I'm glad I did, and Jerry and Paul didn't seem to mind either.

When we returned with the girls for a last day together, Donna was with me. Bob and Robyn, Jerry and Sue, Paul and Shanly, Donna and I—each group of two sort of went its own direction, coming back to the raft now and again to share. Donna and I went swimming in the clear Fortymile, then walked along its gravel beaches.

We all agreed that somewhere downriver we'd have to get together. Now, in ordinary parley, that means so long, but to the six of us, three river rats and three dancehall girls, it was for sure.

Late on July 3 we left Fortymile, hoping to arrive in Eagle, Alaska, for the Fourth of July.

At 5:26 A.M., we drifted into Alaska. One year ago to the minute we were asleep on another border, at the summit of Chilkoot Pass.

I penned in my log:

4 July 1973

05:26 — Crossing U.S.–Canada boundary. The border is simply a clearing, stretching over the hills on either side of us. Same trees on both sides, same water under us. The Yukon has grown a lot in its roaming through Canada, and so have we. . . .

We decided to go to four-hour shifts, at least to try them; there didn't seem to be any reason not to. Without the cold, without the work of threading a thousand islands, it was easy. I think, too, we were getting better at rafting, with six hundred miles of river under our belts. Bob and I worked the four-to-eight morning shift into Eagle.

The Fourth of July festivities in Eagle were old-fashioned and great, so everyone told me. But after being awake all night, I slept right through. I even slept through the first part of our great rendezvous.

Paul's folks, my folks, brothers, sisters, and friends met us in Eagle for their Fourth of July holiday. Paul's parents buzzed us at mast level before landing their Cessna 180 at Eagle's dirt strip. My folks came up the road that had once been the only all-American overland route to the Yukon. The trail has since been improved somewhat—you can now drive it. Dad had our wood cookstove, a victim of modern day delivery schedules. Our siblings and friends followed in a cloud of dust. The Fischers even came by boat. It was a glorious reunion.

We toured Eagle, where law and order first came to Alaska's interior, replacing the miner's meetings in 1901 with the circuit court of pioneer judge James Wickersham; where Billy Mitchell was the telegraph man; where Roald Amundsen wired his word to the world, "I've made a Northwest passage." We roamed the quiet town of 150 at the end of the Eagle trail.

We found time to wax the seams of our wearing-out tent, hoping it would no longer leak, and to lose all our spare change to my dad and Vic Fischer, a family friend, in a poker game. Our moms cooked the first meal on our new wood-burning stove, with fresh vegetables brought in the Crews' plane. Our visitors had a chance to get tired of the raft's latest musical offering, Al Jolson singing "Swanee," "My Mammy," and "Carolina in the Morning" over and over on our battery-operated recorder.

On July 6 everyone went their own direction, by plane, car, boat, and raft. An Alaskan reunion was over.

A short distance downriver from Eagle we passed the striated, twisting Calico Bluff, rising sheer from the river's edge. One hundred and eighty miles of high summer, drifting on a big, fast river still shouldered by hills and bluffs lay between us and the next village, Circle, the first mining community in the interior of Alaska.

We went two for three on the historic sights we sought in that stretch of river, all abandoned. The community of Seventy Mile at the mouth of the Seventy Mile River was gone, washed away, but Nation and Star we found. At Star City, after much looking and searching, we found the remains of seventeen structures hidden back in the brush. Seventy Mile wasn't a complete bust, the river's as clear as ever. We collected fresh, clear water for laundry, and we bathed.

We were complacent in our river running, even casual in our confidence. We hadn't touched bottom yet, except when tying up. We continued to cruise along at more than five miles an hour and traveled at any time of day we wished. But just below Nation we had a shocker that jolted us.

Paul and I were on shift; it was a hot sunshiny day, the thermometer in the mid-seventies. We all lounged on deck, soaking up the sun, taking life easy.

"Is that a rock?" Paul asked. I'd sort of been watching the same bit of ruffle in the river's surface, not really concerned. I looked harder—sure enough, just the barest point of a rock poked above the water.

"Seems it is," I answered. It wasn't any big deal, the river was plenty big enough for us to miss it, but the fact that we'd spotted a rock was novel. We'd seen no obstacle in the two hundred miles since Dawson.

"There's another one to the right!" It was Bob.

We were planning to pass the first rock on the right, now we were committed to going between them. Whether there was enough room or not was moot; it was too late for any other choice. As we closed, we could see that the water dropped behind the rocks into a big whirlpool. We were crossing a reef.

We were lucky, really lucky, squeezing between the rocks with about five feet to spare. But then we dropped on top of the whirlpool, like a big sheet of rubber on a bathtub drain. Immediately we began to spin and sink, sucked down till water was rising above the deck.

"Sweep," Paul yelled. "Break the spin!" It was no use; there was no way we could break it. The force of the whirlpool was far too great.

Momentum bailed us out. After our third revolution we were cast out of the whirlpool and on.

After our adrenalin had a chance to go back where it belonged, Bob broke the ice.

"That's a bad place—a guy could get seasick spinning around, fall right off, and go straight to the bottom!"

All's well that ends well, I suppose, still I don't think I'd like to run into that one with a canoe—I could have looked right down into a black hole.

We kept a better lookout from then on, trying not to be too lulled by the beauty around us, but it was tough. We were hundreds of miles from anywhere with no limit on our schedule but winter, and it was only July!

8 July 1973

22:00 — Just off mouth of the Tatonduk River. I've entered what we found at the site of Star City. All the buildings are about the same size; all the roofs are down, only log walls remain.

I don't think anyone has visited Star for a long time. Its post office was discontinued in 1902. One cabin we found had empty bottles for windows, standing on end with moss chinking between them.

Our wood stove is a real gem; no gas, no racket, coffee's always hot. Today a marvelous beef stew, made from the remains of meat bought in Dawson, green and strong, but excellent. Paul made breakfast of pancakes and bacon, also very good. I did laundry today with clear Seventy Mile water.

Eight-to-ten hour run ahead of us to Slaven's Camp at the mouth of Coal Creek. Woodchopper Creek is 6 miles below Slaven's. Dad worked at a gold mine on Woodchopper during the 1930's when he was going to college. I'd like to look around there a bit.

An old-timer was killed by a grizzly on Woodchopper—so we heard in Eagle—13 miles up the road and over the hill from Coal Creek.

The bear came into his camp and he shot it, but before the bear died, it mauled him badly. The old boy tried to walk to help and made it 7 miles before he expired. Tough way to go. We'll take a rifle if we walk up that way.

Put sourdough aside for hot cakes and *bread* tomorrow. Bob's birthday. Oh, boy!

We passed by both Coal Creek and Woodchopper, held far across the river at the mercy of a contrary wind. We tried sweeping over, to no avail.

We continued traveling all night, and aside from a lively game of pinochle and a short chase just past midnight that ended with Jerry, Paul, and me catching Bob and giving him twenty-seven birthday swats with a canoe paddle, it was a night for thought, I was working something out in my mind.

Not long ago, even in my time, the North was just the North, the national governments of the United States and Canada differed most notably in the fact that the territorial marshal collared you in Alaska, the Mounties in Canada. Life-styles were alike, interests alike, and the world that wasn't the North was just the "outside."

My thoughts were interrupted by the hum of an approaching motorboat. It was coming downriver behind us and drew alongside. Sarge Waller was driving, a roly-poly ex-Marine we'd met in Eagle, the type of guy who somehow gets by by doing about everything, although it seems he doesn't do anything at all. He had two passengers with him. They were dressed for the bush, but in the same way that a European can spot an American, it was easy to see they weren't from the North. We poured coffee—motorboat riding can be cold business—and traded names. Both men were U.S. government employees, one from Washington, D.C., the other from Denver, Colorado. Sarge was hauling them from Eagle to Circle.

They were elated, taken with the beauty around them, excited. The expanse was stupifying to them. They were engaging, interesting, and mostly curious. We related our experiences over refills, then

143

learned the purpose for their trip. On the basis of their short ten-hour visit by boat, the future of the land they saw was to be determined. They would decide what federal system the land should fall under: National Park, Wilderness River, whatever. I went ashen. Oh, it hurt deep down inside to hear that.

They were aboard for half an hour, warming up enough to continue on their journey. As the drone of their motor faded downriver, something clicked.

There is a cleanliness of spirit in the Yukon Territory, a scope of vision that looks into the clear sky, a scope as wide as the horizons. It's a land where anything seems possible, where the government is still a bystander.

Not so in Alaska. Most people look over their shoulders, not to the sky. The sky is murky with the smog of government. Alaska's very future is a national issue and all Alaskans are caught in the crossfire.

A great game is being played between industry and the environmentalists, with Alaska as the game board, from the Brooks range and rime-iced battlements of the Aleutians to the stately forests of the southeast and the silent snows of the Arctic.

It doesn't matter which side wins, or what compromise is struck. Everything that Alaska stands for—the frontier, the place where a man or a woman could go and get away from the mainstream, live a life beyond the rat race, carve his or her own niche—is over. The land that was once so free will now bear "No Trespassing" signs.

Shortly after the sun rose, we cleared the end of our last shouldering hill and moved into the Yukon Flats. The Yukon, as if freed at last, spills into the 15,000-square-mile flats, giving way to caprice. Unfettered, it carves a thousand channels, deposits millions of tons of silt in ever changing bars.

For a thousand miles we had been in the close company of mountains and hills. Now there would be no landmarks, no identifiable promontories to reckon our location from, no bends in the river to identify us—just islands, channels, and bars. We felt naked. There would be decisions everywhere, all the time, the relaxed moments preciously short. The map of the flats, notably the ninety miles from Circle to Fort Yukon, made anything we'd experienced to date look like kid's stuff. No telling where the main channel went, there were dozens of them.

We spied Circle, but for the raft it was too late. Wary of taking

144

any channels leading us away from the main current, we'd missed the "turn."

"Never mind, we're still in the main channel," Jerry reassured us from the crow's nest. "I think Circle made the wrong choice!"

As soon as we could, we tied.

The journey back to Circle, to get mail and have a look around, reminded me of something out of *The African Queen*. Paul, Jerry, and I, with the canoe in tow, waded, paddled, and forded our way back through the myriad channels, around bars, across narrows and shallows, for three miles before Circle came into sight.

Was Circle ever a surprise! There literally wasn't anything to it. Nothing remained of Jack McQuestion's boomtown, the largest log cabin city in the world in 1894; of the "Lost Preacher's Creek" gold found on Birch Creek; of the saloons, where, at the miner's meetings, a free-wheeling, frontier style of justice was molded that suited many of the miners better than the regulations and restraints of the Mounties in Canada.

Circle is at the end of the last road to the Yukon. The trader, postmaster, service-station owner, hotel operator, and general man-about-town, Frank Warren, opened his lounge for us so we could play a game of pool while we waited for the twice-weekly mail plane. The single-engine Cessna came and went, with our mail—three letters from the girls in Dawson. Whoopee!

There is no feeling of actually going anywhere in the flats, except past the next island or back toward the main channel. The world resolves quickly to the sky, the forest, and the Yukon's braided course.

The heart water is something on the order of three miles across, yet in no instance was it possible to see both sides of it; in fact, rarely did we know where the sides were. Our world was one of big islands, small islands, bayous and sloughs, eroding banks, washes, and sluicelike chutes. Where the actual limit was, the farthest bank of the last wayward slough, was impossible to detect; it could only be guessed at. From the masthead, general configurations of islands and channels could sometimes be associated with the map, but in reality we were guessing where we were. Not that it mattered.

The flatness was really borne home shortly after we'd returned to the raft from Circle. A flashing, blustery thundershower was headed our way. We were tied to a great drift log on the edge of a gravel bar, the nearest standing trees half a mile away. Our mast stuck up like a forty-five-foot lightning rod above our cast-iron cookstove and steel tools. Luckily Zeus passed us at a distance.

The wind has free reign over the flats; it is absolutely uninhibited and seems to be strongest at midday. With the maze of islands, bars, and narrow channels to get fouled on, we would learn to be very heedful of the wind. In the flats it really didn't matter which way it blew; sooner or later in our willy-nilly search for the Holy Grail main current we would be bound to come against it.

From the masthead, forty-five feet above the deck, we could see far ahead, a great assistance in making decisions. A simple choice between going to the left or right side of an island could be very important if the left channel split and continued splitting until it petered out and we were high and dry. The view from the crow's nest was glorious. There was just so damned much sky. If I could only have climbed another ten feet I know I'd have seen the curve of the earth. I was in space.

Our general goal was to start with a sense of where the "big water" was—the deepest, strongest current—and we assumed every objective after that would be an attempt to regain it.

We cast off, all four of us on pins and needles lest we get stuck on a sandbar, or worse, end up in one of the sloughs the entrances to which look no different than the thousands of others but which twist far off into the hinterland.

We drifted all through the night of July 12, a golden blend of sunset and sunrise; by mid-morning we had gained some confidence. We guessed ourselves to be about halfway to Fort Yukon, somewhere near Halfway Whirlpool, though far across the river from it, on the left limit. If we were where we figured we were, there were twenty different passages between us and the far bank, three and a half miles away.

We had tie-ups down to an art, now we just maneuvered right into the bank. The fact that we didn't have a double layer of logs in the water, only a single row, made all maneuvering easier for us.

We slept magnificently; the breeze kept the mosquitoes at bay. We had developed a wind gauge, or mosquito gauge, if you prefer. When they announced themselves via that familiar buzzing in the ear, it was time to be out in the river again, away from their forest homes—the wind had died.

With that kind of attitude we had little problem with mosquitoes.

146

In fact, in our whole Yukon experience, the mosquitoes never took on even a semblance of the menace we'd heard so much about. They simply weren't that big a deal. Now, the gnats . . .

We cast off late in the afternoon, heeding our wind gauge. We were in for more random floating, more decisions taken for better or worse, yet we continued to move along at about five miles an hour.

It seemed almost unbelievable that we could clear the first third of the flats without getting hung up on a bar, yet the white radar domes behind Fort Yukon were in view by 2:00 A.M. We'd come nearly ninety miles from Circle without touching bottom! Again we tied, waiting out the wind, and slept.

The last four miles into Fort Yukon took us twelve hours, because we dared the wind. We cartwheeled along a cutbank for a good mile, pressed into it by old Aeolus, chopping and cursing at branch and bush all the way. Thankfully there were no really big trees to foil us. But that wasn't all of it. We were rudely shoved by the howling wind into a tiny channel, maybe fifty yards wide. Up we'd go till the current outmuscled the wind, then we would drift down to its mouth where the wind, waiting for us, slapped us back up our hole. We did that for a while. Sometime during that twelve-hour struggle we crossed the Arctic Circle into the land of the midnight sun.

14 July 1973

22:50 — Ft. Yukon. Tough work, but we made it. I'm ship guard, the others went to town. We want to have somebody aboard all the time here just in case. So far there have been two rafts cut loose, we hear.

Fort Yukon was a disappointment. There were no remains of the original settlement, the Hudson's Bay Company post; it has long since washed into the river. Now all that remains of the original settlers' intrepid advance down the Porcupine to the Yukon River is a weathered concrete memorial stuck in the graveyard in the 1920's.

The Hudson's Bay Company established its fur-trading post at the mouth of the Porcupine in 1847. They knew it was then in Russian America, but they stayed, a sort of colonial gambit. If the Russians asked them to leave, they would play dumb. The Russians didn't.

In 1869, following the U.S. purchase of Russian America, U.S. Army captain Charles W. Raymond, on behalf of Alaska's new owners, took astronomical observations at Fort Yukon that ended any

147

"speculation" about whether Fort Yukon was located in United States territory. The Hudson's Bay Company was invited to leave. The Alaska Commercial Company, a San Francisco outfit that bought out the Russian America Company, quickly occupied the comfortable fort, hanging up their sign. But, to the miners yet to come, there was only one Hudson's Bay Company, its logo, H.B.Co., would always mean "here before Christ."

Fort Yukon is a village of six hundred people, mostly Athabascan Indians. There's a Northern Commercial Company store, an old hotel, and a barge line that pushes freight and fuel up the Porcupine as far as Old Crow in Canada. An Air Force Early Warning Radar site exists on the fringe.

There isn't really anywhere to go or anything to do for a visitor, a few hours of walking takes one over all the town's trails and streets.

Fort Yukon seemed to be made of factions—tiny cliques or communities within the whole, each integrally complete. The teachers stuck with the teachers, the Air Force stayed with the Air Force, the Indians were together. The religious folks—Fort Yukon seemed to have quite a contingent of these—were busy trying to convert the drinkers, an even bigger group. All this we heard second-hand from visitors to our raft, tied just below the town proper.

17 July 1973

21:00 — Ft. Yukon. Haven't done much besides watch the south-westerly blow like hell.

Bought $100 worth of hardware and food at the N.C. store, played a little basketball at the school/community center. Not much to say, not much to do but wait, just wait.

It was hot, really hot. Even the wind was hot. We took refuge inside the tent on our bunks, drowsing off in the shade. The door had to be left open or we'd bake. That posed a problem because horseflies would come in and attack a dozing man, chewing chunks out of him. The horseflies, sometimes a dozen of them, were too stupid to find their way out, and droned around the ridge pole, waiting for the tent to disappear, I guess. Jerry and I watched the horseflies with loathing. It was no use killing them; we'd tried. There was an endless supply of replacements.

Then a hornet flew in. I followed his flight with interest; I've

148

always been friends with hornets. Would he be able to find his way out?

The hornet seemed to look around, taking a special interest in the horseflies. He circled one ugly brute in particular, then, to my amazement, the hornet struck. They wrestled in mid-air, the intrepid little hornet and the great, ugly horsefly, a struggle to the death. To my surprise, the horsefly was no match for the hornet, who proceeded to tear the horsefly's wings off, and, in a coup de grace, tore off its head. The victorious hornet lumbered out of the tent, straining with his load of carnage.

For the rest of the time we were there, we liked to see the horseflies because the hornets cleaned out the tent every time, beating hell out of their larger foes. Justice was served. It offered the same kind of satisfaction you get if you're a Montreal Canadiens fan.

20 July 1973

The Dawson girls have 5 days off; they're going to meet us in Tanana, 300 miles downriver. A charter plane will pick them up at Action Jackson's Boundary Roadhouse, a 70-mile drive from Dawson, and wing them to us across 325 miles of Alaska.

Last night, at the invitation of Major Leon Kirk, the 4 rafters went to the Air Force station for dinner, movies, and a basketball game. The rafters won, the 4 of us against their 4 officers.

The site has 8 officers and 60 or so enlisted men. Their job is to detect enemy aircraft as they come over Alaska, locate them, and direct interceptors to shoot them down.

Major Kirk and "Rocket," their only flight officer, returned the call, visiting the raft this morning.

Our food has been holding out well. Bacon is still good, though we bought 50 lbs. of salt to put it up some more.

The wind is blowing so hard our wood stove won't get hot, so we cook on our Coleman stove inside the tent. I sure hope the wind quits. The wind really can blow—and hard. It's like the great swells in the Pacific with nothing to slow or impede its growth. It can come from anywhere, and roams about in the sky above the flats at will. It's gusting to 40 or more, and it's lasted 6 days. Yesterday it rained like hell. It would be very easy for me to leave Fort Yukon, *now!*

Half past five the next morning found Jerry and me pulling away at the sweeps, all lines neatly coiled on deck. The wind had been down for forty-five minutes; that was enough for us, we were off and inching our way into the mainstream. Our farthest northing was reached; we were heading west.

The channel for the remaining 180 miles of the flats, past Beaver and Steven's Village, is more pronounced, less confusing. But long sloughs are more frequent, the kind that take off from the main river and journey all over the flat country.

We watched the wind attentively. Thankfully, its will with us was limited to two minor groundings and a few short excursions through slack-water sloughs at hardly more than a mile an hour.

The next day I penned in my log:

22 July 1973

12:15 — Close to the village of Beaver. It's tough, bucking the wind. Not only does it slow us down a little, but, as soon as the river's bends put the wind abeam, we have to work like hell to keep out of dead water, out of sloughs, off bars, and away from sweepers. Yesterday we made 50 miles in 15 hours. Today with a more mischievous wind, progress will be even worse, I'm afraid.

Four boats put out from Beaver as we drifted past, easily overtaking us—long, low, aluminum riverboats with outboard motors. The four boatloads of smiling people, we learned, were out for an evening drive, out to check their salmon nets and to visit our floating camp. All over the raft they went, ten kids and half a dozen adults, their four boats tied alongside. We served coffee and juice and swapped yarns, ours mostly about the raft. In going off to check salmon nets, Cliff Adams invited Bob and Jerry to go along with him. In a clatter, the boats were loaded and roared away. In short order they returned with a beautiful King Salmon—fresh fish for us!

They bade us so long about ten that night, and sped off upriver in four smooth wakes, the hum of the outboards still audible after they were gone from sight.

We were once more alone in the Yukon Flats. The sky was clear; we would run all night.

By late July the golden sunrise–sunset of a sun just below the horizon has changed to a longer twilight of dew and a mist you can feel but can't see. The stars are faint, almost shadows. There is something about night traveling, something mysterious, and eerie. So much of the human experience exists between the rising and setting of the sun, yet half of life belongs to the night, and to the night creatures. We saw bats. We were fearful the creeking of our sweeps would give us away.

"Almost four," Paul whispered through the tent door. The last thing I'd remembered was the muffled words of Paul and Bob as I went to sleep sometime after midnight. It was time for Jerry and me to take over. There was a burst of activity from Jerry's end of the bunk. From the time his covers first moved till he was on deck was hardly ever more than twenty seconds. I rustled out and dressed, following him.

The stove was crackling softly. A thin wisp of smoke followed the raft like a kite's tail. The coffee was piping hot. Bob and Paul had baked a cake on their "graveyard" shift and graciously left half for us.

"Good-night, Keith."

"Good-night, Paul."

"Good-night, Jer."

"Nite, Paul."

"Nite, Bob."

"Nite, Paul."

"G'Nite, B.C."

"G'Nite, Paul."

"Good-night, Keith."

"*Shut up!*"

All was quiet; Bob and Paul had been riding close on the south side of the main channel near the forest.

No wind, no clouds, just a little haze on the horizon from a distant forest fire. It was our favorite shift, Jerry's and mine. We'd sit on boxes close to the warm stove and sip coffee, parking our full cups on the stove's top to keep them warm while we contemplated our surroundings. Every once in a while one of us would make a couple strokes with the big sweep so the raft would continue to face downriver. Few words were spoken. There's greatness to that, not needing words while at the same time sharing so much. I'll remember those conversations as some of the finest in my life.

The silence was interrupted by the call of a moose, coming from the near shore, perhaps a quarter mile ahead of us. The call of distress, of anguish, comes through in every language. I looked at Jerry. Once more we heard the call. Two minutes later we heard yelping, a wolf.

There was no more sound from the forest, but far off, across the river, we heard a raven call and soon a pair crossed over us headed toward the sound we'd heard. They landed in a tree; we could see them. Two more ravens came, and a fifth lone raven. All landed in the same spruce tree on the riverbank. Twenty minutes after the moose call the ravens dropped to the ground, out of sight, squabbling.

Twilight. No time carries sound like twilight.

The sun rose like a harvest moon, its hot brilliance subdued by forest-fire smoke, till we saw a huge red orb in a steel and gunsmoke haze.

In silence, we passed Purgatory, one-time steamer landing and home of the Yanert Brothers, turn-of-the-century Alaskan explorers. Nothing stirred here, nothing would. All dead. The Yanerts were good men, Alan Innes-Taylor had told us. In their later years they left a scarecrow hanging from a tree to shock first trippers on the steamboats.

Woodpeckers and squirrels were up with the sun. Though a mile away on shore, they sounded like they were working on the tent frame.

After watching a wolverine chasing a rabbit along the beach, Jerry and I put on a fresh pot of coffee, cooked up a big batch of wheatmobile, and ate our share. Just at eight, we called Paul and Bob for their shift, breakfast and coffee waiting for them.

"Good-night, Keith."

"Good-night, Paul."

"Good-night, Jer."

"Nite, Paul."

"Nite, Paul."

"G'nite, B.C."

"G'nite, Paul."

"Good-night, Keith."

"*Shut up!*"

Three and a half hours of sleep is really quite a bit when you think about it. You get to go to bed twice a day, too.

Jerry and I rose to a hot summer day, a lemonade day (we had the powdered brand). Bob and Paul were clad only in shorts. They'd had an easy time during their shift, avoiding bars and sloughs with little effort.

152

The Rafters Rejoin and Meet the Can-Can Queens

14:40 — It was a pilot error again—we grounded out!

While dealing a hand of pinochle, shift vs. shift, I neglected to watch our course. It took half an hour to get off the bar.

I pulled another good one with the salmon. Paul came up with the idea of smoking it in the stack of our stove, this had worked well between Fort Yukon and Circle. So, half we kept to bake for dinner, half we put into the stovepipe to smoke. Smoked salmon is yummy.

Anyhow, while taking it out of the stack, carefully so I wouldn't drop it, I slipped and was on my way to falling on the hot stove when Jerry grabbed me. Luckily he was right there stirring his laundry which was cooking in the washtub. The washwater made the muddy Yukon look like Lake Tahoe. Half the fish slid down the stove pipe to the damper, the other half ended up in Jerry's wash!

Late that night, after a bit of difficulty navigating behind an island, we poled into Stevens Village. The gravel-beach waterfront was lined with riverboats, wood and aluminum, all flat-bottomed and long. There were assorted fishnets and a great chicken-wire-and-spruce-pole framework—a fish wheel under construction.

We'd seen but one fish wheel in Canada, in the Yukon Territory, but in Alaska we saw them with increasing frequency. They were larger, too. Somewhat like a waterwheel or a paddle wheel on a raft, the fish wheel is an unmanned fish catcher. Two great baskets, either of willow or chicken wire, are attached to a drum or axle. Between the baskets and at right angles to them are two big plank paddles. This "wheel," two scoops and two paddles, rests on a log raft held out in the river from the bank by a boom log and secured to the shore by a steel cable. The current pushes the paddle through the water turning the wheel, and the baskets scoop up the fish. The wheel runs around the clock during the salmon runs, depositing the fish in a hopper emptied daily by the wheel's owner. Salmon are the summer mainstay for people living on the Yukon.

Jerry checked the mail in Stevens Village; we didn't have any.

Into Stevens at 22:00, out by midnight and on our way. We'll leave the flats tonight.

We made 3.3 miles an hour from Fort Yukon to Stevens Village, a distance of 160 miles, our first average of less than four miles an hour. Surely the wind caused some of our slowing down; we'd made about five miles an hour from Circle to Fort Yukon.

24 July 1973

04:00 — We're passing the last of the flats—mountains and rolling hills ahead. They sure look good.

09:00 — For the first time in 1000 miles, for the first time ever on the river, we're drifting with 3 men asleep, 1 on duty, the river a half mile wide in a solid, single channel through rolling hills. There can't be half a dozen islands total between us and Rampart, 80 miles downriver. Yipee!

At five the next morning we pulled into Rampart and promptly turned in, all four of us, till ten-thirty that morning.

Rampart was born as a mining boomtown in 1896, for the gold on Minook Creek, and burgeoned to some fifteen hundred people in 1898–99 before beginning its long decline. Today, Rampart is a town of two dozen sheet-iron, log, and weathered-plank cabins with two notable exceptions—the white schoolhouse on the hill overlooking the town, and the two-story, false-fronted, swayback building with IRA WEISNER TRADING CO. stenciled on the front.

We walked up the stony beach, sun beating down against us, headed for the dirt bank in front of the store. On the way we met a tall, lanky fellow cleaning salmon on a table at the water's edge.

"Hi. About time you got up. I'm Ed Wilson, the school teacher."

We introduced ourselves, I gave him our "short" litany and asked, "No summer vacation for you?"

"Oh, I'm on vacation," he laughed. "I just happen to fish during the summer, like most everybody else around here. Besides fire fighting, fishing is the main source of summer income." He continued talking, cleaning salmon at the same time.

"It's something to do—I don't make much, the buyer makes the money. He flies in every day or so during the run in his float plane, gives fifty cents a pound, then turns around and sells the salmon the same day in Fairbanks for a dollar twenty-eight a pound. Not bad. You going to be around long?"

"Probably leave tomorrow," Bob said.

"Well, stop up at the house later and meet my wife, Sue. We'll have a chat."

We went on up to the store, the inside just as colorful as its exterior. We had to wait for our eyes to adjust; the daylight coming through the windows didn't seem to get very far.

The Rafters Rejoin and Meet the Can-Can Queens

Just inside the door to the right, a partitioned-off corner was labeled U.S. Post Office. A blond woman who couldn't have been thirty-five but owned a face that had seen a century was sitting behind the window filing her nails as if each were her special enemy, an open bottle of beer close at hand. To the left, stacks of beer and cases of whiskey were enclosed in a chicken-wire room, the liquor store.

There were two shelves of groceries: ten-pound sacks of flour, sugar tins of meat and vegetables, basics, a candy counter, and a dusty old filigreed cash register. A drum stove was in the center of the room, and an old pool table was piled high with junk. I don't think you could have found a piece of floor level enough for it anyhow. Along three of the walls, shelves without order held everything from trousers and cotton shirts to pipe fittings and bolts.

"What can I do for you?" an old man said. He was sitting in front of a cluttered government-surplus oak desk under a window, in a swivel chair.

"We're looking around," I said. "We came in on that big raft."

"I'm Weisner, Ira Weisner, but around here they call me Trader Ike." He stood and stuck out a thick hand.

"We're following in my granddad's footsteps; he came downriver in 1901."

Ira Weisner chuckled. "I may look like I've been around that long. No, I came north in 1922. Been in Rampart since 1942."

He was an engaging old codger, and likable.

"I'd like to have been in the gold rush for the easy money," he said. "That's what the gold rush was, easy money. Oh, but times are different now. I had a salmon cannery, did real good, put lots of people here to work, but the government closed me down, and I'm getting too old to work my claims. Betty Ann! Show 'em our nugget."

The postmistress opened the cash register and took out a nugget the size of a small egg. No way would she let loose of it.

"Oh, it's worth a couple thousand dollars, I guess," Weisner said, passing it off. "There's lots more where that came from. You fellows want to buy some claims?"

"No," I laughed, "not now, we'd have to go to work!"

Trader Ike laughed. "No, it ain't like the old days. There's only fifty, sixty people in Rampart now, most of 'em Indians."

"There's old lame-brain up on the hill—he might as well be an Indian," Betty Ann interrupted.

"Now, Betty Ann, you let me tell the story. Anyhow, I get along

155

better with the old-timers, the full bloods, than with these breeds. Now a full blood you can talk to, he'll go along with you as long as you give him a convincing story, you know what I mean?"

I couldn't believe what I was hearing.

"The young breeds are causing the trouble, stirred up by that school teacher. I had to teach one of 'em a lesson a while back. Oh, I hit him a few times, with this."

To my astonishment, he pulled a .45 automatic from the open drawer his hand was resting on.

"Put that away, Ira, you don't know who these boys are!" his blond protégée shrieked.

"Now, Betty Ann, I can tell these boys are all right," he said consolingly. "We'll bring that teacher around, too."

"Ira Weisner, put that away!"

"All right, all right. Drink your beer." It was an order.

He put the pistol away, to everybody's relief, then congenially added, "Oh, it's a nice little village when it's run right."

We didn't have any mail.

That afternoon, we went up to the school, Jerry, Bob, and I. Paul hiked out the road to see Bill Carlo's mining operation.

It was a one-room school, self-sufficient with its own running water and its own power plant for generating electricity. Half of the schoolhouse was an apartment where Ed Wilson, his wife, Sue, and their small child live.

"We came up to Alaska four years ago as Vista volunteers from what laughingly pass as mountains in Pennsylvania," Sue told us.

"They flew us to Little Russian Mission," she continued. "It's on the Kuskokwim River in western Alaska. It's a tiny village, less than a hundred, and few of the Eskimos spoke English. We were supposed to sort of teach them how to accomplish their goals, an in-house Peace Corps, you could call it."

"Was the program successful?" I asked.

"Well, it was successful for us personally," Ed responded, "but as far as the program goes, how the hell am I going to come up here from Pennsylvania and tell some guy who lives on the Kuskokwim how to better his life? I couldn't hunt, had never trapped, and was hardly capable of taking care of myself at twenty below zero, let alone thirty, forty, fifty below. The shoe was really on the other foot; I was the one being taught.

"Now, if you want to come up here and live for twenty years in the same place with the same economic base as the local people, then they might pick up some stuff from you that improves the way they live. They may reject it, but you can't feel bad about that; all you can do is set an example."

Sue Wilson continued, "We were at the bottom of the pecking order in Little Russian Mission, asked to haul water and firewood, until we found out the word 'vista' is very much like the Eskimo word 'bistok' or 'vistok,' meaning slave. When the Little Russian Mission elders signed up for two Vista volunteers, they mistakenly thought they were getting two slaves!"

The Wilsons left Vista for teaching jobs. After a spell at Point Hope, on the Arctic Coast, they landed at Rampart, where Ed is the sole teacher.

"There's one real advantage to teaching in Rampart," Ed told us. "It started as a mining community. English is the only language that's been spoken here since the village was founded. The result is that I have a much easier time here than I would, say, at Point Hope. I don't have any language difficulties."

"I hear you're making trouble for Ira Weisner," I said.

"Ole Trader Ike? You bet," Ed said easily. "He was friendly when we got here; don't let that fool you. He said we should work to get along. Then I found an auxiliary fuel line leading from the school's fuel supply down the hill to his place. He was accustomed to running his light plant at school expense. I stopped that, and from then on it's been war.

"Weisner runs the store, liquor store, post office, and town radio. He gives out credit and cashes checks. In effect, he controls everything. He knows who you write to, who you talk to on the radio. If he doesn't want you to use the radio, it's conveniently broken. If you write to a store in Fairbanks to have your food shipped out rather than paying the prices Weisner charges, he conveniently loses your letter; it never gets mailed. I know, it's happened to me."

It was a real live, twentieth-century Hatfields-versus-McCoys feud. Ed and Sue Wilson, products of the motorcycle sixties, had found another cause. It was their goal to first get the radio moved, then the post office.

"It isn't easy," Ed told us. "As long as Weisner has the liquor store he'll always have his stoolies; people will say what he wants. Booze talks. I want to get that closed down, too. It's the key."

The Wilsons were trying to bring the wheels of law and order to bear on the Rampart czar, but, just like any other wheels in the Alaskan bush, they don't always work the way they're supposed to. The courts, but for a local magistrate, are in Fairbanks. The lone peace officer for the region is stationed seventy-five miles downriver in Tanana. Modern law and order, with its complicated procedures and requirements, has yet to hit the bush.

Alaska state trooper Gary Harding was in Rampart gathering information in a pistol-whipping case. That evening he came down to visit the raft.

"It's really rough," Trooper Harding told us. "Sometimes I wonder why I stay in the Troopers. By the time I get to a village, all the stories are worked out. I know they're not telling me all, or they're telling me what they've been bribed to tell me, but what can I do? If there was a trooper right here, ready to investigate law breaking immediately, things would be different."

Gary was also planning to fly along the river on his return to Tanana, looking for the body of an Indian man presumed drowned. His boat had been found, run up on a gravel bar. A cigarette lighter lay open in the bottom of the boat. Gary figured the man stood up to light a cigarette, lost his balance in the moving boat, and fell out. The last people to see him said he'd been drinking.

Gary Harding was a nice sort, working hard against an attitude that was suspect of the law, of anything that emanated from Fairbanks and Anchorage. We offered to take him on our raft to Tanana, so he could look for the drowned man along the way.

When we pulled out of Rampart that evening, leaving the feud behind, Gary was aboard. Feud or no feud, we learned that we should pass Rampart Rapids on the left.

Gary fit in well, picking up the arts of rafting, especially the sweeping part, easily. He offered to pitch in where and as needed. We didn't worry having him aboard—if anyone should be able to take care of himself, it ought to be a trooper.

We drifted for five hours that evening, the overcast sky making it difficult to see that a medium sort of wind, coupled with the rapids somewhere ahead, would soon force us to tie up. We were tied for four hours.

At 4:30 an event I'd been waiting for happened. The "barge" passed us, heading up river. I felt it pulsing, then heard the throbbing long before I saw it, lit up like an ocean liner. Three decks, if you count the pilot house on the powerful diesel tug, doors and railings, lights—a river ship pushing a great steel barge full of fuel, covered with bulk goods for the river communities.

We'd passed the only roads to the Yukon at Circle and Eagle, far behind us. With the exception of the pipeline haul road that had reached Yukon between Stevens Village and Rampart, the only way goods were transported on the Alaskan Yukon was either by air or by water. In Alaska the next generation of boats, after the stern-wheelers, ply their trade hauling freight from the rail head at Nenana, 180 miles up the Tanana River, to the Yukon river communities.

Another difference between the Canadian part of the river and the Alaskan side began to gel in my head. The river was now alive. People still live and work on the Alaskan Yukon, ship goods on it, travel it from place to place in their kicker boats, harvest its fish during the summer. It isn't a museum; it didn't die with the gold era. It may have slowed down, most of the miners having left or passed away, but the Alaskan natives who were there before the gold era are still there, getting by.

The barge pushed upriver and out of sight, making its way toward Fort Yukon. I could hear it for a long time after.

Rampart Rapids proved to be a real bore. We were so far from the boulder reef that created the rapids that we could hardly see them. We'd even fixed up a big energy breakfast for the occasion: bacon, sourdoughs, and eggs that Ed Wilson had donated in Rampart. Very good, but totally unnecessary.

It rained off and on. The wax job we did on the edges of our worn-out tent in Eagle was a disaster. The water ran down the canvas, but instead of over the edge and off, it stopped when it hit our wax and soaked through the tent, dripping down inside the walls.

Below the rapids we received two boatloads of visitors. Seeing our rig floating along, they came out to check us out.

Our first visitors gave us a side of dry caribou ribs for munching on, a gift well received. The second visitors—three gals, a young man, and an older gent known as Willie Grouse—had firewood in their boat. They'd picked it up along the beach.

"Here, here," said Jerry, after we'd offered coffee around on that gray, damp afternoon. "Where're you headed with all that firewood?"

Willie Grouse was on to us right away and answered, "What you got for trade?"

"Beans!" Paul replied. That was good for a laugh. There were no takers on the beans.

"I got dry fish, too!" Willie Grouse said, bringing out a paper sack of dried salmon strips.

"How about some bacon?" Jerry asked.

"Sure enough," Willie Grouse answered.

The deal was struck, some of our furry bacon that seemed to have been around just about long enough, for their wood and fish.

Firewood wasn't really a problem unless we traveled round the clock; then our supply of about a rick would run low after a day or three.

We landed at Tanana at midnight. Gary went home, the rest of us to bed.

Tanana, a village of five hundred, sits on the Yukon's bank across from the mouth of the Tanana River, the Yukon's greatest tributary. The Tanana stretches southward and east into the heart of Alaska. Called Nuklukayet before the Europeans came, it was a major Indian trading community.

Four decades before the gold rush, when Karl Marx had a job in London and Europe was trying to adjust to the French Republican ideals, the Russians, pushing up the Yukon from their post at Nulato, met Hudson's Bay Company men working down from Fort Yukon. Neither established a post, yet both traded there. They had little in common, the Russians and British. What little contact there was between them happened at the mouth of the Tanana. After all, they were rival traders.

It was Arthur Harper, the pioneer trader, who established an Alaskan Commercial Company trading post there in 1880, and, in 1891, an Episcopal mission was opened. In 1897 the settlement was called Tanana Station. There were three trading companies there.

It was up the Tanana where Felix Pedro was prospecting in 1901, up the Tanana where Burnette figured in starting a trading post. The two men came together, one with gold, the other with goods, and the Fairbanks strike was hit—the biggest event of interior Alaska gold history, a strike in proportion to Dawson and Nome, one of the three great finds in the far North.

During the gold days, Tanana was an important transfer point for trade. For twenty years goods came up the Yukon from the mouth or down from Dawson to Tanana, then up to Fairbanks. With the coming of the railroad from Seward to Fairbanks in 1922, the flow reversed: Goods left the railhead at Nenana, 180 miles up the Tanana, and came down to the Yukon by barge. Either way, Tanana was the transfer point, as it is today.

In Tanana I noticed something different, something new, for the first time in any river community since Whitehorse. Tanana seemed to have little historical perspective, little concern with the past. It seemed to have continually updated itself. The only old buildings along Tanana's waterfront were in the process of being torn down. Two false-fronted relics stood, one wearing the faded label "Post Office." Those are signs of a living community with a future. Ghost towns happen when, at some point, the inhabitants give up on renewing paint, changing building designs, remodeling. Time stops at the time of demise. Tanana is still a transfer point for the Yutana Barge Lines, with its headquarters up the Tanana at Nenana on the Alaska Railroad, and there is a good government payroll at the small Public Health Service hospital with its staff of doctors, an FAA contingent that runs the airport, and a weather station.

Our first day in Tanana was a lazy one; we looked around a bit but stuck mostly to the raft and gave it a good cleaning. That evening we had dinner with the Hardings: Gary, his wife, Joanne, and son, Chris. We had fried chicken, corn on the cob, and blueberry muffins! The Hardings lived in a nice modern trailer house with electricity, a flush toilet, the whole works, even carpeting! We felt strangely uncomfortable.

Ah, but not for long. The downriver reunion with our Dawson girlfriends, pledged at Fortymile, was set for Tanana.

The girls, Shanly, Sue, and Donna, showed up Sunday, all looking downright gorgeous, our own favorite dancehall girls!

We met them on the gravel airstrip and walked down to the raft.

We had five days to share. Five days for walks in the forests, meals and evenings aboard the raft, tight but loving quarters inside the tent. Bob—poor Bob—slept alone.

"This is for the birds!" he said early Monday morning, packing his bag.

"What?" I asked.

"This is for the birds! I'm heading for Whitehorse to visit Robyn. I'll be back in a week."

Bob was off on Tanana Air Taxi's scheduled flight to Fairbanks, a single-engine Cherokee Six.

We spent five glorious days together, the dancers and the river rats. At the far end of town, in an open birch forest, the Episcopal mission waited to rot away. We spent a lot of time up there, picking berries, lying in the sun, picnicking.

One evening, as we sat sunning ourselves on the deck, Gary came down to the raft. We were tied out of sight of town, behind bushes.

"Can I get one of you to give me a hand?" he asked.

"Sure." Paul and I both volunteered.

"We're going to take a short boat ride."

I figured it out when I saw the body bag.

"He's floating by the front of town," Gary told us as we headed out in his riverboat. So he was, bobbing along spread-eagle, Levis like sausage casing.

I'd never done anything quite like it. We pulled his arms in so he'd fit in the plastic body bag. Water came out of his mouth in little bubbles. His fingers were all shrivelled like they'd been too long in the bathtub, except his were coming unraveled. We took him up to the hospital; they have a cold room. It didn't take long, but that short affair gave the river a new significance for me.

Meanwhile the six of us took turns with all the chores and did a bit of baking. We even found a real piece of the past, the Pan House, run by an old Indian and his wife. Pan, short for Pangingue, is a traditional Alaskan gold-camp card game, seldom played anymore. The Pan House's chief feature was a big round table, where the card game, something like rummy, is played. Nine packs of cards make a Pan deck. It's a very fast game, with everyone seemingly playing simultaneously. From morning till late at night they played Pan, players joining or leaving after each hand. As we talked with Gregory Kokrine, the proprietor, the clink of chips and shuffle of cards never ceased. Gregory Kokrine had been in on the Ruby gold rush, and the last rushes of the era to Flat and Iditarod. He'd known Gordon Bettles, the early trader who founded the town named after him up the Koyukuk River.

The old man sat in the back of the Pan House. His wife ran the game, playing most of the time. A naked light bulb hung over the table's center. Gregory Kokrine didn't play, he told us, because he had bad luck!

"In the early days when they were rushing to Nome they called this the tobacco trail; there was tobacco juice right clean down to

Nome. If you lost the trail, when you got back to that tobacco you were on the trail to Nome," Kokrine told us.

His dad was named Hakara, a Fin trader—his stock, muzzle loaders, powder, and caps.

"I don't know why they called him Kokrine," he told us. "Then they named those hills 'Kokrine.' I used to spend a lot of time in the hills," he continued, but, "now, in my eighties, I have no business out in the hills, I'm ready for the boneyard." He chuckled. "Yah, ready for the boneyard."

The tent was confusing, but the girls fit right in, even to the psychological space we had long since divided.

It was a peaceful time with our ladies, but all too soon it was over. Their charter plane came to take them away, back through Fairbanks, back to the Action Jackson's Boundary Roadhouse with its hillside gravel strip, back to the waiting car and the seventy-mile drive to Dawson. It was a real farewell. At the end of the season they would leave Dawson for the South—Ontario and points between; they weren't even sure where. We would be up north, our future just as unpredictable. Why is it always that way on the road?

The fly-in visit of two friends from Anchorage, Ken Peterson and Mike Renfro, in their light plane lifted our spirits. Bob returned, and our plans gelled.

August was upon us, seven hundred river miles separated us from the Bering Sea. We decided to raft down to Holy Cross, a bit more than four hundred miles. We would load on our winter supplies there. Somewhere below Holy Cross we would pull ashore for the last time, take our raft apart, and build a cabin from it. We would wait until the freeze, snug in our cabin, then ski to the Bering Sea in mid-winter, on the thick ice of the Yukon.

When we left Tanana, a freak night low of 28 degrees Fahrenheit that left frost on the deck went a long way in convincing us we should make haste. We would confirm our plan with *Geographic* from Ruby, 125 miles downriver, and order our winter gear from Galena, 55 miles below Ruby.

14 August

13:40 — Thirty miles above Ruby. Paul and Jerry took first shift this morning, casting lines at 05:30. Bob and I took over at 09:30, we've just changed again. Big dinner planned for tonight, we'll have candied ham (canned) with a basting of honey, brown sugar, and cloves, baked spuds, cooked cabbage Norwegian-style, corn on the cob, and yes, fresh cornbread! Fresh food purchased at the Tanana N.C. store.

We passed the empty town of Kokrines, named for Gregory Kokrine's father. We were traveling along the Kokrine Hills, a mini-mountain group rising from the right bank of the river.

The story goes that the Catholic priest, Father Jette, after witnessing acts of desecration in his church at Kokrines, closed it in rage, leaving a curse that grass would cover the site before the church would return. He was right, only one of the handful of rickety cabins appeared to be inhabited, smoke coming from its stack.

The wind was sharp. Bob and I swept hard throughout our shift, trying to keep off the left bank, only to take the grand tour down the slough behind Ham Island. We cartwheeled and spun our way along the bank for about a mile, wrapping our flags tightly around the mast in the process. There was no damage, but Jerry and Paul had been busy with the axes, clearing the branches as we hit them.

As night came on, the wind died. We decided to drift around the clock once more, though we now had a bona-fide night. The sky was cloudless; it wouldn't be jet-black. The river was big and straight, with one great sweeping bend into Ruby. We would also have a new moon.

The darkness dropped over us slowly, allowing us to adjust to it; we could make out shore easily enough, and stayed off it. It was a cool night; I had the collar of my wool coat turned up, my wool watch cap pulled down over my ears. Our cookstove puffed and crackled. When we weren't sweeping we stood around it warming our fingers, drinking hot tea.

We came to bluffs along the left bank and moved in close, less than a hundred feet. The current was good along the rocky shore below the bluffs.

Notches clove down through the bluffs, tiny creeks and streams in them. Cold fog poured from the notches onto the Yukon's surface. we would drift into the damp, eerie clouds and vanish until we emerged below them. A chill wind carried the fog from the land and when we could see we found ourselves pushed out from shore. Bob and I swept back in to drift along the bluffs.

"Do you hear that?" Bob asked.

"Yes." I could barely hear a baleful groaning coming from somewhere ahead, then a splash. We were in a fog. As we emerged a black shadow loomed before us, nearly on our course.

"Fish wheel," I whispered.

Sure enough, a moonbeam lit up the wheel as it turned, and the great baskets rose and dropped, groaning and heaving. It was a prehistoric monster, feeding on the bottom, its head dipping and rising, the great baskets its cavernous maw.

We swept out to miss it, passing it close by, then moved back in to drift slowly along the bluffs.

For two hours we passed monster after monster, anchored to the stony shore, in fog, in black shadow, flashing in the moonlight, all moaning piteously. Above, the first northern lights of the season, faint green shimmerings in space, competed with the moon.

By the time we reached Ruby, nestled into one of the notches in the bluff, perhaps a quarter mile long, it was four o'clock and light enough to read.

Ruby was struck in 1911, a small sunset movement in the great American orchestration of the gold rush. By then Oscar and Charlie Tryck had been through Dawson, down the Yukon, and on to Nome. After Nome it was Fairbanks, sometimes mining, sometimes freighting with horses or hauling firewood, doing whatever they could. When they saved up a grubstake, they prospected.

Oscar was mining at Tenderfoot, south of Fairbanks on the Richardson trail, in 1911. He had good prospects, but the gold was deep, and there was too much overburden; it was more than a hundred feet to bedrock and the pay streak. Charlie was up along the Yukon prospecting at the time the rush started to Long Creek some thirty miles back off the Yukon River. Ruby came to be as its supply town.

Ruby wasn't named after a girl or because of the presence of the valuable gemstone. There are two basic auriferous sands, black sand (mostly iron), and ruby sand, which has a high concentrate of garnet, the poor man's ruby. Garnet abounds in the Ruby mining district.

Charlie and Oscar and one of their original partners, Oscar Lundine, joined together to take a "lay" on Long Creek. Under the lay system, the original discoverer of gold lets someone else mine his claim for a percentage of the profit. They stayed, their wandering over for a while.

In 1913 a different kind of bug bit my grandfather. He left Ruby for the "outside," by way of Nome, took the steamer to Seattle, then the rails to Michigan, to his childhood sweetheart, Blanche Tipping. They married. He returned with his bride in the dead of winter over the Richardson Trail from Valdez to Fairbanks, the same route the Richardson Highway was to follow, and later the Trans-Alaska Pipeline.

He brought with him crates of fresh eggs. He knew the trail well, as he'd freighted on it after the Fairbanks strike. He brought a wife and eggs, both wrapped in warm bearskin robes, into the heart of Alaska by dog team—without freezing, breaking, or otherwise disturbing any of his delicate cargo! The eggs sold for a dollar apiece in Fairbanks. Grandpa paid his return fare with the proceeds. After breakup they boarded a stern-wheeler bound for Ruby.

Ruby was good to them; there was gold all about on numerous creeks and work for miners, even after the boom toned down. In 1914, my uncle was born in Ruby.

Charlie, not so tied down, found time to prospect, and was in on the discovery of a galena deposit downriver some fifty miles.

World War I came and galena, a source of lead, was in demand. The brothers mined it. Along about the end of the war the price of lead went to hell—the generals didn't need any more bullets—so the galena mining slacked off. The mill burned down; there was no reason to rebuild it.

About that time, my grandfather Oscar received an offer to be superintendent of a hard rock gold mine in the Willow mining district far to the south, below the Alaska Range. He left Ruby, the Yukon, and the interior of Alaska. His brother stayed on.

My grandfather made only one trip back to the Yukon and Ruby—in 1953, to settle the affairs of his brother's estate: a handful of traps, some claims long since unworked, a cabin; the effects of an old bachelor.

Out on the road from Ruby, built by the Alaska Road Commission, the mines on the creeks kept pumping out gold, hiring miners and woodcutters, blacksmiths and cooks. Charlie's specialty was drift mining, pick and shovel work. Drift miners tunnelled along the bedrock, hoisting up the pay dirt by windlass so it could be sluiced for its gold. By the late thirties, heavy equipment—cats, draglines, tractors—put an end to drift mining. It was cheaper just to move the overburden than to tunnel under it.

Charlie was getting along in years then, as was his partner, Harry Boland. They still prospected during the summers, but long-hair fur brought top prices in those days, and they relied more and more on trapping during the winters for their income.

World War II came, and the government requisitioned the heavy equipment on the creeks for the war effort; Executive Order L-208 in effect stopped gold mining. The industry shut down. It was pretty hard to start up after the war; the price of gold stayed fixed at thirty-five dollars an ounce, and operating costs climbed. Gold mining became a wildcat affair, no longer a major industry. That's the way it is now. Most miners are going over old ground. A handful of miners, all with family operations, keep at it in the Ruby district.

The place to start out from in a town like Ruby is the store. Always on the waterfront, this one was an affair of time-warped logs and bent timbers that seemed to have conformed to the land. There was a boardwalk out front and benches, but the town seemed a little past the point where the old-timers hung around the store, sat on the benches out front, and watched the river go by. Everything was right for it, but the old-timers were all dead or gone.

The Ruby Trading Company was a family affair, owned and operated by Harold Esmailka, a forty-year-old vim-and-vigor type who couldn't seem to move from one end of the old glass-topped counter to the other without trying to do it as quickly as he could. If he did slow down it was because he was thinking too hard to worry about how he got anywhere. Harold also ran a bush plane outfit, Harold's Air Service. In one wing of the long building was the Esmailka home, a combination "bus" station, airline terminal, radio shack, office, and home that his wife, Florence, moved in and through like a dervish— serving coffee, doing laundry, answering the radio, and somehow tending to the needs of her five kids all the while. Everyone was going somewhere, doing something simultaneously.

"What can I do for you?" Harold asked, smiling over his owly glasses from behind the counter.

I told him my name and explained that I'd like to meet anyone who knew my uncle.

"You can start right here," he said, pointing to a tall, slim man.

167

"Johnny May, meet Keith Tryck."

Johnny May returned to Ruby after World War II, with a new steel plate in his head, recurring malaria, and a diet of straight milk. He had purchased the store from Northern Commercial and then sold it to Harold. He'd known Charlie quite well, he told me.

"I miss those old fellows. He was one of the best, he really liked the kids. His house is gone now, it was right next to mine. I own his claim at thirteen mile on the road. He and Harry Boland had a galena prospect there, and their trapping cabin. It's pretty near fallen in, but you can go out there and look at it if you want.

"And you should see Charlie Carlo; he knew your uncle."

Charlie Carlo lived on the hill in an old but neat frame house. It was a nice place, Ruby.

Charlie was in his shop/garage working on his "light plant," a small generator. There was no community electricity.

"This is my second one," he informed me. "I already have the first going good, but if it quits when I'm gone, they'll need to use this one.

"I met Charlie Tryck back in 1931," he said, wiping the grease from his hands. "That's a long time ago. I worked with your uncle at Long Creek," he continued, "drift mining—five dollars a day in those days. Damn glad to get it, too. There were jobs then working underground. But when the equipment came, I switched and learned to operate cats. Charlie was old then, so he started taking it easy. They kept a neat house, him and Harry Boland, just down the street there by Johnny May's. They didn't get out much in their last years; he and Harry Boland used to stay at home. Made good home brew, Charlie Tryck did; all the old-timers used to go up there."

Charlie Carlo's family was the first Indian family to come to Ruby, in 1931 from Rampart. It was his brother, Bill Carlo, who was placer mining at Rampart. Charlie Carlo was one of the last men to make the winter mail run by dog team into Ruby. When the switch was made to airplane, he went to work for the outfit with the mail contract. Now in his sixties, he makes his living as a heavy-equipment operator, a job that takes him all over Alaska during the summer construction season. There's little opportunity for work in Ruby; the school employs one or two local people, and Harold hires one or two outside his family. The health aide has a job, and Johnny May runs the Standard Oil outlet, getting his fuel from the barge. There's work for two on the road crew, and summer work for some fighting forest fires. The rest, mostly natives, fish and trap and live on food stamps and welfare. That accounts for Ruby's 175 residents.

One real old-timer who still lives in Ruby is Dolly Yrjana. She was born Dolly Fischer in Dawson, and came down the Yukon in 1914 with her family. Her father set up a roadhouse in Ruby, and Dolly has been there ever since. Dolly knew my grandfather and his brother when they stayed in Ruby during World War I. Dolly's husband, Albert Yrjana, came to Ruby in the thirties and worked as a woodcutter and freighter for the miners before taking a job with the Alaska Road Commission maintaining the road to the mines. Later, when the Road Commission became the Bureau of Public Roads, it was known affectionately in Ruby as the "Bureau of Parallel Ruts."

"Everyone liked Charlie," Dolly said, when I visited her home, which reminded me of my grandfather's. It had a big fenced-in garden; the dogs for Albert's trapline team were staked out in the yard.

"He never leaned on anybody or drank too much, and whatever he wanted he paid for in cash. You couldn't say that about everyone," she said. Dolly had a smile that was infectious.

"I stayed with Charlie when I went to and from my camp," Albert told me, a twinkle in his eye. "So, you're his relative . . . and as welcome as the flowers in May. That's Charlie's expression."

Albert went on. "I got along fine with the old fellow. He had breakfast for me in the morning, and he wouldn't let me help; he did it all. The line between our traplines was on the ridge, the divide. I trapped on one side and he was on the other. We never encroached on the other guy's line. I stopped at his cabin on the way out and hauled his groceries. I'd bring 'em in and he'd put me up for the night. I couldn't make it in one day unless the trail was broke, so I would stay with him. I liked to just visit; we'd talk to beat hell late into the night!"

In the afternoon Bob and I returned to the store and arranged to link through Harold's radio to Fairbanks, then by phone link to D.C. and *Geographic*. That's how we learned we had received a go-ahead on our plan to build a cabin; they would grubstake us.

In the morning we left for Galena. We needed to make time, but I knew I'd return to Ruby. I'd only scratched the surface.

Albert Yrjana was the last to visit us before we left. He came by in his boat on his way back from checking his fish wheel, one of those we'd passed the night before. He brought us two fresh salmon.

"Can't have you fellers going hungry. What would Charlie say?"

The wind blew. It continued overcast and drizzled thick enough to start dripping inside the tent. We finally beat the wind, hoisting our sail for the first time that season and sailing downriver into Galena. We didn't make especially good time, but it sure lifted our spirits to be making headway.

Galena was established in 1919 to supply the mine Charlie Tryck had helped find. The Air Force base that keeps it alive was built as a relay field for lend-lease planes going from the U.S. to Russia during World War II.

We were ready to order what we figured we'd need for winter and then get moving, but we ran into a bit of a delay. Someone had heisted the post office the same night we came in; we couldn't get our mail till the postal inspector came. When he arrived, he figured we might have had something to do with it, until someone reported a boat had been stolen. The bandit had taken to the water; we were clean.

We made one trip to Hobo's, the only bar open on a regular basis for the entire length of the Alaskan Yukon. The first thing I noticed were the murals on the walls; the second, bullet holes. We had a beer and returned to the raft.

The gear and food we'd ordered would meet us in Holy Cross, mailed general delivery or sent air freight. We would load it aboard and continue on, seeking a place to convert our raft into a cabin.

When we left Galena, we'd had enough of visiting towns for a while. We passed Koyukuk at the mouth of the Koyukuk River and didn't slow for Nulato either, other than for Jerry and me to race in by canoe and check the mail.

We were now in the country first explored by Russians. Nulato was their farthest upriver trading post, established in 1838 by a Russian Creole trader, Malakhov. Every time he left, the Indians burned him out, and, to hear the trooper in Galena, Wayne Selden, talk, things hadn't changed much.

"You think Galena is wild," Wayne warned us, the North's answers to "Dodge City and Tombstone are waiting for you in Koyukuk and Nulato!"

The Rafters Rejoin and Meet the Can-Can Queens

Two days after we left Galena, Selden had a triple murder-suicide on his hands.

At Kaltag, barely a hundred miles from the Bering Sea and at the eastern end of the portage route to Nome, the Yukon turns. We began the long southern dive, traveling nearly due south, almost to the latitude of Lake Laberge, far behind us.

We sailed when we could and even made what turned out to be our ultimate use of the sail just below Kaltag. The wind blew upriver, so we chose a spot on the shore and deftly sailed in, turning against the current at the last and using the wind to drive us upstream till we nudged into a great root wad on the shore. Jerry tied us to it without so much as stepping off the raft.

Our progress diminished day by day. Where once we dreaded the thought of an average of less than four miles an hour we now revelled in anything greater than three miles an hour and were happy enough with two. Getting a wind assist was a real thrill.

It was a long, trying stretch of river from Kaltag to Holy Cross. We would pass the villages of Anvik and Grayling in the 175 miles. Decks in the morning were damp; we almost always moved out into fog. Though the leaves were turning once more, the general scheme of things seemed to be drab, gray river and a gray sky overpowering all else. The wind blew; it seemed most of the time we worked against it.

Today is Sunday. Bob and I drifted out into fog at 5:30. I've made my concession to the coming autumn and now wear my wool long johns in the morning. If the sun, bless it, comes out at all, and if there isn't any wind, by midday I have to take them off. But those days will be fewer and fewer.

Yesterday we made 21 miles in 19 hours, struggling the whole way. Paul and Jerry had a terrible go during their second shift, 300 yards in 4 hours, by far the worst shift to date. They tried sweeping, sailing, pushing, poling, kedging in a lot of different combinations. They were foiled by a combination of slack water, shallows, a strong shore-bound wind, and a healthy eddy ever circling upstream. What a bummer.

The raft has been in the water for 2 months, some of the logs 2½ months; it floats measurably lower. All the logs are below the surface of the water now. It's time to think cabin.

We had used up all our gift food—the salmon, moose meat, and ducks given to us in Galena—and we were back to beans and bacon, the same bacon we bought in Canada; we had to scrape off the mold and soak out the salt to use it. Sometimes we had bread, most often bannock or biscuits. It was good fare, if uncomplicated, with a lot of energy in it. We needed it.

Every four-hour shift was work; there wasn't much of the high-summer, easy duty that had spoiled us. If we weren't on our toes, we could screw up badly. It seemed we were clawing our way downriver mile by mile. The sail was a real asset, but the wind often blew us into the outside of a bend and into the cutbanks.

If the wind got too strong, driving us relentlessly ashore, we tied. If we didn't, the consequences could be perilous. We spent hour after grating hour tied, waiting for the wind to slacken so we could again make progress. Wind, wind, wind! Not only from the sky was it an enemy. For days it had kicked up waves on the Yukon, increasing tenfold the cutting action of the river against soft earth banks. Great trees toppled like jack straws, massive chunks of bank dropped into the river with great reports like cannon fire. We stayed away from the cutbanks; we never tied under them. In the night, we could hear them blasting into the river.

Inside the tent there was peace, relief from the elements and the responsibility of the helm. Each of us knew the peace and used it in his own way. Each of us was reluctant to call to the tent for assistance while on duty, yet it had to happen many times. Sometimes it was just a warning that you might be needed, but more often it was a simple, "How about a hand on deck?" which got immediate response. Any of us could put a fireman to shame, we were so quick in reaching the deck to raise or lower sail, wield an ax at branches and snags, or take over on a sweep. "All hands on deck!" meant big trouble. There was never time to talk; in the instant it took to reach the deck you must see where you were needed and jump to it.

Jerry and Paul canoed into Anvik for our mail. It was late in the evening and our light was almost gone. Bob and I stayed aboard. We were making progress; the wind had died.

There wasn't any mail.

It was time to make for shore, but we didn't. We would make a last all-night run. The map showed a long, straight section of river ahead, beyond the next bend. We were in the center of the one-half-mile-wide river. By the time we turned the corner and drifted to the end of the straight stretch it would be light enough to handle the bend ahead of that. The sky was clear but for clouds far to the west. We knew we could make out the shore and keep away from it in the starlight. The wind was negligible. Everything should have gone all right, but by the time we figured out it wasn't going to, it was too late.

As our light slowly faded, the wind picked up, but only by whispers—never enough to suggest we couldn't handle it. We lost track of the clouds to the west and didn't know they were rapidly coming our way.

When we turned the bend into the straight stretch, the wind hit us. The last inkling of light vanished as the clouds swept over us, blocking out the sky.

Bob and I were on duty.

"Christ, we're in for it this time," I said. We couldn't have seen as far as the end of the raft if it weren't for the lantern burning in the tent.

There wasn't anything to do but wait. We had no idea which way we were going or where the shore was. If the wind put us ashore we would tie up, simple as that; if not, we would continue through the night on pins and needles.

The wind increased, kicking up one-, then two-foot waves. We began to pitch and yaw, as we rode in and out of the wave troughs. Our Coleman lantern, set in a Blazo box reflector, cast its light with little effect. We got the sail ready in case we needed it in a hurry.

"Listen!" Bob exclaimed.

Above the groaning of the raft and splash of waves against it, we heard another noise—waves against the shore. The wind was carrying us slowly toward the noise. We aimed our makeshift searchlight. Nothing.

"We're taking a long time," I said. "The wind must be angling to the shore."

We waited—there was nothing else we could do. As we drew closer, we heard something else that rattled us but good. We could hear big trees slamming into the river—we were closing in on a cutbank. The old adrenalin started pumping through me right then.

"Let's get the sail up!" I shouted. Paul was on deck in a flash, Jerry right after him.

The sail was set awfully fast and trimmed just as quickly for as much angle as we could get. It helped, but not enough.

"Shore!" Bob yelled.

I could just make it out, no more than seventy-five feet away.

The bank was at least twenty feet high; tall cottonwood trees stretched along its brink. The soft bank was literally melting away before the combined action of wave and current. Bob and I were sweeping now, helping the sail. Still it wasn't enough. As we slipped along parallel to the beach, losing inch by inch our battle to stay off the shore, we witnessed the awesome destruction. Trees leaned far over the river, ready to fall. Some trees were already down but were being held to the shore by their roots. Trees that had fallen long before jutted at all angles from the river's surface like the broken and shattered masts of a thousand sunken ships. We had to get to shore. There wasn't any way we could drift through the snags.

"Head her in!" I said. "I'll take a line with the canoe." There wasn't any need for discussion—it was obvious what we had to do, cutbank or no cutbank.

It was a sickening feeling when we closed within reach of the overhanging trees. Any one of them would smash us flat if it dropped on us. Using the sail as a brake, we eased along the shore till we found a place that had just sloughed. I took a line upstream by canoe, securing it to a snag.

Far across the river we could hear a barge pushing its way upstream, the beam of its powerful searchlight periodically checking the shore in flashes like lightning. We flashed our feeble "lantern in a box" at him. He acknowledged us, then turned his light back to the far shore. I thought about the pilot. He, too, was feeling his way, but he was warm and cozy in his pilot house thirty feet above the water.

I turned in, shivering. The canvas wall of the tent did little to block out the sounds of the storm. The booming and crashing of sloughing banks and falling trees made my sleep fitful at best.

Paul and Jerry rose at 5:00 A.M. The storm hadn't eased, and the wind continued to blow upriver. But they were able to use it to advantage and sail out beyond the reach of the snags and sweepers.

Once in mid-channel, I dozed back off.

"Let's have a hand with the sail!"

In a daze I stumbled into my jacket, pants, and boots, and rushed on deck.

"Take the tiller," Paul panted. "If the seas take us broadside, we'll lose our decks!"

The river's temper knew no bounds. Angry waves pushed high by wind and current at loggerheads crashed over the deck, washing to the tent. I was immediately soaked from the knees down. We were blown against the current, the power of the wind so great the sweep was like lead in the water. I struggled to hold us true. Even so, the grip of the current was stronger than the force of the wind, and we continued to move downstream.

The mast leaned a crazy twenty degrees, our guy lines taut to the point of breaking. Jerry and Paul were forward, struggling with the sail, trying to rescue it before it could be carried away. They got it furled, and as we lost headway the sweep became more manageable. Paul came back, took over his sweep. We were plowing into ugly, gray, five-foot waves and were rolling like a ship at sea.

The biting wind had thoroughly chilled me; I hadn't time for wool underwear or socks—not even a shirt. I shivered back to bed. It was eight o'clock, an hour and a half before Bob and I would face the storm.

Bob was still in bed, but wide awake and laughing! As the waves rolled under the tent floor, jets of water, like tiny fountains, spurted up waist-high through the cracks.

I dozed off, only an hour and a half till our turn.

"Nine-thirty, up and at 'em!"

I was dressed for the North Sea in winter when I hit the deck, Bob right behind me.

The wind had slackened, the storm had eased. We were back to just ordinary clawing for every mile. By the end of the day we could show eight miles of progress for a dozen hours of hard work.

We'd learned a lot about rafting in two seasons and fifteen hundred miles, a lot about the nature of the Yukon. We had sailed the lakes, P and P'd, run the canyons. We'd threaded the Yukon's mazes, learned our lessons on bars and shoals. We had dueled the wind. But before we got to Holy Cross we had used every trick we knew to keep us moving. It was like a great trial planned just for us, a warning not to forget who called the shots.

We limped into Holy Cross late in the evening on the last day of August. The sky was clear, the air crisp; stars riddled the heavens. The storm had passed. The next morning we had frost on the deck. It wasn't a freak freeze. It was that time of year again.

To say we were busy in Holy Cross is an understatement. We had shipments of winter clothing from three different sources dribbling in at the post office, hardware we would need in cabin building coming from Anchorage, food for the winter also arriving from Anchorage.

Harry Turner, retired storekeeper, is the Wien Air Alaska agent. The tall, gray bank of dials, knobs, and dipping needles, the HF radio, Holy Cross's communication link with the rest of the world, screeched and squawked in his living room. His thirty-year-old Army surplus four-by-four hauled the freight and mail from the gravel strip to town. Turner, an easy-going man in his late forties, half Indian and half gold-rush trader, knew where all our gear was; his happy-go-lucky wife, Lucy, laughed as we gathered it all on the raft.

Winter clothes from Anchorage, down clothing from Seattle, trail food, hardware, staples from Anchorage—all had been coming into Holy Cross in bits and pieces for a week.

We had too much food. Our raft looked like a grocery store warehouse without walls, it was piled so high with boxes of "essentials." You should never order a winter's supply of grub on an empty stomach.

There was no course but to sell some. We spread the word, and on a sunny afternoon opened our bazaar, selling off grub at the price we paid to whoever would buy. It's my guess that a third of Holy Cross's hundred residents came down for a look at the bargain basement. We sold off four hundred dollars worth of grub, cash and carry!

Harry and Lucy thought it was great fun. They were down on the raft the afternoon after the bazaar. When they learned of our plans to build a cabin somewhere between Holy Cross and Russian Mission, ninety miles downriver, Harry suggested we build near Tucker Slough, forty miles below Holy Cross. As usual, we did a lot of talking about our adventures. Harry was a good storyteller, so in turn we learned a bit about Holy Cross and the country up the Innoko River where Harry was born, and where his dad traded. The conversation turned back to today.

"I've been thinking," Harry said, "you should fly over that country downriver, sort of pick out a place to aim for. Pretty hard to run this raft back upriver if you pass all the good spots for a cabin. There's no charter service here, but Chet Clark comes over from Aniak quite a bit. That's Aniak Flying Service. You could have him take you up for a look."

"Sounds good," Bob said. "I could take some pictures, too."

176

"Who's that?" I asked, changing the subject. A boat was headed our way, hell bent for election.

"Looks like the teacher, Bill Brown," Harry answered. The light was just about gone, so it was hard to tell.

Something was wrong. The boat was coming right up to the raft. There was nothing graceful or planned about the approach; he was getting to us as fast as he could.

"Gunshot wound!" the teacher yelled.

Two young boys, teenagers, sat in the front of the boat utterly lost to shock and despair. A third lay still in the bottom on a pile of jackets, a tarp over him.

Jerry and I quickly tied the boat between raft and shore and stepped into the boat.

"Did you stop the bleeding?" I asked. Jerry was carefully sliding the tarp back.

"Yes, I think so," he answered. The boy was ashen.

A bandage of some sort was wrapped around the boy's middle. It seemed to be working; little blood was seeping through it. We didn't move him. Paul showed up with two warm sleeping bags to put over the boy. Bob took the two other boys inside the tent, put warm jackets on them, and sat there with them. They couldn't have done anything for themselves.

The three boys had gone goose hunting, cruising along the river in their boat checking out the points of bars and islands where the geese rest in their long flight south. They'd spotted some, and in their hurry to get ashore and out of the boat, a twelve-gauge shotgun had accidentally discharged. Point-blank range, left side of the boy's back.

Bill Brown had seen the boys waving from shore. They couldn't get their motor going. Bill picked them up.

An hour had already passed since the accident. Jerry felt for a pulse, said nothing. I felt for a pulse. None. I didn't want the responsibility.

I looked at Harry. Harry looked at me.

"Better call the doctor," Harry said, and left for his radio. Lucy Turner stayed.

Twenty minutes passed, Harry returned.

"He's on his way from Aniak, be here in about an hour," he told us.

It was dark.

177

People began to appear, shadows in the willows on the riverbank. Wise old Indians, men and women, young people. All quiet. An Alaskan vigil. Two women came for their sons.

"That's his father," Lucy Turner whispered to me. He had gray hair and stood tall and straight. He looked into my eyes, seeking. I wouldn't lie. I couldn't say, "He'll pull through," not even with my eyes.

I sought the pulse again. None. Jerry softly raised the boy's eyelid, then turned to me. The father watched us.

I faced him, standing on the riverbank not ten feet away. In the softest, gentlest way I knew how, I shook my head. "No," it said. "God above, I'm sorry."

His eyes were still on mine as his head dropped ever so slightly. "I had to know," it said. Then he turned away.

We saw the plane, its landing light a moving star to the south. Gradually it grew, we saw the red and green running lights, then heard its long engine.

Harry left for the runway. There weren't any landing lights on the gravel strip, the headlights from Harry's four-by-four would have to do the job. They'd done it before.

The young doctor confirmed what we knew, had a cup of coffee, and left, flying alone in the night back to Aniak.

Our gear continued to dribble into Holy Cross. We waited for it impatiently; time was awasting, and it ran out on Paul.

The professional ski-racing season was fast approaching; he had to prepare for it. He planned to walk the forty-mile portage from the Yukon over to the Kuskokwim, raft down to Bethel, and fly to Anchorage. We would sorely miss him.

We waited four more days in Holy Cross. On September 6, we decided the hell with it, and pulled out. Harry and Lucy, ever helpful, would bring down anything that came for us, including mail, by boat, sometime before freeze-up.

6

From Raft to Cabin; By Skis to the Bering Sea

"Watch the propeller!" Bob yelled.

The orange-and-white Cessna 180 floatplane taxied toward us. We needn't have worried; the pilot deftly gauged his speed, cut the power, and drifted serenely to the raft, a perfect three-point docking. The pilot stepped easily to the plane's float, then to our deck. We were drifting in mid-river, five miles below Holy Cross.

"Geez, Harry said I shouldn't have any trouble finding you, but this is the first time I've had a charter like this! I'm Chet Clark."

Chet Clark, in his early thirties, is part owner and chief pilot of Aniak Flying Service. Aniak, a small community on the Kuskokwim River, is about a hundred miles south of Holy Cross. We explained we wanted to have a look downriver for a good place to build a cabin.

Jerry and I went up first. The ancient who put a finger on perspective would have come unglued if he had an airplane. To lift above the mast beyond the river's banks, being so long on the raft, was breathtaking and spellbinding.

We flew beside the Paimiut hills, locating what we thought were good places for cabins, where mountain brooks met the Yukon. We would check them by canoe, then float the raft to the site we had selected.

On the return we spied the raft and saw it anew, a naked spot on a great river that flowed in majestic arcs. And the Yukon took its humble place in the expanse of Alaska.

We returned to the raft as expertly as before. We were gone just twenty minutes.

179

I shook my head.

"This is my baby," Chet said proudly, slapping the dash. I believed. His plane seemed to fly like it was alive, effortlessly, just for him.

Bob climbed aboard for a combination look-see and picture-taking run. Chet turned upstream and was off, water streaming from the floats, tiny rivulets suspended in air.

"Well, you think we've got it covered?" Jerry asked.

"I hope so," I answered. "Good forest, fresh water, dry land, southern exposure for the low winter sun, hills at our backs to hike in—I hope so."

They were back soon; Bob was in agreement. We would build along the Paimiut Hills on the north bank of the Yukon.

We made arrangements for Chet to fly in just before freeze-up with supplies and mail. Then, with little fanfare, he was gone.

The wind had one last dance with us, fetching us to the south shore of the Yukon thirty-five miles below Holy Cross. We waited three days for calm. When it came, it took us two hours to sweep across the river, the three of us rotating at the sweeps.

That evening, September 9, with the raft securely tied, the three of us canoed down the shore, checking for a cabin site.

None of the clear brooks offered a nearby cabin site, but about a quarter mile below the last one, at the toe of the hills, three-quarters of a mile above the entrance to Tucker's Slough, we found a spot in an open birch grove. The ground was dry, and the lift for the logs to the cabin site not unreasonable. But there was no clear-water brook.

"What the hell," Bob said. "We've been drinking the muddy Yukon for two summers already and haven't died." It was settled. Just as well, too; we could have spent a month of Sundays looking for an ideal cabin site.

We paddled back up to the raft and, in the last waning light, slipped our moorings. We stayed close to the stony beach. Above us the hills were crimson, the leaves on the birch trees anchored in the close rocks were yellowing, the grassy forest floor at our sides had turned tawny brown.

The final voyage of our faithful raft was a quiet one, a thoughtful one. It had been home for nearly 1800 miles of Yukon voyaging, had seen us safely through thick and thin, storm and fair weather. It had gone through half a dozen transformations, each an improvement.

Our great sweeps were our sixth and seventh ones, nicely balanced and proportioned. Just enough firewood for the cookstove was stacked along the tent, all the right little niches for the right things had been built into the kitchen, where everything hung or was neatly stored. The decks were shiny from bare feet and rubber boots. We now knew something about rafting, I thought, reflecting. Ah, but cabin building. I slipped into my raft-borne bed for the last time. Before I would again be comfortable, I would be in a cabin.

The morning of September 10, the raft's metamorphosis began. Our trusty wood stove hardly missed a puff in its transfer from the raft to our camp ashore. By nightfall, the raft had been stripped to its bare logs, everything else was on the beach: cases of food under canvas, tools, a stack of cabin hardware, boardwalk decking and graded lumber in separate mounds, duffels, packs, gas box "drawers" inside our transferred tent.

"Tomorrow the work starts," Bob remarked grimly as we turned in.

None of us had built a log cabin before, but we'd seen cabins all along the river; they became our "plans." Forty-seven single logs made up our raft, a dozen twenty-five feet or longer, most of them eighteen feet in length. They would become the walls of our cabin. Decking would become the floor; planking, tent frame, and scraps would make, in order of priority, an outhouse, door, bunks, shelves, porch, and cache. We would make a roof of poles, cover the poles with canvas from the tent, then cover all with a thick layer of sod.

First things first: Under Jerry's direction, we raised a shortened mast for a spar tree. Every bit of lift we could get for the logs would be a help, but no matter how we figured it, lifting the logs to the cabin site would be rough work. One at a time, using block and tackle, we would skid the logs into the edge of the forest, ten feet above and fifty feet from the river, and stack them. From the deck we would select logs as needed for our cabin walls, re-rigging the spar tree just behind the cabin site for the purpose.

Late in the afternoon we spied a canoe coming downriver with a lone occupant. He landed above camp and walked down to the site of our activity.

"I guess I missed it," he said contemplatively.

"Missed what?" Bob asked.

"I put in at Johnson's Crossing on the Teslin and ever since

Dawson I've been behind you. I wanted to see the raft I've heard so much about."

"That's too bad," Bob said. "But I'll tell you what, if you stick around a couple days you can see how one raft of said characteristics is converted into a comfy cabin, and we provide room and board!"

That couple of days turned out to be nearly three weeks. Greg Gibbons, a husky, soft-spoken Minnesota man joined us in our windy, flapping tent, and took his turn in our makeshift kitchen.

Getting the big logs up took a lot of work, and every bit of trickery we knew. Over slick logs, along inclined plane—you name it—up they went to the landing by block and tackle, as we charged down the same bank applying our body weight as well as muscle to the haul line. My hands cracked from constantly being in and out of the river, working the logs. Greasing my boots barehanded with a concoction of mink oil, Neat's Foot Oil, and pine tar expertly mixed by Jerry, shaped my hands right up. Did my boots some good, too.

We leveled a spot for the cabin on an ever-so-slight knoll surrounded by white birch trees. We laid two great foundation logs and began the walls. As most of our logs were eighteen feet long, that became the wall length. The interior would measure sixteen feet square.

We shaped the logs, chopping off knots and high spots by ax, notching them carefully at the cabin's corners. They fit like interlocking fingers, with no gaps.

When satisfied with a log's fit, we laid moss in the notches and along the bottom log and rolled it into place. As the walls rose, one of us was busy hammering more moss chinking between the logs already laid, to ensure a tight, warm cabin.

The moss came into camp gunnysack by gunnysack. One sack was enough for one log. On moss trips we explored around our cabin site. The best moss for our purposes came from the edge of a marsh a quarter of a mile away. It was a continuous job; a sharp report sometimes meant the gatherer was also bringing back a spruce hen for the bean pot.

When the walls rose too high to clamber over easily, we cut a hole for the door and laid the floor.

25 September
Temporary camp. Would give the time but my clock ran down and

we don't need it anyway. 26° last night. That's the only time we need to know.

"Plane!" Bob called. We were working on the gables.

It was Chet's 180. He landed and taxied up to our beach.

"How are you fixed for meat?" he asked.

"We could use some," Jerry answered.

"I've spotted a big moose not far from here. Give me a hand getting it, and we'll share the meat."

Jerry went with him and brought back enough fresh meat to last us till mid-winter.

We hoisted the purlins and ridge pole. We would have a six-foot overhang, a real Yukon porch.

The world changed around us as we worked. Not so you'd notice it day by day, yet it became apparent. We'd begun construction in an early autumn forest; now we were surrounded by bare, spindly trees, the soft forest floor a blanket of dry leaves that crackled underfoot. The Yukon dropped eight feet, its edge a hundred yards away over a gradually sloping muddy beach. Our view from the cabin was splendid with the leaves gone.

Greg left; winter was getting near and he still had 250 miles to go to the sea. We loaded him up with grub and an extra pair of wool long johns and watched him paddle back to his journey. We would miss him.

One month from the time we eased the raft into its last tie-up, the three of us were sitting on the porch in front of our snug cabin. None too soon, either. Our first snow came the day we finished hauling sod onto the roof. Everything came out just right; we had lumber left over and logs to the measure of a cord and a half of firewood.

Our cabin was about the size of a large master bedroom. Along the east wall we built in four sturdy bunks, one for visitors. I drew the deuce of hearts and ended up with the upper with Bob below me. Jerry drew the lower bunk away from the door. We fixed up our "digs"—shelves, a place for knickknacks, a candle holder for reading at night, each to his own tastes.

Our kitchen, a long counter with shelves below for dishes, pots, and pans, was along the east wall. Above the counter one of our two windows, fashioned from clear plastic, overlooked the forest and river to the east. Our second window, in the door, faced the river.

184

The stove was at room's center. The wall next to the door was one of shelves for staples; flour, rice, spices, oatmeal, dried fruit, etc. A book shelf and desk filled the last corner.

The ceiling was high, high enough for Jerry to move about without hitting his head—with one exception. We couldn't resist hanging our lantern at eye level; the cabin wouldn't have been right if it wasn't there to run into!

As in building the raft, the little things—the finishing touches—seemed to take the most time: building a door, putting in windows, adding the shelves and kitchen, sorting the gear and neatening up our yard. We idled along at these tasks as the fall closed down around us; after all, the cabin was finished. Occasional hunters visited, most of them downriver trying to get their moose for winter meat. Harry and Lucy Turner brought mail down from Holy Cross; two kayakers stopped for a spell.

One morning we rose to a crisp clear day and ice on the river. Great sheets of ice, fragile as window panes, drifted by. There would be no more visiting hunters, no more river travel until the river was frozen solid. We'd entered the northern limbo, not winter, not fall, but freeze-up.

We were all set in the grub department, our cabin stocked, as well as our cache. The porch was stacked high with firewood.

We decided on a routine. Each of us would be responsible for all household chores for three days in a row, leaving the other two free to do as they wished. That worked well. It was agreed that the cabin would be kept clean, wood brought in from the woodpiles every evening, garbage and slop pails emptied, lanterns filled, dishes done, kitchen cleaned up, water hauled from the river, floor swept. You could do them in any order you wanted, when you wanted, as long as they were done before you went to bed.

Each man was king in the kitchen during his shift, his chance to be the Galloping Gourmet. Jerry's biscuits and pies reigned supreme, Bob's fudge, brownies, and cinnamon rolls were superb. I baked bread, slowly progressing toward a loaf I could be proud of. And, I don't care what the vegetarians say, there's nothing like a luscious moose steak for breakfast, moose roast, spuds, and onions for supper, a little chunk of moose, smothered in garlic, thrown in for lunch.

14 October

Yesterday afternoon I took a bath. I heated water in the laundry tub, then climbed in, so to speak, legs sticking out! I did my laundry, too. Like my body, it hadn't been "done" for a month. Wow! It sure felt good. Still got one load of dirty clothes simmering away. That ought to do it for a while.

When we first noticed the scurrying of tiny feet we were happy, glad to know somebody else opted for our home as opposed to the out of doors. The field mice, cute furry little fellas, were welcome. But it only took about three nights before Jerry and Bob were fed up with the little critters running through their hair, across their faces, under their pillows. From then on it was war. We kept shoes and a ball and other such missiles to throw at them as they scurried from haven to haven along the floor, darting out from behind the kitchen, running along the open no-man's land below the door. The thump, whack, bounce of varmint missiles became as commonplace as sirens in Washington, D.C. They had a fair chance, if they could run the gauntlet and survive. More power to them.

Mice turds on the floor, mice turds in the rice, and holes in the biscuits forced an escalation of the war, one new tactic being to use our flashlights to temporarily blind the little beasts. Once caught in the spotlight, all kinds of things would fly their way. Even so, they had a good survival rate; it seemed the ones who survived taught the others how to stay away from searchlights, how to run like little sons-a'- bitches in open ground, and that daytime operations were generally carried on against us at great loss to their forces.

The bravest mice of all, the ones we admired most, raided the "refrigerator," a box nailed up outside the door on the cabin wall. We kept cut up moose and bacon in it; they loved the fat. Through the window we could watch them climb up and over the cardboard door into the trove. All it took was any shift in the door to force their exit; those buggers could jump at least a foot straight up. Some of them survived as many as five close calls before getting it. They were the aces.

The situation at night took on dire proportions. Bob and Jerry, losing gradually, banded together, one as spotter with a flashlight, the other as gunner. That worked for a while, until the mice kept away from all light. Then the ultimate weapon was introduced—Jerry kept the .22 rifle handy, and blasted away at them!

It was great fun for me, being above it all in the penthouse, till a mouse climbed in bed with me. That wasn't much fun. And the last laugh was on me. One family of mice moved in on the roof, between the sod and the canvas, precisely above my head, just two feet away. They pawed and scratched around all night, and I proved to be no more humane or patient in the long run than Jerry and Bob. I finally fashioned a pin to jab up between the roof pole trying to evict my tormenters. It didn't work; I just got used to the scratching.

15 October 1973

Yesterday a plane flew over and dropped a loaf of cheese and some powdered eggs. We don't know who it was, but thanks, whoever you are! Finding the dropped package was our excitement for the day.

Bob streaks on at pinochle. Tomorrow I cook.

As snow became a more frequent companion, and took longer each time to melt away, we conceived the idea of building a toboggan run. We stacked snow high in banked turns, smoothed its twisty course from the cabin to the beach. We hauled water from the river and iced the banks, then added a starting chute, a plank sloping sharply to the cabin roof. Bits of plastic became our toboggans, as the three of us in various combinations merrily returned to preadolescence.

19 October 1973

The cabin leaks in two places along the walls where the canvas didn't overlap the wall logs enough.

Pretty tight cabin—in fact, too tight. We've got three auger holes, two at Jerry's end, one at mine, for ventilation but I still feel groggy sometimes. Now, with the door nearly done and that hole closed, we'll probably drill some more.

My ass hurts from tobogganing!

The days shortened, the sun surrendering quickly to the sky. Kerosene lamps, our gas lantern, and candles provided evening light and shadows inside.

One stormy night we took turns reading short stories out loud.

It was a marvelous idea, so we began one of our favorite pastimes, a journey through a condensed version of the *Arabian Nights*.

Being read to sleep and waking up to coffee in bed was first-class living.

27 October 1973

The last three days have been rain and drizzle, making it miserable to go too far from home. A couple days ago we had a 10-hour pinochle session which ended with all of us swearing off pinochle for a while.

Today I donned my wetsuit and splashed around in the river among the icebergs like a walrus. Great fun, stayed warm everywhere except for my fingers, even with wetsuit gloves. I'll have to get some wetsuit mittens.

This evening before bed, the fluffy stuff started dropping down. I took out the slops and garbage bare-shouldered, the tingling of the snowflakes on my skin sure felt good.

The temperature dropped slowly but steadily as the sun gave us less and less of its warmth. The ice running in the river grew thicker and its rumbling louder.

28 October 1973

Four inches of new powder snow and a river fog awaited us this morning when we awoke. By noon it was clear and sunny and we all went sliding on our toboggan run. Laughing, falling—it was great. Boy, my ass hurts sitting here writing! I got going so fast once that I flew into the air at the second bank and missed the ramp. Thank God for the pillow I was sitting on. Then we walked down to the river and ventured out on some of the icebergs frozen in place along our beach and sat in the sun.

Our beach, now vast, made for excellent walking in times of solitude, which we all needed now and then. A favorite hike was the mile-and-a-quarter jaunt down to the mouth of Tucker Slough, whose sides grew steeper and steeper as the river dropped.

Tucker Slough was first to freeze over, opening a new world to explore—the great island beyond. Jerry and I headed for it during Bob's shift. The temperatures had settled in the twenties. The morning we chose for the hike was gorgeously refreshing, just right for walking briskly without being forced to bundle up. We took our rifles, perhaps we would get a crack at a moose. All was still.

Tucker Island was a new world, a land of long, narrow, open fields separated by bands of trees, the oxbows of the slough. We followed the oxbows and frozen marshes for miles, crossed the slough, and forced our way through knee-deep snow on the trail of a big bull moose till we were atop a third and last ridge, fully ten miles from the cabin. Before us were mind-boggling miles of white country and moose tracks going cold. The bull had picked up a cow on the ridge top and they'd both tromped around in a huge circle, effectively covering the direction of their exit.

We reached the cabin in the starlight.

Jerry and I returned to the island the next day. As we broke out in the open on the first meadow, a movement caught my eye.

"Jer, we're being followed."

Hot on our trail was a fox. He had the white-tipped tail of a red fox all right, but where the red should have been, he was shiny black! We stayed totally still till his curiosity got the best of him, and he came to within a foot or so of us before backing off. For the next twenty minutes he explored with us, sometimes following, sometimes leading, perhaps hoping he might get some leftovers if we were hunting like just about all the other predators he knew.

We pushed ahead to a new field, miles long, untracked. In the distance we saw what looked like ravens, half a dozen of them, but they never flew. As we closed, we could see they were not ravens but land otters. We were walking on a lake. When they figured we were too close, they dove through two holes in the ice. There were tracks all about; it looked like they'd been having a picnic. When we reached the first hole an otter popped up and hissed at us from the second hole, about fifty feet away. When we walked to the second one, the otter went to the first one! Smart otter!

"We'll fix him," Jerry said. "Wait here."

He returned to the first hole. Ah, but the otter was smarter than that. He must have heard Jerry's footsteps on the ice because he never came up. We waited long, but he'd probably played the game before with more serious hunters. It made no difference to him that we only wanted a look. We returned home in the starlight.

I woke up with a start. Morning. Something didn't seem right, but I couldn't put a finger on it. Jerry had already made the fire and was out on the porch. He returned with an armload of stove wood and some news.

"It's stopped. The river's frozen over."

That's what it was. The groaning and rumbling of the ice-choked river had become part of everything. No longer. The thermometer had plummeted two days before. The sky had remained clear; no clouds held the warm air in. The wind came up hard from the north, and the temperature was below zero. Winter had vanquished the Yukon.

The next day we had visitors, men from Holy Cross and Kalskag, a Kuskokwim River community to the south. They were tracking the frozen highway in search of eels. Lucy Turner's brother, Pat Aloyisius, from Holy Cross; his uncle, Alek Aloyisius; and Alek's son, Alek; from Kalskag, were in the group. We heard their snow machines from afar, coming downriver.

The lamprey eels come every fall and have for eons been a source of food for the lower river people. Certain conditions are best for eeling. If the ice is free of snow they can be spotted beneath it. In the old days, the villagers, mostly the old women, maintained a watch on the ice. Once the eels were seen, the word spread from village to village up the river. The rich eels make both good people fare and excellent dog food. Somewhere above Holy Cross the ice becomes too thick and they become impossible to hunt.

Alek said that the eels had been spotted near Russian Mission, forty miles downriver, three days before, and he figured they'd be near us now. After a warm-up, we bundled up and headed to the river. The wind howled. Much of the ice was clear of snow and gleamed in the low afternoon sun.

We spread out over the ice, which was two or three inches thick, looking through it into the river below. A hole was chopped through the ice where they guessed the eels might travel, and John probed with a long pole, moving it back and forth.

"Those eels down there, you bump into them with the pole," he explained. "Feel them, even if you can't see them. They swim in a school under the ice, like a big snake, maybe a half mile long, tubelike, so tight you couldn't push a stick through them."

John demonstrated the method of catching them with his pole. "You take a stick and drive nails through it, then move it up like this and pull them out. They used to wait all night and all day for eels. It's not like that anymore," Pat continued. "Sit on the ice and just watch."

Unsuccessful, the men departed, the two Aleks across country to the south, to Kalskag, Pat upriver to Holy Cross.

We later learned the eels made good their escape; the Holy Cross folks missed them.

Chet flew in, landing his plane on skis, on the river ice out front. As he explained, he "happened to be in the area" and dropped in for a cup of coffee. He also "happened" to have our mail and a gift from him and his wife, Shirley—fresh fruit and vegetables!

The river's conversion to a highway brought yet another pleasant surprise. We had a neighbor, two miles away across the Yukon at the mouth of twelve-mile slough. We'd seen a plane flying over the mouth of the slough and suspected someone was there, but the ice-choked river prevented our crossing till freeze-up.

Our neighbor, Charlie Fitka, Jr., was an Eskimo from Marshall, a village downriver some eighty miles. Charlie was trapping from his fall camp, a canvas-wall tent, by dog team. We became friends with the affable Eskimo, as every three or four days he mushed by our place, usually about dinner time!

When he first came over, he was down to his last tea and biscuits, but, as he said, "I got lots of moose meat left. What I could really use is some tobacco. I got no smokes."

Bob shared his cigars with Charlie. Jer and I offered snuff, but Charlie declined. "I'm not that hard up," he said. "Wait till the cigars are gone."

22 November 1973

19:10 — Blizzard outside, but warm and cozy here!

We had our Thanksgiving feast at four, and a treat it was. Yesterday Jerry made two apple pies, and I baked two loaves of white bread that actually rose! This morning Jerry made two pumpkin pies. I put in the canned ham, and after hors d'oeuvres—pickled white fish (September vintage), raw carrots from Chet, sardines, biscuits, and pickled onions—we prepared to dig in.

Ah, but wait! Out of the blowing snow staggered a weary trapper, only his rifle for a companion. . . . It was Charlie, come on foot from his camp.

We had played a joke on him. He liked our cooking and was always so easy to convince to stay for grub that we were absolutely sure he would show up for Thanksgiving. So, not saying anything, we prepared a feast for four, even setting his place at the table. When he saw that, we all had a good laugh, and our meal was heartily devoured, beginning with Bob's two salads, thousand island dressing with our last egg boiled and sliced in and Italian garlic with our own homemade croutons. Last of all, four pies!

After supper we all sat around with distended stomachs, belching and picking our teeth—four fat, happy cats!

In his mid-thirties, Charlie was the mayor of Marshall, a one-time mining community a hundred miles downriver. His Eskimo wife and two daughters were there, waiting for him. Now, with the river frozen, he was preparing to return home.

Charlie invited us to a Christmas celebration at Marshall.

"You've got plenty of time to make it," he said. "Many of our people are Russian Orthodox, and we celebrate Christmas by the Julian calendar—January 7 in your book." Charlie took the spare bunk that night; we all turned in satisfied.

When I opened my eyes, the sun's early rays were on the counter. She was with me. I would rise, make the fire, warm the house. I snuggled down under the covers to her again.

Nothing. She'd rolled to the edge of the bed.

Reality came down on me in an avalanche of soul-chilling disappointment. I was depressed for two days.

In mid-December we started sorting and packing again. There were 275 frozen miles of river between us and the Bering Sea. We would ski the distance, carrying what we needed on our backs. We planned to ski from village to village, camping between them as needed.

None of us had ever made a journey of these proportions in the middle of a Yukon winter before. Everything would be new. I was getting that itchy, excited feeling again.

I read one last time from the *Arabian Nights*. The characters from that faraway world and time had become our friends, the rascal Haroun Er Rashid, who was forever getting into and out of one jam or another, was our favorite. When I finished reading, the bookmark was at the end of night number 646. I wondered when I would take it up again and where we would be.

I looked around in the lantern glow. Bob and Jer seemed to be asleep. Our rope chair was without rope, a wood skeleton. We no longer had bedding, but slept on foam mats under our warm sleeping bags. Our packs leaned against our bunks.

I climbed up to my bunk for the last time in the dark. I felt the logs, ran my toes along the roof poles. We'd been through a lot with the raft, the trees, the logs, the cabin under us and now over and around us.

"It's been nice, hasn't it?" Jerry said softly.

"Uhhmm," Bob replied.

We rose early but didn't leave till nearly noon. After a long breakfast we shuffled and equalized the loads, all groaningly heavy.

"Jethro," Bob called from the porch. He didn't come, nor did Max or Shorty, our camp robber friends. We wanted to say good-bye. The friendly jays have long been the companions of men in the northern woods, ghosts of miners past, come to give company round the lonely fire. We left them a last offering and skied away, our home and a lot of memories behind us in the cabin on the riverbank. It was twenty below zero, calm and clear.

The Yukon was a white desert. Bars that had been hidden obstacles to navigation in summer were high rolling domes, the surface of the ice as much as twenty feet below their summits. Islands were castles, their steep banks parapets.

We took turns breaking trail—tough work. When the light faded, we were only eight miles from the cabin after four hours of skiing.

We pitched the tent, cooked our first trail dinner of freeze-dried grub, rolled out our bags, and turned in, tired.

In the morning when we rose the mercury stood at minus 36 degrees Fahrenheit. We were quick about breaking camp, eager to be skiing to warm up.

The going improved when we hit Charlie's trail. With the wind at our backs we slipped into Dogfish Village and a lone cabin Charlie had told us about. His brother, Nick, was trapping from it and made us welcome for the night, our bedrolls on the floor. We'd come twenty miles from our cabin in two days; it was about fifteen more miles to Russian Mission.

It was beautiful when we pulled out of Dogfish Village the next morning, crystal clear. Though the wind had covered the trail with snow, we could see its faint shadow, feel it under our skis. The going was good.

At midday we lighted our tiny camp stove and cooked up a spot of tea. Our meals were breakfast and dinner; at lunchtime we munched on bacon bars or chocolate.

We skied through the sunset and into the night. The sky was cloudless, and the starlight lit our way. We hit a fresh snow machine trail and followed it around the last bluff and up the bank to Russian Mission.

Dogs barked, announcing our coming as we skied into the village. Our packs creaked and groaned as they shifted with our moving bodies, skis clattering on hard-packed snow.

On the hill behind town we saw the school; next to it was a long trailer house. Larry Smith, the teacher, had known we were coming. We clattered to the door, kicked off our skis, and lowered our packs. The porch light flashed on—wow, electricity—and Larry Smith came to the door.

"Welcome, welcome," he beamed. "Come in, get out of the cold."

We introduced ourselves, met Jackie, Larry's wife, and their two small children. Smith's home was like Disneyland, it was paneled, had wall-to-wall carpet, soft couches, and electric lamps—all kinds of things. It would take some readjusting to. It was exciting, talking to somebody new, and not a little befuddling. Our words among ourselves had grown fewer and fewer; we had learned to communicate without them. Our sentences were incomplete, disjointed. It was hard to concentrate. I think we were what they call "bushed."

Larry and Jackie both taught, though Larry has the added responsibility of being principal for the two-room school where thirty-five Russian Mission children attend the first through eighth grades. The Smiths, the only white residents in the village of eighty-five souls, had taught there for two years and were happy with their bush post. Larry and Jackie are both private pilots and keep their family plane parked at the Russian Mission strip.

There was a spare room in the school building, Larry told us, where we could make ourselves at home. The school kitchen, used primarily for hot lunches, would be at our disposal. As long as we cleaned up after ourselves and didn't conflict with the school's requirements, we were welcome. We would have running water and a flush toilet and a bathtub! We were tired, but before turning in we wanted to weigh our packs. Larry pulled out the bathroom scales. Our packs weighed from seventy-nine to eighty-four pounds!

"That's going to change," Bob said as Larry walked us over to the school.

We agreed we would make no plans for two days. Our shakedown journey had given us something to think about. Obviously, we must lighten our loads. That could start with footgear.

We had tried three different kinds of footgear. Jerry wore shoe packs, Bob wore canvas mukluks, and I wore Army surplus K-boots, a heavy rubber boot designed for winter use.

Mukluks, we agreed, were the best. We were to receive three pair in the mail at Russian Mission—sealskin boots made for us by Eskimo women.

All but the clothes on our backs would be sent ahead, along with a lot of food.

The first thing I noticed upon waking the next day was the church. It sat on the hill, its cross unmistakable, the symbol of orthodoxy. Russian Mission proper sort of poured down the hill toward the Yukon. Wisps of smoke rose; columns of ice fog wandering toward the sky in the chill sunrise. In contrast to the nightless high summer, a midwinter day was a short filler between sunrise and sunset. Winter and night go hand-in-hand in the high latitudes; the sun makes just a quick lurch over the horizon.

Russian Mission owes its existence to its being the early choice, in 1851, for the site of the Petrovska Mission, the first Russian Orthodox religious facility in the interior of Alaska. Most of the Russian Mission's residents are Russian Orthodox, and their Russian Orthodox Christmas ceremonies begin January 7. Yet some folks, like the Smiths, celebrate on December 25. To resolve this problem, everyone celebrates both!

The Smiths invited us to spend their Christmas with them. After Christmas we would ski over the old Wilson Creek trail to Marshall for Orthodox Christmas! It was something like thirty-five miles overland; we would save more than twenty miles of skiing by cutting off a great bend in the river—the most southerly penetration of the Yukon in Alaska, the "Devil's Elbow."

Jerry and I, at Jackie's suggestion, took advantage of the Smiths' washer and dryer, giving our wool shirts their first real cleaning. The end result wasn't what we'd planned: Harvey Pitka, a jovial eighth grader and the biggest kid in the school, became the proud owner of two newly shrunken wool shirts.

Harvey was a gem. He realized that the store in town didn't customarily cater to the needs of visitors. There was an acute lack of meats for sale, so he brought us a great chunk of moose meat that tided us over during our stay.

One day we learned from the kids that a movie would be shown that evening in Trader Pete Peteroff's hall. We went down, taking

Harvey as our guest. Harvey was always short of cash. The hall, a log building, sat perhaps thirty on folding chairs for the double feature. Kids were everywhere. It was a real treat: first, a 1930's western, with the actors reading their lines above the camera; and then a 1959 Gregory Peck war movie.

We later learned that Pete kept the movies around, charging one dollar on the first night, then seventy-five cents, then fifty cents, and so on till he broke even on the rental!

Russian Mission is a low-key, friendly community content to let traditional ways perpetuate. It was a rare event and a real accomplishment for a student to leave Russian Mission for high school. Larry told us he knew of few Russian Mission high school graduates. For most, after eighth grade, it was back into village life to learn the necessary skills for bush living, to marry, and to raise a family.

Perhaps because of that, creations of the hand and eye were superb. John Changsak and his eighth grade classmates put excellent, practical leather patches on our packs for attaching gear. At this writing, they seem likely to outlast the packs.

Our sealskin mukluks came, delivered by bush pilot Myron Wright from St. Mary's. He'd undertaken their ordering. We took them down to show to Abbie Stephanoff, who lives in a cozy two-room house just down from the school. She is the epitome of good spirits. She has been the health aide for twenty-one years. For Abbie, progress was measured by the fact that she'd had no new cases of tuberculosis in two years. Tuberculosis, the scourge of the Arctic clime for a century, now seemed in check.

She was sitting on the floor skinning a marten that her husband, Enakenty, had brought in from the trapline.

"Nice boots," she said, admiringly. "But you got to get grass, put it in the bottom—keep your feet real warm." Then, with a twinkle in her eye, she said, "You boys better marry Eskimo girls—white girls can't make boots like this for you!"

There was a potlatch at the school Christmas Eve, December 24, with all the people in the village bringing a food contribution. The kids sang Christmas carols in English, and Eskimo dancing followed. Under the Christmas tree was a mound of gifts; it seemed everyone brought something for everybody else.

That night Bob and I finally found a way to get at Jerry for the

196

fact that he made such excellent biscuits and gave us hell every time ours went flat. We volunteered his biscuits as our contribution to the potlatch. Poor Jer made biscuits for a hundred people, much to the delight of the Eskimo women.

"I'll get even, just wait," said ole Jer, the biscuit maker. He loved it.

24 December 1973

We've just finished Christmas potlatch. All the village people delivered and received gifts from under the school's Christmas tree. And there was something under the tree for each of us, stockings filled with candy and toys. Everybody knew but us. From the Stephanoffs. Abbie is a love.

All my friends, everywhere, on this Christmas Eve, may peace truly be with you.

"018, Kalskag." Kalskag radio calling Chet's plane.
"018."
"Yah, Chet, Merry Christmas."
"Thanks, George, Merry Christmas to you."
"Kalskag."
"018."

The airwaves were full of Christmas chatter. No telephones, just the big old radios used by the bush plane operators, the airline agents, the health aides. People sharing, some of whom in twenty or more years of talking to each other had never met. We listened in on Larry's radio, waiting our turn. There was a pause.

"Hurry," Larry said.

I pushed the mike button, "Wien Holy Cross, KMT8 Russian Mission."

"Russian Mission, go ahead." It was Harry Turner.

"This is Keith, Harry, Merry Christmas!"

Everybody in western Alaska was listening.

"You guys make it all right?"

"You bet, Harry. Thanks for everything."

"OK, Wien Holy Cross."

I was just getting ready to cut off. I was supposed to say, simply "KMT8 Russian Mission." You've got to say it just right like you've done it all your life, like the old hands, like Harry and Chet.

But before I could do it, "KMT8 Russian Mission. 018."

I was flustered, no one was supposed to call us. I sort of handled it.

"KMT8, go ahead." Jerry and Bob were rolling on Smith's floor laughing at my consternation, my confused, helpless looks to Larry. Larry was laughing too; I just wanted to be rid of the radio.

"Merry Christmas, you guys."

"Thanks, Chet, Merry Christmas to you and Shirley."

Then out of the blue, "Hey, when you guys gonna quit laying around Russian Mission and come to Marshall? After breakup?"

Oh, no. It was Don Hunter, the Marshall Wien agent. We only knew him by radio. He was having a great Christmas Day.

"Hi, Don. We'll be there by New Year's."

"Not if you don't get started."

I didn't know what to say, I just knew everybody in western Alaska was laughing with him.

"Uh, yah. Merry Christmas!"

Jerry and Bob were howling. I knew I could master the damn thing, but I was sure in a corner. I mean, hundreds of towns were on the air, each interested in getting a chance to say something on Christmas.

"Roger, Merry Christmas to you fellows. Wien Marshall."

"KMT8 Russian Mission." Whew. . . . It was neat, but I was glad it was over.

We waxed our skis. We repacked our gear, lightening our packs by more than twenty pounds each, sending much extra gear ahead to Marshall. Enakenty Stephanoff broke trail out for us till we could follow the old blazes, as the old trail was little used.

As we prepared to leave, old Pete Gleaskok imparted some Eskimo advice. "When freezing, all cold everywhere, and sit down, and pretty soon freeze—drink urine even if it taste bad, you close your eye and just swallow. It make your insides warm. And start to warm you all up to your heart beat faster and you can go. Even if you heat water from snow or river it's no good. Urine, it's real good."

We left on December 29 under ominous skies. A front had moved in, raising the temperature to the point of thawing.

We had previously packed out three or four miles of trail, maybe a mile beyond Enakenty's snow go-track, to be sure we were following the blazes. The old Eskimo knew the country like the proverbial back of his hand, but when we showed him a map, hoping for an indication of our route, he was lost. The land wasn't maps to him, but living things, and real hills and knolls that he knew; the trail was a succession of forks, creek crossings, lakes, and marshes, each memorized through life's journeys in the outback.

The snow was deep. As we pressed beyond the trail, it wasn't as bad. We would each break trail for half an hour or so, rest, then catch up in the track. As the temperature rose above the freezing point, the snow softened and lost its structural base. We, in turn, sank deeper and deeper till we were shoving our way through six to eight inches of thick, clinging mashed potatoes. Four hours was enough, evening was upon us. We made camp near a small knoll beside the trail. We pitched the tent and built a nice fire of crackly spruce. Above us, thick gray clouds would hold in the warmth.

We ate our freeze-dried dinner (the hiker's answer to TV dinners) around the fire, and then made ready for bed. Jerry and I slept inside the tent, Bob elected to sleep outside. Too bad, Bob, but our plight was little better. Sometime early in the dark morning the gray clouds burst. One thing people don't count on much in the middle of Alaska in winter is rain. Rain robs your clothing of its insulating quality. Down sleeping bags soak up, become soggy, leaden, and cold. Nobody takes rain gear on a winter expedition.

At first the patter of rain was fun, especially because we could laugh at Bob outside, but before long he joined us in the tent, grumbling. Our tent, without a rain fly, leaked. Not spectacularly—as the drops hit no little rivers appeared—but the tent just diffused the drops through it till a damp cloud perpetually surrounded us.

We stayed in bed, wishing it would somehow go away. When we rose at first light, our mukluks, hung from the tent pole when we took them off, were dripping. If our down sleeping bags hadn't been so fluffy, they too would have been soaked through instead of being only half soaked!

We were soon on our way again, knowing our miserably wet dispositions would have to improve from the warmth of exercise. *That* there was plenty of. The snow was now the consistency of pudding. We sank to our knees, even on skis, and literally took turns pushing through the slush leg by leg, sometimes only a hundred yards at a time. All day we sloshed along for a gain of maybe five miles.

Bedtime turned out to be a repeat of the previous night's

scenario. At two, Bob and Jerry were out of bed, sitting around a blazing fire. I lasted till five—my bag was thicker—but in the end I made the same choice. It's not easy to sleep in a lake! After daylight we were again on our disgruntled way.

On the other side of a large creek, which we disappointedly had to admit was probably Engineer Creek, putting us twenty miles from Marshall, we heard the unmistakable sound of a snow machine. It was none other than Charlie Fitka, Jr., checking his marten traps.

He pulled up to us, shaking his head. We must have been a sight.

"Want a lift?" he asked, pointing to the sled behind his iron dog.

We all eyed it, but none wanted to ride, after having made it so far on our own.

"How about if I take your packs?" he asked.

"That's it," Bob said; compromise was struck.

"See you in Marshall tonight." He was gone.

It was full night when we reached the Yukon, skiing down the long, gradual bank from the forest to the river's edge six miles above Marshall.

Freed from the forest, out in the open, I felt like an interloper in a mysterious natural light show. The half moon, muted by thin wispy clouds, gave off an eerie glow, while the river's basin and the forest were impenetrably black. It was surreal; a perfect elimination of shadow. The snow shone an awful white; all else was void, indefinable as the space between the stars. A dark spot could be a house-sized boulder far away, your partner resting quietly twenty feet ahead, or a bit of a stump hardly past the tips of your skis.

The Yukon was a glossy black mirror; rain-shined ice and glassy, still rain water in depressions on the river ice's surface. You couldn't tell which was which unless you jabbed it with a ski pole. Here and there on the frozen river, patches of snow glowed as if under a black light.

There were only two measures of distance, what you could touch and infinity.

Skiing along the side-hill bank lost its charm in short order; mukluks have no support, and we had to edge continually to keep from slipping to the river. We doggedly scraped ourselves along, finally leaving the grotesquely enchanting river for the lights of Marshall and the Fitka home.

Charlie's mother, Exenia, met us at the door of the weathered two-story frame house with the simple word, "Hungry?"

We were famished, and in moments set to devouring a great moose roast. We finished just in time to head with Charlie to the hall and the New Year's Eve dance!

Next morning we explored Marshall with Charlie, meeting a good many of the riverside village's 175 residents. The community of two-score frame or log houses has three "roads," two dirt tracks that parallel the Yukon, and the frozen river itself, which becomes a freeway for snowmobiles, and a convenient airport in the winter.

"Meet my gussuk friends!" was Charlie's standard introduction for us. Gussuk, the Eskimo word for white man, is a corruption of cossack, a legacy from czarist Russia's 127-year hegemony in Alaska.

At every village gathering point—the two stores, the community center, the pool hall, the health clinic, and the post office—there was an air of expectancy. The men were in from traplines, from tending their fishnets under the river ice.

The Russian Orthodox Christmas, known simply as "Slavi" in Marshall, would soon be on us.

"We follow the star just as the Three Wise Men followed it to Bethlehem," Charlie explained, "and in each house we proclaim the coming of Jesus. You are our friends, and you are welcome to join us."

Slavi, three symbolic days of ceremony, can actually take a week, Charlie told us. On the first "day" of Slavi, the star, a beautiful decoration of wood and gilt paper and the celebration's focus, begins its journey through Marshall. Each home in turn is visited by the star, carried in a procession led by the town's religious leaders. In the homes, the entourage sings traditional Christmas carols, first in Eskimo then Russian, and then continues to the next house till the whole village is visited.

The second "day" is a repeat of the first, but after the ceremony proclaiming the coming of Jesus, the host family serves a warm beverage, such as tea or coffee, and perhaps cookies. When all have partaken, the star moves on.

The third "day," the day of feast, is Slavi's highlight. Again the star and elders begin at one end of town, but in each home, after the religious ceremony and caroling, host and hostess humbly serve food to all in the true spirit of giving. First the elders, the religious men,

201

are seated, and as each finishes his meal, someone takes his place. One by one, the villagers are all served.

During the celebration in Marshall, as a family served and each guest waited his turn, every sitting and leaning space in the home was occupied by waiting people, children laughing and playing, mothers with tiny tots, old men sleeping. Five or six hours per house was normal, as around the clock the star moved through the town.

It was a glorious experience. Everyone talked to everybody else; it was a yearly reunion, when all other worries were put aside.

The Fitkas, our hosts, prepared long for their turn. Great pots of moose stew, mounds of freshly baked bread, cisterns of coffee were made ready. Daughters Rose, Olga, and Ellen helped their gracious mother; Charlie, Sr., and the boys pitched in as needed for the traditional feast. Charlie, Jr., his wife, Alice, and his two little daughters lived next door and were busy with their own preparations.

During Slavi, Bob, Jerry, and I lived like kings on the marvelous fare—moose soups, king salmon, fresh biscuits, dry fish. . . . A special highlight of Slavi for us was "aguduk," or Eskimo ice cream. We couldn't get enough of it. Seal oil, berries, and boned fish are the major ingredients. Yum, yum. Exenia Fitka's aguduk was best.

In our travels with the star, we met many wonderful people while waiting and visiting in the mostly one-room log homes of the cordial Eskimos.

Nick Andrew, maintenance man at the school and one of two appointed Russian Orthodox readers, explained the soft, melodious Eskimo caroling to me as we waited our turns.

"Caroling just like American Christmas, same kind," he told me, "but in this village we sing mostly Eskimo so, ah, the people here they can understand better Slavi. Those other villages, they sing them mostly by Russian. They sound good, but nobody understand the words."

"You don't sing any in English?" I asked.

"No. Some of these people don't even understand English yet," Nick said. "But we're going to start in English. Eskimo talking is quite a bit slower than English, these Eskimo words little bit longer. Say something in Eskimo it be longer, say it in English, it be shorter. My kids talk Eskimo, but they don't like. They probably think it's easier to talk English. Faster."

"Is the feasting traditional?" I asked.

"No," he answered. "That's not come from church. These are Eskimo, they like to feed the people when they come."

In another home, a village elder, spry and happy, told us about the upriver Indians who tried to shoot a shaman living inland from an abandoned village just downriver. That village and Ohagamiut, also now abandoned, were the biggest sources of the native population here. The inhabitants were forced to move to Marshall by the schooling requirements imposed on them by the government in the 1940's. The shaman had a pair of magic suspenders with the power to prevent any harm from arrows or bullets to the wearer. Nine Indians tried to kill the shaman but he wasn't hurt and he slew them all, marked their graves, and buried them, then came to Marshall and turned himself in to the territorial marshall. He was released; all the deaths had resulted from the old man defending himself. "The grave markers are still back there," I was told.

An old gent, one of the Orthodox leaders, told me more.

The shaman would sit in the steam house, pull off his parka (in those days made of skin), and lay it on the floor. Then he would talk to it and it would rise. Then he would speak to it, conjure answers from it. The old man remembered they were far more often right than wrong with their information.

A form of reincarnation is believed in. As the old pass on, their souls return in the newborn so that a child may have two names, his given one and the name of the deceased whose soul he possesses. In fact, the youth is often showered with gifts and affection from the deceased's family on the deceased's birthday, etc. Boys can be named after old women and girls after old men. Occasionally the young say and do startling things that show no relation to their present family but relate to their deceased name-giver. They make trancelike references to their soul's former abode.

Another Eskimo custom is the open giving of children from a prolific family to a barren one. The Eskimo society is well adjusted to this practice and no repercussions whatever occur as the child grows up, knowing his real parents live next door.

Eskimos have a strong, contemporary, working society that flourishes, embracing those aspects of the white man's way that make living by the Eskimo ways easier.

On January 13, after a six-day Slavi, the star returned to the church. It was over.

The thaw that ushered us into Marshall continued till the river was completely free of snow. When the cool came the river returned to plate glass, polished by the wind. Whoever heard of a winter in the interior of Alaska without snow? The ice was difficult enough to walk on, with each toe trying to grip the ice through the bottom of your skin boots, but it would be just plain ludicrous to attempt to ski. However, the old adage, "He who waits for good weather in Alaska will get nowhere," began to eat away at us. We finally changed our plan and enlisted Charlie's aid. He would take us the sixty miles downriver to St. Mary's by dog team. Perhaps skiing would be a more realistic way to travel from there.

The night before our departure the village held a dance for us in the community hall. An old phonograph played a handful of scratchy records—the Virginia reel, polkas, schottisches, waltzes. It was fantastic to see young and old squiring away in the most uninhibiting ballroom in the world. A one-time transfer point between upriver steamboats and downriver steamboats, the mining town of Marshall had hosted many stranded travelers in the old days. This was its legacy, with an all Eskimo cast. We joined right in. It was one of the best dances I've ever been to.

On January 18 we mushed out of Marshall, three of us, our gear, and Charlie in a twelve-foot freight sled pulled by eleven husky dogs. Dog teams are the only way to travel if you have to go any distance or are required to carry supplies of any amount. As Charlie said, "It's pretty hard to sleep and stay warm in a blizzard with a snow machine, and hard to eat one when the grub is gone."

We took turns, two riding in the sled, or "basket," one on the other runner with Charlie. Riding on the runner was a joy, watching the winter wonderland slipping by, sharing the spirit of dogs that love to run.

At one point, Charlie interrupted a particularly long silence.

"Do you know what's the difference between a sled and a sledge?" I didn't, and, as it happens, it was something I had wondered about.

"What?" I asked, interested.

He looked at me seriously, then his round cheeks rose to his eyes in a smile. "Well, you can't say sledge with a mouth full of tobacco!"

We both laughed as we sped along, free in spirit.

From Raft to Cabin; by Skis to the Bering Sea

We made the sixty-mile journey, including an overnight stop at Pilot Station, with little effort, and with no sound but the patter of dogs' feet.

At St. Mary's we bade so long to our indefatigable friend, Charlie Fitka, Jr., who hitched up and headed home.

Again we were delayed for lack of snow. We stayed in the junior high school boys' dormitory at St. Mary's Mission, a Catholic Jesuit school established late in the nineteenth century, last in a chain of Jesuit missions which diligently pushed north from Mexican origins in the sixteenth century.

During our stay we had an opportunity to see the mission school in action. They keep it together on a shoestring, barely meeting their operating expenses. The keys are love and faith and round the clock devotion to the goal of education. They have the finest academic record of any school serving bush students in Alaska, so we learned, and they are proud of it.

One day I was asked by a teacher, Fred Ali, to put my surveying experience to work and explain the concept of land ownership to his Eskimo high school students. As they passed from youth into the mainstream of Alaskan life, they would constantly be confronted with the Alaska Native Claims Settlement Act, passed in 1971 by the U.S. Congress, giving forty million acres of Alaska and $900 million to Alaska's natives in recognition of their aboriginal right to the land.

Trying to explain something as simple as the division of property, the corners of ownership, to young people who had no experience with that kind of thinking, was heartbreaking. It isn't that the native people had all the land in Alaska and wanted it back, but rather that no one thought about having it or owning it; land was for everybody, like the ocean. The idea of giving out even forty million acres—which sounds like a lot of land—to the natives of Alaska just doesn't hold water. It's like telling a falcon he can have any kind of leash he wants, be it gold braid or silk, a foot long or a mile long, but he will have to wear a leash. And the money, almost a billion dollars, was another tough "gift" to explain. It seems axiomatic in our economic system that eventually all money either gravitates back to the government or flows to the coffers of those few adept at gathering it. I think you can give any group of people in America a billion dollars and directly measure their economic sophistication by the length of time before the money is gone. If anything, the land settlement established what land doesn't belong to the first Alaskans, and what their price for that concession was.

We each made the final improvements on our clothing and adjustments in our equipment. Our packs stayed at about sixty pounds. We'd used up much of our trail food, but we'd added some too. Dried native salmon became our midday staple, as well as our emergency food. As an energy booster, ounce for ounce, it had proven better than anything the mountaineering/backpacking nutritionists had come up with.

While skiing we wore strictly cottons and woolens; their ability to insulate and at the same time allow for the passage of moisture away from the body make them ideal. Sealskin mukluks, the Eskimo skin boots, beat any other footgear hands down. I purchased an Army-surplus camouflage shell of sturdy double-layered cotton from the mission and had it fashioned into a kuskpuk, an Eskimo pullover parka without a zipper. It would make an excellent windbreaker and still pass sweat away from my body as I skied along. While my nylon shell blocked the wind out famously, it prevented all moisture coming off my body from leaving my clothing, and, when I rested, the damp clothing quickly chilled me. Lena George, a cheerful Eskimo woman, sewed a ruff of wolverine fur around the hood to keep my face warm. It was a fortuitous move.

Finally, for two straight days it was windless. The mercury dropped to minus 45 degrees Fahrenheit, but 45 degrees below zero and calm is a lot warmer than 30 below with a stiff wind. During those calm days, frost was deposited on the glare ice like a crystal mold. We could ski on it.

The following morning, February 9, we left St. Mary's for Mountain Village, the last community before the empty, barren delta. Six miles out, eighteen miles from Mountain Village, we hit the wind. It came from the northeast, hitting us nearly head on. It took our frost away.

As the afternoon wore on, with our senses dulled as the chill factor dropped to somewhere around 70 degrees below, the lights of Mountain Village came into view. But before we could reach the village, protected behind the last rise before the delta, I came to hate the lights. They mocked us. Hour after hour we skied straight toward them, never seeming to get any closer. The wind was holding us back till pushing ahead on skis was hardly any better than walking. Jerry finally threw his skis over his shoulder; we followed suit and marched into Mountain Village. It wasn't as good a way to travel as skiing, but changing method certainly helped our spirits.

From Mountain Village it was ninety miles to salt water, seventy-five to Emmonak on the Kwiguk Pass, the last village on our route, fifteen miles from the Bering Sea ice.

The Yukon Delta, thousands of square miles in area, has been pushed into Norton Sound over the eons. For fifty miles past Mountain Village, the river holds a major channel, then it splays like a fan thirty-five miles to the sea. The Eskimos likened the delta to a great hand, its channels the fingers. But for the river, the delta is fruitless; barren trees and brush squat along the waterways only.

We learned of three cabins, each about twenty miles apart. They were summer fish camps and were not insulated, but would at least offer us shelter. Once we rounded the corner at Mountain Village nothing stood between us and the northeast wind coming off the Bering Sea pack ice.

Peter Moses, a mountain village Eskimo, and I set out stores at the cabins, by snow machine. I noted where they lay in the featureless delta and left a gallon of gas and five days food at each. If a storm should overtake us it would be folly to travel afoot, we would have to be able to wait it out. We hoped the food we carried and the caches would be ample for a forced halt. If all went according to Hoyle, we'd find them.

It was neither clear nor cloudy when we left; it was snowing, but the sun shone. Somewhere far out on the Bering Sea ice, the wind had picked up the snow in a great blizzard. Now the tiny specks twinkled about us like weightless diamonds.

Five miles from Mountain Village we passed the last people we were to see for a while, an elderly Eskimo couple, checking their fishnet under the ice. They smiled at us, the old woman hugged herself, shivered, then pointed downriver. We returned their wordless greeting and skied on.

We were protected at first in a narrow slough with high banks, but there was no question that we were venturing into a new world, the delta.

The slough joined a larger one that carried wind through it. The thermometer was somewhere in the minus twenties, the wind biting. At least the February days were longer.

There was no trail to follow, no trail to break, only hard patches of snow and great fields of glare ice. The snow patches turned out to be blessings; one didn't have to grip the ice like a cat to keep from blowing over.

Three miles from the first of the fish camps, Patsy's Cabin, we joined the main river, behind an island. There the wind hit us full force. We didn't dare look into it for long; our faces would freeze.

I hunched down, hood pulled to my eyes, and peered through the protective wolverine hairs of my ruff. I wore a scarf wound round my face, over a wool face mask. Every so often I would glance up, aim, then lower my head and watch my feet, keeping my course by the feel of the wind on my body. The cold was great, but the psychological strain of having to look down, seeing only your feet shuffling along is not to be made light of. There was no other choice. At times the wind was so strong it took every ounce of effort to make the simplest forward movement.

We were a collage of three individual efforts. Every step was planned, was itself part of an overall plan—an instinctive and absolutely essential pattern—which alternated exercise and rest. There was no communication between us.

In this way we reached Patsy's Cabin. We fired up the wood stove, then our own gas stove, but the wind literally sucked the heat away from the cabin through the walls. We were never able to warm it up enough to drive the frost from the ceiling! Still, it seemed like Honolulu to us. The wind didn't get in.

The wind eased during the night, but was howling the next morning. We stayed put at Patsy's Cabin the next day. We had a long twenty miles to Fish Village, all of it on the main river; no islands, no sloughs to hide behind.

The following morning when we rose to make the fire, it was minus 40 degrees and calm. We waited till sunup, trying to outguess the wind, and opted to move on.

We moved beyond any semblance of forest. The river was a shallow draw, more than a mile wide and fifteen feet below the barren land. The ice was covered with sand and gravel ripped from the frozen banks by the wind. In some places the ice was rough and choppy, like coarse broken glass. But even if our skis were sanded bare by rough ice and grit, the two or three or four inches of grudging slide gained in each step made their erosion worth it.

For two hours we had relative calm, then the wind came. It gained force; we were once more driven into our "cocoon" form of foot-watching travel, wiggling fingers inside the great gauntleted mitts just to be sure they were there and unfrozen. I learned that being cool (if you live in Florida you might call it "cold") isn't really bad at all. Keeping a rapport with cold things is where it's at. I like the feeling for its lesson that all systems are still good. It's when you lose that contact, that sense of coolness, that fingers, toes, face are freezing.

By early afternoon we'd made just eight miles. We were near the only sizable concentration of snow we'd seen, a solitary drift sloping off the bank. Rather than backtrack to the cabin or push on into a night that would take the thermometer down toward fifty below, we elected to bivouac.

We burrowed into the drift, carving snow blocks from it to build an entrance. Not being masters of the igloo, we covered the blocks with our tent and skis and piled snow on top till we had a cozy half igloo, half snow cave. We spent our warmest night of the delta trek in there, listening to the wind reach a force absolutely incompatible with us, as the thermometer plunged to minus 40 degrees. Yet it was downright delightful in our snow house, a foot of block snow between us and the elements. Bob was "Chef Boyardee" for the night. Our meal, chili and beans, was gulped by candlelight from the communal pot.

The next day was glorious. There was no wind, no blowing snow. At one point we all took a breather together, lying back on our packs facing the sun. We were fully clothed, but could feel the warm rays on our cheeks. We were sunbathing at a balmy minus 8 degrees Fahrenheit.

Fish Village is haunted, according to many lower river people, who claim that when you go to sleep you may not wake up. Apparently that had happened twice, until everyone left town. Well, we didn't die at Fish Village, though Jerry thought he might. Nothing gives a more false security than the shell of a house in really cold weather. Bob and I sandwiched him between us, and he was still cold. When we woke it was minus 40 degrees inside. We were quickly on the trail at sunrise, the temperature minus 48 degrees Fahrenheit.

18 February 1974

Simion Harpak's Cabin.

Left Fish Village yesterday morning at 10:00 on a beautiful day. We cruised along at 2-hour stretches with 5-minute breaks in-between. After 4 hours total we were 2½ miles out. Not bad. Over 3 mph. The snow was pretty good in stretches with the frosted, chopped snow machine trail the best going. Still had lots of slow going in windblown parts, though.

The last 3 hours was the psychologically tough and slow part. I remembered the distance to the cabin as 15 miles, not 18½. When we figured it to be 15 there wasn't a slough in sight. Thoughts of having passed it up dogged us as we trudged on, unsure of ourselves with the prospect of a −50°F. night in the barren delta. Luckily we found the slough and pushed into the cabin. We were all strong and running well into here—the last 20 to Emmonak looms but with no forebodings.

"The only way out for you, lady, is the window."

"No. . . ." Even found a portable radio. We thawed it in the oven and just found KICY Radio Nome and "The Shadow!"

Slept warm last night; temperature only about −45°. Our speedometer doesn't register below −40° but the stem is there and we guess. Radio predicts −50°'s for the lower Yukon tonight. May be even colder here.

Last night we talked about the cold weather and our expedition experiences in general. It was a good chat, all huddled around the Noble wood stove which is about the same size as our kitchen stove was but so much better. Even so, burning the wood stove, covering the door and windows, blocking off half the cabin and burning Harpak's Coleman 2 burner, it's +30° in here. Daytime temperature warms up to about −20° outside. If, please, we can have no wind, we'll do well into Emmonak. Then on to the Bering Sea.

"Who knows what evil lurks in the hearts of men. The Shadow knows. Ha, ha, ha, ha!"

Next day we pushed into Emmonak, where a local school teacher put us up for two nights. On the third morning, as we prepared to leave, he tucked something beneath Jerry's parka.

"Champagne," he said with a grin. "I was saving it for a very special occasion. Seems to me this is it. Good luck!"

If anything, it was hard to push, to hurry; I didn't want it to end. What did it all mean, the Chilkoot Pass, the raft, two thousand miles of river, two summers, the cabin, the winter?

From Raft to Cabin; by Skis to the Bering Sea

It was calm, sunny mid-afternoon when we hit the sea. The Bering Sea had been our goal, but our summits were scattered all along the Yukon.

We should have been elated I guess, but it didn't work out that way. We drank our champagne, shook each other's hands, and were silent.

My reward was in Jerry's eyes, Bob's smile. As for what was in our hearts, Robert Service said it all in his *The Spell of the Yukon:*

> There's a land where the mountains are nameless,
> And the rivers all run God knows where;
> There are lives that are erring and aimless,
> And deaths that just hang by a hair;
> There are hardships that nobody reckons;
> There are valleys unpeopled and still;
> There's a land—oh, it beckons and beckons,
> And I want to go back—and I will.

Epilogue

Before leaving Emmonak we radioed Myron Wright, our bush pilot friend in St. Mary's, to land on the ice and pick us up when we got to the Bering Sea. His timing was perfect; we hardly had a chance to cool off before we were airborne, winging our way inland. Looking back over the ice, stretching on and on toward sun and horizon no matter how high we rose in the sky, I couldn't help wondering whether or not we'd gotten anywhere at all.

From St. Mary's our goal was Anchorage, and we each chose a different way to get there. Jerry would take a scheduled flight to Anchorage by way of Bethel; Bob planned to fly direct to Anchorage with Myron; I elected to backtrack up the Yukon, village by village, to Holy Cross, then fly through Aniak to Anchorage. I hitchhiked by bush plane and snow machine, visiting as I went and picking up cached equipment we'd left behind. I hit Anchorage ten days after leaving St. Mary's. Jerry was there waiting; Bob was a few more days coming because of bad weather.

The three of us hung around the Anchorage area batching (as in bachelor) and generally enjoying the easy life till our grub was gone. For Jerry, that meant it was time to head south to big timber country and a timber felling job. Bob and I were off to Washington, D.C., and the offices of *National Geographic* magazine.

We were there for ten days of meetings that resulted in another season on the Yukon for Bob and me. We spent that summer traveling from Whitehorse to Marshall by outboard-powered riverboat, filling in material gaps for our magazine article. We were finished in September and returned to Anchorage, where I jumped into writing my story for *Geographic*. Pictures done, Bob was off to Whitehorse to visit Robyn. By Christmas my story was in Washington and accepted, just in time, too (I was broke).

Construction of the Trans-Alaska Pipeline from Prudhoe Bay in the Arctic to the ice-free port of Valdez on the south coast was in full swing. Twenty thousand men and women were working on the line, and just as many were using every angle conceivable to land a job on the line. As luck would have it, a long-time friend in the surveying business needed a three-man survey crew in Prudhoe Bay. Bob, my life-long friend and fellow surveyor Maynard Taylor III, and I were available and ready. We got the job. The day after New Year's I was on the long dark flight into the Arctic night, Bob and Maynard already waiting at Prudhoe Bay.

Our home was a series of two-room trailer units, interconnected with heated halls and complete with dining room, kitchen, and showers for the three hundred or so men living there. The camp, ARCO II, was one of many; five thousand men and women were working at Prudhoe Bay that winter.

Day in, day out, twelve hours or more a day we surveyed locations for the googol of pilings needed to support the compressor plants, pump stations, buildings, and miles upon miles of pipe of all sizes that had to be in place before any oil could flow to America. Most of our work was done under lights, especially in the darkest months: the headlights from our Chevy Suburban survey rig, flashlights, lanterns, and especially our portable light plant. Whenever we worked to the edge of the lights we just moved them all ahead and went back to work. Bundled up in our Arctic gear, we were forever trying to accomplish simple tasks with thick, fumbling mittens on!

By May, even with a couple of "R and R" trips to Anchorage and a short stint at Pump Station Four in the Brooks Range for Maynard and me, we'd had enough. Besides, our pockets were a-jingle with pipeline money; summer was coming on, and we were going back into the bush prospecting.

We decided on a remote portion of the upper Stewart River, one of the major tributaries to the Yukon in Canada. Jerry, back up north after a good season falling timber, and Paul, who'd taken time off from skiing to catch some of that pipeline money working construction on the southern section of the line, took a rain check on prospecting. They'd concocted an adventure of their own, a raft trip down the Pelly River to the Yukon, then to Dawson and beyond, this time with their girl friends! No dummies, those boys. We agreed to meet in Dawson for Discovery Days in late August.

Jerry drove us over to the town of Mayo, in the Yukon, where Bob, Maynard, and I chartered a float plane to the upper Stewart. We made camp on the banks of the Stewart at the mouth of a small brook and worked out of it all summer, lining our small inflatable boat up the Stewart, roaming back through the hills and valleys on foot, panning for gold.

We saw only three other people all summer, fellow prospectors winding their way upriver in an aluminum skiff they'd carried around Frazer Falls, following their own intuitions toward a hoped-for silver strike.

We didn't have much luck prospecting, but, now that I know a bit more about the art, I'd go back up there today.

In mid-August we floated down the Stewart, portaging around the falls. We left our rubber boat in Mayo and hitched into Dawson for Discovery Days and our reunion.

Discovery Days, Dawson's late-summer festival, celebrates the discovery of gold in 1896. There were softball games and canoe races, gold-panning and greased-pole contests, a wood cutting competition which Jerry won against Paul in the finals, and the Yukon tug-of-war championships, which we won. It was good to be together again. We talked about adventuring some more on the Yukon. *National Geographic* had professed an interest in making a documentary film of our adventure. We four agreed it was time to pursue the opening.

After a very busy winter and spring we found ourselves once again at the foot of the Chilkoot Trail. Same guys, but in addition to the four of us and our packs, our party included a film crew with a producer, cameraman, soundman, grip, two guide-helpers for them, four packers on foot, two wranglers, and four horses!

Again we rafted the lakes under sail and drifted downriver, not without our share of excitement, including some very tense minutes in Five Finger Rapids. We again built a cabin, this time twenty-five miles upriver from Ruby, and traded a ski-exit for a six-hundred-mile dog team journey in December and January down the frozen Yukon to Marshall. The "Filmies" from New York and we four "Rafties"

215

became good friends: We learned a bit about their lives and filming; they learned a bit about us and the North Country. The resulting *National Geographic*–WQED Pittsburgh Special *Yukon Passage* was a fine achievement for us all.

After the film expedition I returned to the cabin at the Big Eddy, twenty-five miles upriver from Ruby. Our friend Randy Jones stayed at the cabin while we were traveling downriver; he and I finished out the winter at Big Eddy. Randy was off to work in Mt. McKinley Park after breakup of the Yukon's ice; I stayed on.

In mid-June, John Honea and his family came up from Ruby to their fish camp at Big Eddy. We had built the cabin on Johnny's land. That summer, local man Art Pitka and I built a fine log cabin next door for the Honeas.

In September, Maynard came out to trap with me. We got our feet wet, so to speak, in the business, learning our trapping by word of mouth and trial and error. When February rolled around we went into Anchorage to sell our fur. We had made just enough money to cover a little bit of fun in the big city!

I was back at Big Eddy after breakup with a new outboard motor, or "kicker," and fixed up an old riverboat to put it on. After helping Johnny Honea get his fish wheels going, I headed upriver for Dawson, 850 river miles.

Paul and his new bride were passing through Dawson on their way to Anchorage, and Jerry and his girl, Gail, were there. Bob was in Whitehorse with Robyn, and they didn't make it down to Dawson. Nonetheless, a fine time was had by all.

For Jerry, Gail, and me, Dawson was but a prelude. They returned downriver with me to the cabin, new partners for the trapping season. The three of us helped the Honeas fish their wheels that fall. We cut firewood for them, firewood for ourselves, and firewood to raft down and sell in Ruby.

Now, you might have some reservations about how it would work out, two guys and one girl winter-bound in a cozy log cabin. Well, you're right. I had some thoughts about that too, and the *only* thing I could figure, short of sleeping in the outhouse, was for *me* to have a roommate. The upshot was that Sam, a lady I'd been seeing in Dawson, arrived in Ruby in early October, barely ahead of freezeup. Now things were better. Jerry and Gail stayed in the Honeas' cabin—

the Honeas had gone down to Ruby for the winter—and Sam and I bunked in the little one.

Snow came right on Sam's heels, and we set out our traps on skis. When we weren't on trapline, skinning or stretching marten, wolverine, or mink fur, we were off in the hills behind the cabin skiing for fun, or at home visiting, reading out loud to one another. Jerry and I spent a lot of time telling each other lots of new stories, mostly lies, while playing cribbage. It's a good thing we cut a lot of firewood, because every time I turned around it seemed I was in the sauna. I hardly had time to grow a new skin before I was back in the sauna scrubbing it off for another one. As Sam explained, I could sleep on the floor any time I didn't feel like bathing! Life at the Big Eddy for us was a grand time of hard work and good living. Mid-December came all too soon, and with it, packing. We went separate ways at Christmas, Sam back to Canada, Jer and Gail to their families in the Northwest for the holidays. I stayed in Anchorage with my family. Our fur catch had been pretty good and the prices were up, but not enough to keep me from having to go to work after the holidays.

Back to the Arctic I went, again surveying, though not to Prudhoe Bay or the pipeline, but to Camp Lonely in the Arctic and from there out to the vast National Petroleum Reserve, surveying construction sites for exploratory wells. When a site was ready for the drill rig, with runway and parking aprons built; drill pad, reserve pit, and containment dikes up; and campsite completed; our cat train just hitched up and headed out across the frozen Arctic tundra like the wagon trains of old. Offices, sleeping units, maintenance units, power plant, kitchen—the whole caboodle, in structures like mobile homes with ski runners instead of wheels, was hitched behind the bulldozers and moved out, heading for the next location.

I was rooming with Bob for a while at Camp Lisburne—he'd been hitting the Arctic pretty regularly. That was in March, just before I pulled out with my latest grubstake. April 1979 that was; now it's mid-winter.

Jerry is down in the big timber country, filling his pockets with sawdust and, I hope, some money, too. I know he's eating all right; if not, he'd be up here mooching off me!

Paul, in addition to running his own helicopter ski-guiding outfit out of Anchorage into the mountains of Alaska, is coaching alpine skiing for Alaska's junior racers at Mt. Alyeska, thirty-five miles south of Anchorage. At the moment he's on loan to the U.S. National Alpine Ski Team, coaching downhillers in Europe.

Bob is in Whitehorse with Robyn. They were married last fall and all of us met in Whitehorse for the wedding. We keep pretty close tabs on one another; you never know what might come up.

So, here I am in Fairbanks, pounding on a typewriter before heading back out to camp. I say camp: I don't live at Big Eddy any more, I've moved my residence fifty miles back in the hills south of Ruby, into what once was gold mining country. Home is a 12 by 14 foot shack sitting on an old tailing pile left over from the last gold miner, and, though I'm not living alongside the Yukon but next to a sliver of a creek seeping down an old mining cut, that's all right. All I need is enough water to swizzle a gold pan in and to fill a coffee pot. All the good ground has been staked and held since the gold rush, but I just know they couldn't have gotten it all, I just know they couldn't have.

February 1980
Fairbanks, Alaska

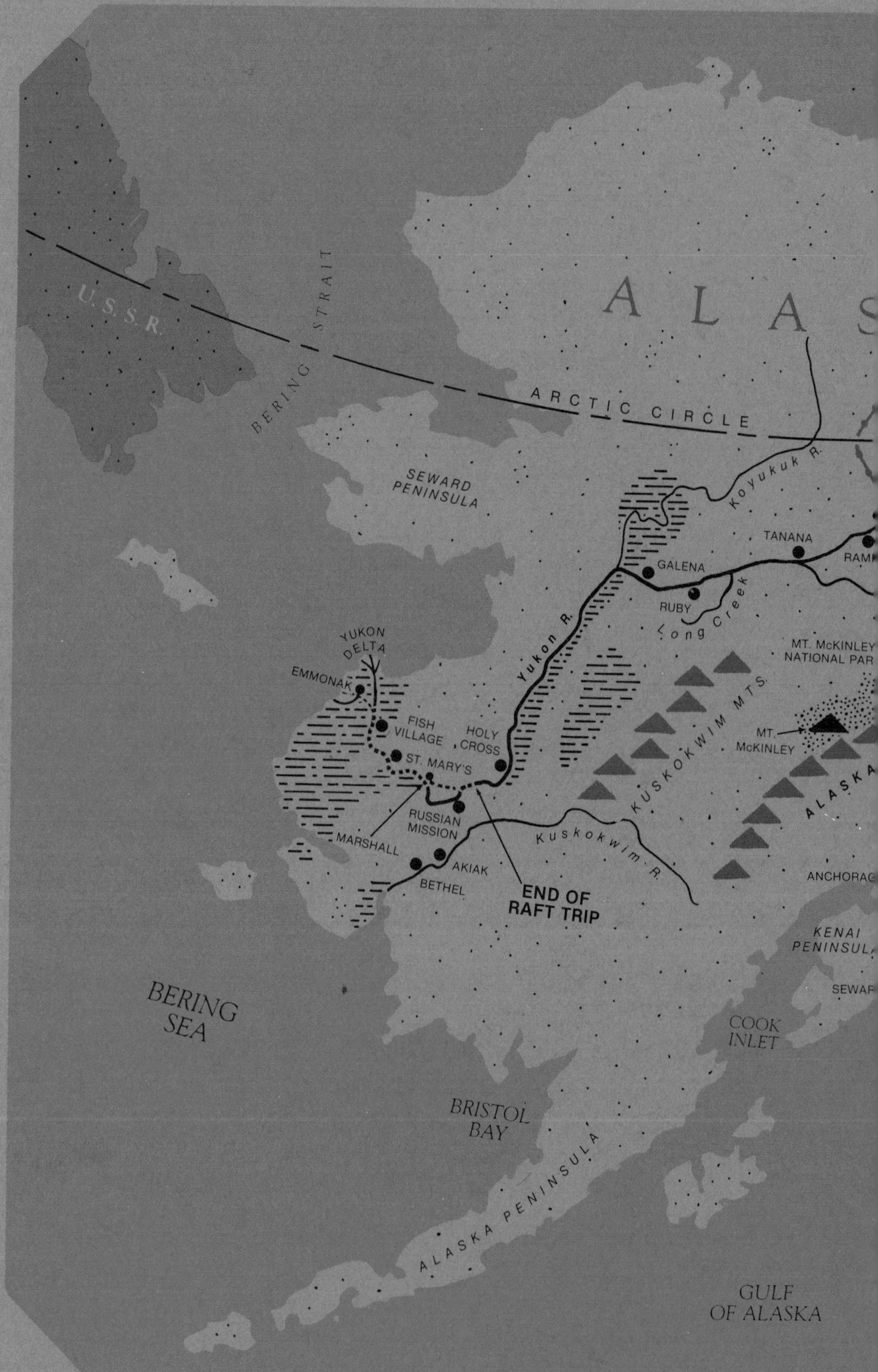

U.S.S.R.
BERING STRAIT
ARCTIC CIRCLE
ALAS
SEWARD PENINSULA
Koyukuk R.
TANANA
RAM
GALENA
RUBY
Long Creek
Yukon R.
YUKON DELTA
EMMONAK
FISH VILLAGE
HOLY CROSS
ST. MARY'S
RUSSIAN MISSION
MARSHALL
AKIAK
BETHEL
END OF RAFT TRIP
Kuskokwim R.
KUSKOKWIM MTS.
MT. McKINLEY NATIONAL PAR
MT. McKINLEY
ALASKA
ANCHORAG
KENAI PENINSUL
SEWAR
COOK INLET
BERING SEA
BRISTOL BAY
ALASKA PENINSULA
GULF OF ALASKA